Alban Butler

The lives of the saints of Egypt

Together with the Principal of the European Saints, According to the Roman

Catholic Church

Alban Butler

The lives of the saints of Egypt
Together with the Principal of the European Saints, According to the Roman Catholic Church

ISBN/EAN: 9783744777162

Printed in Europe, USA, Canada, Australia, Japan

Cover: Foto ©Lupo / pixelio.de

More available books at **www.hansebooks.com**

THE

LIVES

OF THE

SAINTS OF EGYPT,

TOGETHER WITH THE

PRINCIPAL OF THE EUROPEAN SAINTS,

ACCORDING TO THE

Roman Catholic Church:

SELECTED FROM THE REV. ALBAN BUTLER'S

Lives of the Saints,

WHICH HAVE BEEN

PUBLISHED WITH THE APPROBATION OF THE ROMAN CATHOLIC
BISHOPS OF PHILADELPHIA AND BALTIMORE.

WITH THE APPROBATION OF THE
RT. REV. BISHOP NEUMAN, OF PHILADELPHIA

PHILADELPHIA:
1863.

Entered, according to an Act of Congress, in the Clerk's Office, of the Eastern District of Pennsylvania, by C. GRATE, April 20th, 1858.

THE PUBLISHER'S PREFACE.

IN publishing the "Lives of the Saints of Egypt," by the Rev. ALBAN BUTLER, the undersigned cannot but persuade himself that he is conferring upon the Catholic public of America a favour, which all those, who are acquainted with the merits of the work, will appreciate. Though this publication contains but a portion of the "Lives of the Saints," considered as an entire work, yet, as the principal lives are included in it, and as it is printed in a large, clear type, adapted to all eyes, it possesses many advantages for spreading wholesome information among all classes of readers. The large editions of the "Lives of the Saints," published some twenty-five years ago in Philadelphia, was too expensive for the poorer classes, by reason of its bulky size; and that which was published in Baltimore, in numbers, ten years ago, too much condensed, by the small print, for old and weak eyes. To obviate these two objections, the present form was fixed upon as the most proper for the great body of the people. Here the reader is presented with a beautiful book, in a convenient form, well adapted for the centre-table in the parlour—where it may often be taken up by the worldly-minded, of both sexes, merely to while away a moment; and well shall it be for their souls, if, during that moment, they shall catch the spirit of piety which it contains, and, induced by the large clear print, (not difficult to the eye,) continue to read on till they have finished the life of a St. Francis of Sales, or a St. Francis Borgia, or a St. Antony, or a Mary of Egypt. They may thus become saints themselves, by mere accident, as many have done before them. St. Austin mentions two courtiers, who were moved on the spot to forsake the world, and became fervent monks, by accidentally reading the life of St. Antony. St. John Columbin, from a rich, covetous, and passionate nobleman, was changed into a saint, by casually reading the life of St. Mary of Egypt. The Duke of Joyeuse, Marshal of France, owed his conversion to the reading of the Life of St. Francis Borgia, which his servant had laid one evening on the table. It is unnecessary to multiply examples, as many more might be adduced, of a similar character, not to mention that of St. Ignatius Loyola, who, from a worldly-minded young man, became a great saint himself, by reading the "Lives of the Saints," while confined to his bed by sickness.

To lead such lives as we see here recorded, would perhaps not be practicable in this country, nor at this time; yet this is no reason why they may not be read with great advantage by persons in secular employments. The chief virtues, which characterized these saints in their retirement from the world, were humility, patience, and charity. All these virtues may also be practised, in a high degree, in the world; and those who practise them the most, shall be the most happy, both here and hereafter. We are told in the Bible that humility and charity are necessary to salvation—so much so, that none can enter heaven without them. By the humility and charity of the saints, we can see how deficient we are in these virtues; and by comparing their mortifications and privations, which they wilfully underwent, for the sake of Christ, we have reason to blush for ourselves, when we fret at the little that we sometimes suffer.

The lives of the saints show how much human beings, of the same frail mould with ourselves, may be elevated in the soul, by having the carnal nature subdued; how they may, in a manner, have a glimpse of heaven, while in the body. Some of these saints, as we read in their lives, were at a former period great sinners. This should give us courage, who are yet so deficient in virtue, inasmuch as it is a signal proof that Christ is willing to forgive former transgressions, provided we leave off our sins and take to a life of virtue.

To lead a life of piety, even great piety, we need not retire into a wilderness, nor enter a cloister. We may remain in the world, in any honest station, exposed as it may be to temptations, and yet lead a life of piety. Where there is such room for the exercise of all the nobler virtues, as there is in the world, there the soul may be made to shine forth in its full lustre; and though our sanctity may not be so established, by the working of miracles, as among the saints in the desert, yet shall we be the no less near to heaven, by our lives of piety, nor the less sure of a heavenly crown. Nothing can be more beneficial, in order to practise such piety, than the frequent reading of the lives of the saints.

St. Francis of Sales and St. Francis Borgia, &c. were not saints of Egypt, yet the publisher thought proper to insert their lives in this volume, as they are so useful for all classes of readers, and have such tendency to instil sentiments of piety.   C. GRATE.

PHILADELPHIA, *September* 16, 1853.

THE
LIVES OF SAINTS.

ST. PAUL, THE FIRST HERMIT.

From his life, compiled by St. Jerom, in 365. Pope Gelasius I., in his learned Roman council, in 494, commends this authentic history.

A. D. 342.

ELIAS and St. John the Baptist sanctified the deserts, and Jesus Christ himself was a model of the eremitical state during his forty days' fast in the wilderness; neither is it to be questioned but the Holy Ghost conducted the saint of this day, though young, into the desert, and was to him an instructor there; but it is no less certain, that an entire solitude and total sequestration of one's self from human society, is one of those extraordinary ways by which God leads souls to himself, and is more worthy of our admiration than calculated for imitation and practice; it is a state which ought only to be embraced by such as are already well experienced in the practices of virtue and contemplation, and who can resist sloth and other temptations, lest, instead of being a help, it prove a snare and stumbling-block in their way to heaven.

This saint was a native of the Lower Thebais, in Egypt, and had lost both his parents when he was but fifteen years of age; nevertheless he was a great proficient in the Greek and Egyptian learning, was mild and modest, and feared God from his earliest youth. The bloody persecution of Decius disturbed the peace of the church in 250; and what was most dreadful, Satan, by his ministers, sought not so much to kill the bodies, as by subtle artifices and tedious tortures to destroy the souls of men. Two instances are sufficient to show his malice in this respect. A soldier of Christ, who had already triumphed over the racks and tortures, had his whole body rubbed over with honey, and was then laid on his back in the sun, with his hands tied behind him, that the flies and wasps, which are quite intolerable in hot countries, might torment and gall him with their stings. Another was bound with silk cords on a bed of down, in a delightful garden, where a lascivious woman was employed to entice him to sin; the martyr, sensible of his danger, bit off part of his tongue and spit it in her face, that the horror of such an action might put her to flight, and the smart occasioned by it be a means to prevent, in his own heart, any manner of consent to carnal pleasure. During these times of danger Paul kept himself concealed in the house of another; but finding that a brother-in-law was inclined to betray him that he might enjoy his estate, he fled into the deserts. There he found many spacious caverns, in a rock, which were said to have been the retreat of money-coiners in the days of Cleopatra, queen of Egypt. He chose for his dwelling a cave in this place, near which were a palm-tree[1] and a clear spring; the former by its leaves furnished him with raiment, and by its fruit with food; and the latter supplied him with water for his drink.

Paul was twenty-two years old when he entered the desert. His first intention was to enjoy the liberty of serving God till the persecution should cease; but relishing the sweets of heavenly contem-

---

[1] Pliny recounts thirty-nine different sorts of palm-trees, and says that the best grow in Egypt, which are ever green, have leaves thick enough to make ropes, and a fruit which serves in some places to make bread.

plation and penance, and learning the spiritual advantages of holy solitude, he resolved to return no more among men, or concern himself in the least with human affairs, and what passed in the world: it was enough for him to know that there was a world, and to pray that it might be improved in goodness. The saint lived on the fruit of this tree till he was forty-three years of age, and from that time till his death, like Elias, he was miraculously fed with bread brought him every day by a raven. His method of life, and what he did in this place during ninety years, is unknown to us; but God was pleased to make his servant known a little before his death.

The great St. Antony, who was then ninety years of age, was tempted to vanity, as if no one had served God so long in the wilderness as he had done, imagining himself also to be the first example of a life so recluse from human conversation. But the contrary was discovered to him in a dream the night following, and the saint was at the same time commanded, by Almighty God, to set out forthwith in quest of a perfect servant of his, concealed in the more remote parts of those deserts. The holy old man set out the next morning in search of the unknown hermit. St. Jerom relates, from his authors, that he met a centaur, or creature not with the nature and properties, but with something of the mixed shape of man and horse,[1] and that this monster, or phantom of the devil (St. Jerom pretends not to determine which it was), upon his making the sign of the cross, fled away, after having pointed out the way to the saint. Our author adds that St. Antony soon after met a satyr,[2] who gave him to understand that

---

[1] Pliny, 1. 7. c. 3, and others, assure us that such monsters have been seen. Consult the note of Rosweide.
[2] The heathens might feign their gods of the woods, from certain monsters sometimes seen. Plutarch, in his life of Sylla, says, that a satyr was brought to that general at Athens; and St. Jerom tells us, that one was shown alive at Alexandria, and after its death was salted and embalmed, and sent to Antioch, that Constantine the Great might see it.

he was an inhabitant of those deserts, and one of that sort whom the deluded Gentiles adored for gods. St. Antony, after two days and a night spent in the search, discovered the saint's abode by a light that was in it, which he made up to. Having long begged admittance at the door of this cell, St. Paul at last opened it with a smile: they embraced, called each other by their names, which they knew by divine revelation. St. Paul then inquired whether idolatry still reigned in the world. While they were discoursing together, a raven flew toward them, and dropped a loaf of bread before them. Upon which St. Paul said, "Our good God has sent us a dinner. In this manner have I received half a loaf every day these sixty years past; now you are come to see me, Christ has doubled his provision for his servants." Having given thanks to God, they both sat down by the fountain; but a little contest arose between them who should break the bread: St. Antony alleged St. Paul's greater age, and St. Paul pleaded that Antony was the stranger: both agreed at last to take up their parts together. Having refreshed themselves at the spring, they spent the night in prayer. The next morning St. Paul told his guest that the time of his death approached, and that he was sent to bury him, adding, "Go and fetch the cloak given you by St. Athanasius, bishop of Alexandria, in which I desire you to wrap my body." This he might say with the intent of being left alone in prayer whilst he expected to be called out of this world, as also that he might testify his veneration for St. Athanasius, and his high regard for the faith and communion of the catholic church, on account of which that holy bishop was then a great sufferer. St. Antony was surprised to hear him mention the cloak, which he could not have know but by divine revelation. Whatever was his motive for desiring to be buried in it, St. Antony acquiesced to what was asked of him: so, after mutual embraces, he hastened to his monastery to comply with St. Paul's request.

He told his monks that he, a sinner, falsely bore the name of a servant of God; but that he had seen Elias and John the Baptist in the wilderness,—even Paul in Paradise. Having taken the cloak, he returned with it in all haste, fearing lest the holy hermit might be dead, as it happened. Whilst on his road, he saw his happy soul carried up to heaven, attended by choirs of angels, prophets, and apostles. St. Antony, though he rejoiced on St. Paul's account, could not help lamenting on his own, for having lost a treasure so lately discovered. As soon as his sorrow would permit he arose, pursued his journey, and came to the cave. Going in, he found the body kneeling and the hands stretched out. Full of joy, and supposing him yet alive, he knelt down to pray with him, but by his silence soon perceived he was dead. Having paid his last respects to the holy corpse, he carried it out of the cave. Whilst he stood perplexed how to dig a grave, two lions came up quietly, and as it were mourning, and tearing up the ground, made a hole large enough for the reception of a human body. St. Antony then buried the corpse, singing hymns and psalms according to what was usual and appointed by the church on that occasion. After this he returned home, praising God, and related to his monks what he had seen and done. He always kept as a great treasure, and wore himself on great festivals, the garment of St. Paul, of palm-tree leaves patched together. St. Paul died in the year of our Lord 342, the hundred and thirteenth year of his age, and the ninetieth of his solitude, and is usually called the *first hermit*, to distinguish him from others of that name. The body of this saint is said to have been conveyed to Constantinople by the Emperor Michael Comnenus, in the twelfth century, and from thence to Venice in 1240.[1] Lewis I., king of Hungary, procured it from that republic, and de-

---

[1] See the whole history of this translation, published from an original MS. by F. Gamans, a Jesuit, inserted by Bollandus in his collection.

posited it at Buda, where a congregation of hermits under his name, which still subsists in Hungary, Poland, and Austria, was instituted by blessed Eusebius of Strigonium, a nobleman, who having distributed his whole estate among the poor retired into the forests, and being followed by others, built the monastery of Pisilia, under the rule of the regular canons of St. Austin. He died in that house January the 20th, 1270.

St. Paul, the hermit, is commemorated in several ancient western Martyrologies on the 10th of January, but in the Romanon the 15th, on which he is honoured in the anthologium of the Greeks.

An eminent contemplative draws the following portraiture of this great model of an eremitical life:[1] St. Paul, the hermit, not being called by God to the external duties of an active life, remained alone, conversing only with God, in a vast wilderness, for the space of near a hundred years, ignorant of all that passed in the world—both the progress of sciences, the establishment of religion, and the revolutions of states and empires; indifferent even as to those things without which he could not live—as the air which he breathed, the water he drank, and the miraculous bread with which he supported life. What did he do? say the inhabitants of this busy world, who think they could not live without being in a perpetual hurry of restless projects; what was his employment all this while? Alas! ought we not rather to put this question to them; what are you doing whilst you are not taken up in doing the will of God, which occupies the heavens and the earth in all their motions? Do you call that doing nothing which is the great end God proposed to himself in giving us a being, that is, to be employed in contemplating, adoring, and praising him? Is it to be idle and useless in the world, to be entirely taken up in that which is the

---

[1] F. Ambrose de Lombez, Capucin, Fr. de la Paix Intérieure, (Paris, 1758, p. 372.)

eternal occupation of God himself, and of the blessed inhabitants of heaven? What employment is better, more just, more sublime, or more advantageous than this, when done in suitable circumstances? To be employed in any thing else, how great or noble soever it may appear in the eyes of men, unless it be referred to God, and be the accomplishment of his holy will, who in all our actions demands our hearts more than our hand, what is it, but to turn ourselves away from our end, to lose our time, and voluntarily to return again to that state of nothing out of which we were formed, or rather into a far worse state?

ST. ISIDORE, P. H.

HE was priest of Scété, and hermit in that vast desert. He excelled in an unparalleled gift of meekness, continency, prayer, and recollection. Once perceiving in himself some motions of anger to rise, he that instant threw down certain baskets he was carrying to market, and ran away to avoid the occasion.[1] When, in his old age, others persuaded him to abate something in his labour, he answered: "If we consider what the Son of God hath done for us, we can never allow ourselves any indulgence in sloth. Were my body burnt and my ashes scattered in the air, it would be nothing."[2] Whenever the enemy tempted him to despair, he said, "Were I to be damned, thou wouldst yet be below me in hell; nor would I cease to labour in the service of God, though assured that this was to be my lot." If he was tempted to vain-glory, he reproached and confounded himself with the thought how far, even in his exterior exercises, he fell short of the servants of God, Antony, Pambo, and others.[3] Being asked the reason of his

---

[1] Cotellier, Mon. Gr. t. 1, p. 487.
[2] Ib. p. 686, Rosweide, l. 5, c. 7.
[3] Cotel. ib. t. 2, p. 48. Rosweide, l. 3, c. 101; l. 7, c. 11.

abundant tears, he answered: "I weep for my sins: if we had only once offended God, we could never sufficiently bewail this misfortune." He died a little before the year 391. His name stands in the Roman Martyrology, on the fifteenth of January. See Sassian. coll. 18, c. 15 and 16. Tillem. t. 8, p. 440.

ST. MACARIUS, THE ELDER, OF EGYPT.
A. D. 390.

St. Macarius, the Elder, was born in Upper Egypt, about the year 300, and brought up in the country in tending cattle. In his childhood, in company with some others, he once stole a few figs, and ate one of them; but from his conversion to his death, he never ceased to weep bitterly for his sin.[1] By a powerful call of divine grace he retired from the world in his youth, and dwelling in a little cell in a village, made mats, in continual prayer and great austerities. A wicked woman falsely accused him of having deflowred her, for which supposed crime he was dragged through the streets, beaten, and insulted, as a base hypocrite under the garb of a monk. He suffered all with patience, and sent the woman what he earned by his work, saying to himself: "Well, Macarius, having now another to provide for, thou must work the harder." But God discovered his innocency: for the woman falling in labour lay in extreme anguish, and could not be delivered till she had named the true father of her child. The people converted their rage into the greatest admiration of the humility and patience of the saint.[2] To shun the esteem of men he fled into the vast hideous desert of Scété, being then about thirty years of age. In this solitude he lived sixty years, and became the spiritual parent of in

---

[1] Bolland. 15 Jan. p. 1011, § 39. Cotel. Mon. Gr. t. 1, p. 546.
[2] Cotel. ib. p. 525. Rosweide, Vit. Patr. l. 3, c. 99; l. 5, c. 15, § 25 p. 523.

numerable holy persons, who put themselves under his direction, and were governed by the rules he prescribed them; but all dwelt in separate hermitages. St. Macarius admitted only one disciple with him, to entertain strangers. He was compelled by an Egyptian bishop to receive the order of priesthood, about the year 340—the fortieth of his age—that he might celebrate the divine mysteries for the convenience of this holy colony. When the desert became better peopled there were four churches built in it, which were served by so many priests. The austerities of St. Macarius were excessive; he usually eat but once a week. Evagrius, his disciple, once asked him leave to drink a little water, under a parching thirst; but Macarius bade him to content himself with reposing a little in the shade, saying: "For these twenty years I have never once eat, drank, or slept as much as nature required."[1] His face was very pale, and his body weak and parched up. To deny his own will, he did not refuse to drink a little wine when others desired him, but then he would punish himself for this indulgence by abstaining two or three days from all manner of drink; and it was for this reason, that his disciple desired strangers never to tender unto him a drop of wine.[2] He delivered his instructions in few words, and principally inculcated silence, humility, mortification, retirement, and continual prayer, especially the last, to all sorts of people. He used to say, "In prayer, you need not use many or lofty words. You can often repeat with a sincere heart, Lord, show me mercy as thou knowest best. Or, Assist me, O God!"[3] He was much delighted with this ejaculation of perfect resignation and love: "O Lord, have mercy on me, as thou pleasest and knowest best in thy goodness!" His mildness and patience were invincible, and occasioned the conver-

---

[1] Socrates, l. 4, c. 23.
[2] Rosweide, Vit. Patr. l. 3, § 3, p. 505; l. 5, c. 4, § 26, p. 569.
[3] Rosweide, l. 3, c. 20; l. 5, c. 12. Cotel. p. 537.

sion of a heathen priest, and many others.[1] The devil told him one day, "I can surpass thee in watching, fasting, and many other things; but humility conquers and disarms me."[2] A young man applying to St. Macarius for spiritual advice, he directed him to go to a burying-place and upbraid the dead, and after to go and flatter them. When he came back, the saint asked him what answer the dead had made. "None at all," said the other, "either to reproaches or praises." "Then," replied Macarius, "go, and learn neither to be moved with injuries nor flatteries. If you die to the world and to yourself, you will begin to live to Christ." He said to another: "Receive, from the hand of God, poverty as cheerfully as riches; hunger and want as plenty; and you will conquer the devil and subdue all your passions."[3] A certain monk complained to him, that in solitude he was always tempted to break his fast, whereas in the monastery he could fast the whole week cheerfully. "Vain-glory is the reason," replied the saint; "fasting pleases when men see you, but seems intolerable when that passion is not gratified."[4] One came to consult him who was molested with temptations to impurity. The saint examining into the source found it to be sloth, and advised him never to eat before sunset, to meditate fervently at his work, and to labour vigorously, without sloth, the whole day. The other faithfully complied, and was freed from his enemy. God revealed to St. Macarius that he had not attained the perfection of two married women, who lived in a certain town. He made them a visit, and learned the means by which they sanctified themselves. They were extremely careful never to speak any idle or rash words; they lived in the constant practice of humility, patience, meekness, charity, resignation, mortification of their own will, and con-

---

[1] Rosweide, l. 3, c. 127.   Cotel. t. 1, p. 547.
[2] Rosweide, l. 5, c. 15.
[3] Rosweide, l. 7, c. 38.   Cotel. t. 1, p. 537.   Rosweide, ib. § 9.
[4] Cassian, Collat. 5, c. 32.

formity to the humors of their husbands and others, where the divine law did not interpose; in a spirit of recollection they sanctified all their actions by ardent ejaculations, by which they strove to praise God, and most fervently to consecrate to the divine glory all the powers of their soul and body.[1]

A subtle heretic of the sect of the Hieracites, called so from Hierax, who in the reign of Dioclesian denied the resurrection of the dead, had, by his sophisms, caused some to stagger in their faith. St. Macarius, to confirm them in the truth, raised a dead man to life, as Socrates, Sozomen, Palladius, and Rufinus relate. Cassian says, that he only made a dead corpse to speak for that purpose; then bade it rest till the resurrection. Lucius, the Arian usurper of the see of Alexandria, who had expelled Peter, the successor of St. Athanasius, in 376 sent troops into the deserts to disperse the zealous monks, several of whom sealed their faith with their blood; the chiefs, namely, the two Macaliuses, Isidore, Pambo, and some others, by the authority of the Emperor Valens, were banished into a little isle of Egypt, surrounded with great marshes. The inhabitants, who were pagans, were all converted to the faith by the confessors.[2] The public indignation of the whole empire obliged Lucius to suffer them to return to their cells. Our saint knowing that his end drew near, made a visit to the monks of Nitria, and exhorted them to compunction and tears so pathetically, that they all fell weeping at his feet. "Let us weep, brethren," said he, "and let our eyes pour forth floods of tears before we go hence, lest we fall into that place where tears will only increase the flames in which we shall burn."[3] He went to receive the reward of his labours in the

---

[1] Rosweide, l. 3, c. 97; l. 6, c. 3, § 17, p. 657.
[2] Theodoret. l. 4, c. 18, 19. Socr, l. 4, c. 22. Sozom. l. 6, c. 19, 20. Rufin. l. 2, c. 3. S. Hier. in Chron. Oros. l. 7, c. 33. Pallad. Lausiac. c. 117.
[3] Rosweide, Vit. Patr. l. 5, c. 3, § 9. Cotel. Mon. Gr. p. 545.

year 390, and of his age the ninetieth, having spent sixty years in the desert of Scété.[1]

He seems to have been the first anchoret who inhabited this vast wilderness; and this Cassian affirms.[2] Some style him a disciple of St. Antony; but that quality rather suits St. Macarius of Alexandria; for, by the history of our saint's life, it appears that he could not have lived under the direction of St. Antony before he retired into the desert of Scété But he afterward paid a visit, if not several, to that holy patriarch of monks, whose dwelling was fifteen days' journey distant.[3] This glorious saint is honoured in the Roman Martyrology on the 15th of January; in the Greek Menæa on the 19th. An ancient monastic rule, and an epistle addressed to monks, written in sentences like the book of Proverbs, are ascribed to St. Macarius. Tillemont thinks them more probably the works of St. Macarius of Alexandria, who had under his inspection at Nitria five thousand monks.[4] Gennadius[5] says, that St. Macarius wrote nothing but this letter. This may be understood of St. Macarius of Alexandria, though one who wrote in Gaul might not have seen all the works of an author, whose country was so remote, and language different. Fifty spiritual homilies are ascribed, in the first edition, and in some manuscripts, to St. Macarius of Egypt; yet F. Possin[6] thinks they rather belong to Macarius of Pispir, who attended St. Antony at his death, and seems to have been some years older than the two great Macariuses, though some have thought him the same with the Alexandrian.

---

[1] Pallad. Lausiac. c. 19.
[2] Cassian. Collat. 15, c. 13. Tilem. Note 3, p. 806.
[3] Rosw. Vit. Patr. l. 5, c. 7, § 9. Cotel. Apophthegm. Patr. 530. Tillem. art. 4, p. 591, and Note 4, p. 806.
[4] See Tillem. Note 3, p. 806.
[5] Gennad. Cat. c. 10.
[6] Possin. Ascet. pr. p. 17.

SAINT ANTONY, ABBOT,

PATRIARCH OF MONKS.

From his Life, compiled by the great St. Athanasius.

A. D. 356.

St. Antony was born at Coma, a village near Heraclea, or great Heracleopolis, in Upper Egypt, on the borders of Arcadia, or Middle Egypt, in 251. His parents, who were Christians, and rich, to prevent his being tainted by bad example and vicious conversation, kept him always at home; so that he grew up unacquainted with any branch of human literature, and could read no language but his own. He was remarkable from his childhood for his temperance, a close attendance on church duties, and a punctual obedience to his parents. By their death he found himself possessed of a very considerable estate, and charged with the care of a younger sister, before he was twenty years of age. Near six months after, he heard read in the church those words of Christ to the rich young man: *Go sell what thou hast, and give it to the poor, and thou shalt have treasure in heaven.*[1] He considered these words as addressed to himself; going home, he made over to his neighbours three hundred *aruras*, that is, above one hundred and twenty acres of good land, that he and his sister might be free for ever from all public taxes and burdens. The rest of his estate he sold, and gave the price to the poor, except what he thought necessary for himself and his sister. Soon after, hearing in the church those other words of Christ: *Be not solicitous for to-morrow:*[2] he also distributed in alms the movables

---

[1] Matt. xix. 21. [2] Ibid. vi. 34.

which he had reserved; and placed his sister in a house of virgins, which most moderns take to be the first instance mentioned in history of a nunnery. She was afterward intrusted with the care and direction of others in that holy way of life. Antony himself retired into a solitude, near his village, in imitation of a certain old man, who led the life of a hermit in the neighbourhood of Coma. Manual labour, prayer, and pious reading were his whole occupation; and such was his fervour, that if he heard of any virtuous recluse, he sought him out, and endeavoured to make the best advantage of his example and instructions. He saw nothing practised by any other in the service of God, which he did not imitate: thus he soon became a perfect model of humility, Christian condescension, charity, prayer, and all virtues.

The devil assailed him by various temptations: first, he represented to him divers good works he might have been able to do with his estate in the world, and the difficulties of his present condition: a common artifice of the enemy, whereby he strives to make a soul slothful or dissatisfied in her vocation, in which God expects to be glorified by her. Being discovered and repulsed by the young novice, he varied his method of attack, and annoyed him night and day with filthy thoughts and obscene imaginations. Antony opposed to his assaults the strictest watchfulness over his senses, austere fasts, humility, and prayer, till Satan, appearing in a visible form, first of a woman coming to seduce him, then of a black boy to terrify him, at length confessed himself vanquished. The saint's food was only bread, with a little salt, and he drank nothing but water; he never eat before sunset, and sometimes only once in two or four days: he lay on a rush mat, or on the bare floor. In quest of a more remote solitude, he withdrew farther from Coma, and hid himself in an old sepulchre; whither a friend brought him from time to time a little bread. Satan was here again permitted to assault him in a visible manner, to terrify him with dismal noises;

and once he so grievously beat him, that he lay almost dead, covered with bruises and wounds; and in this condition he was one day found by his friend, who visited him from time to time to supply him with bread, during all the time he lived in the ruinous sepulchre. When he began to come to himself, though not yet able to stand, he cried out to the devils, while he yet lay on the floor, "Behold! here I am; do all you are able against me: nothing shall ever separate me from Christ my Lord." Hereupon the fiends, appearing again, renewed the attack, and alarmed him with terrible clamours, and a variety of spectres, in hideous shapes of the most frightful wild beasts, which they assumed to dismay and terrify him; till a ray of heavenly light breaking in upon him chased them away, and caused him to cry out: "Where wast thou, my Lord and my Master? Why wast thou not here, from the beginning of my conflict, to assuage my pains!" A voice answered: "Antony, I was here the whole time: I stood by thee, and beheld thy combat; and because thou hast manfully withstood thy enemies, I will always protect thee, and will render thy name famous throughout the earth." At these words the saint arose, much cheered and strengthened, to pray and return thanks to his deliverer. Hitherto the saint, ever since his retreat in 272, had lived in solitary places not very far from his village; and St. Athanasius observes, that before him many fervent persons led retired lives in penance and contemplation, near the towns; others remaining in the towns imitated the same manner of life. Both were called ascetics, from their being entirely devoted to the most perfect exercises of mortification and prayer, according to the import of the Greek word. Before St. Athanasius, we find frequent mention made of such ascetics; and Origen about the year 249[1] says, they always abstained from flesh, no less than the disciples of Pythagoras. Eusebius tells us, that St.

---

[1] Orig. lib. 5, p. 264.

Peter of Alexandria practised austerities equal to those of the ascetics; he says the same of Pamphilus; and St. Jerom uses the same expression of Pierius. St. Antony had led this manner of life near Coma, till resolving to withdraw into the deserts about the year 285, the thirty-fifth of his age, he crossed the eastern branch of the Nile, and took up his abode in the ruins of an old castle on the top of the mountains; in which close solitude he lived almost twenty years, very rarely seeing any man, except one who brought him bread every six months.

To satisfy the importunities of others, about the year 305, the fifty-fifth of his age, he came down from his mountain, and founded his first monastery at Phaium. The dissipation occasioned by this undertaking led him into a temptation of despair, which he overcame by prayer and hard manual labour. In this new manner of life his daily refection was six ounces of bread soaked in water, with a little salt; to which he sometimes added a few dates. He took it generally after sunset, but on some days at three o'clock; and in his old age he added a little oil. Sometimes he eat only once in three or four days, yet appeared vigorous, and always cheerful; strangers knew him from among his disciples by the joy which was always painted on his countenance, resulting from the inward peace and composure of his soul. Retirement in his cell was his delight, and divine contemplation and prayer his perpetual occupation. Coming to take his refection, he often burst into tears, and was obliged to leave his brethren and the table without touching any nourishment, reflecting on the employment of the blessed spirits in heaven, who praise God without ceasing.[1] He exhorted his brethren to allot the least time they possibly could to the care of the body. Notwithstanding which, he was very careful never to place perfection in mortification, as Cassian observes, but in charity, in which it was his whole study

---

[1] St. Athan. Vt. Anton. n. 45, p. 830.

continually to improve his soul. His under-garment was sackcloth, over which he wore a white coat of sheepskin, with a girdle. He instructed his monks to have eternity always present to their minds, and to reflect every morning that perhaps they might not live till night, and every evening that perhaps they might never see the morning; and to perform every action, as if it were the last of their lives, with all the fervour of their souls, to please God. He often exhorted them to watch against temptations, and to resist the devil with vigour: and spoke admirably of his weakness, saying: "He dreads fasting, prayer, humility, and good works: he is not able even to stop my mouth who speak against him. The illusions of the devil soon vanish, especially if a man arms himself with the sign of the cross.[1] The devils tremble at the sign of the cross of our Lord, by which he triumphed over and disarmed them."[2] He told them in what manner the fiend in his rage had assaulted him by visible phantoms, but that these disappeared while he persevered in prayer. He told them, that once when the devil appeared to him in glory, and said, "Ask what you please; I am the power of God;" he invoked the holy name of Jesus, and he vanished. Maximinus renewed the persecution in 311: St. Antony, hoping to receive the crown of martyrdom, went to Alexandria, served and encouraged martyrs in the mines and dungeons, before the tribunals, and at the places of execution. He publicly wore his white monastic habit, and appeared in the sight of the governor; yet took care never presumptuously to provoke the judges, or impeach himself, as some rashly did. In 312, the persecution being abated, he returned to his monastery, and immured himself in his cell. Some time after, he built another monastery, called Pispir, near the Nile; but he chose, for the most part, to shut himself up in a remote cell upon a mountain of difficult access, with Macarius,

---

[1] P. 814.   [2] P. 823, ed. Ben.

a disciple, who entertained strangers. If he found them to be *Hierosolymites*, or spiritual men, St. Antony himself sat with them in discourse; if Egyptians. (by which name they meant worldly persons,) then Macarius entertained them, and St. Antony only appeared to give them a short exhortation. Once the saint saw in a vision the whole earth covered so thick with snares that it seemed scarce possible to set down a foot without falling into them. At this sight he cried out, trembling: "Who, O Lord, can escape them all?" A voice answered him: "Humility, O Antony!" St. Antony always looked upon himself as the least and the very outcast of mankind; he listened to the advice of every one, and professed that he received benefit from that of the meanest person. He cultivated and pruned a little garden on his desert mountain, that he might have herbs always at hand, to present a refreshment to those who, on coming to see him, were always weary by travelling over a vast wilderness and inhospitable mountain, as St. Athanasius mentions. This tillage was not the only manual labour in which St. Antony employed himself. The same venerable author speaks of his making mats as an ordinary occupation. We are told that he once fell into dejection, finding uninterrupted contemplation above his strength; but was taught to apply himself at intervals to manual labour, by a vision of an angel who appeared platting mats of palm-tree leaves, then rising to pray, and after some time sitting down again to work; and who at length said to him, "Do thus, and thou shalt be saved." But St. Athanasius informs us, that our saint continued in some degree to pray while he was at work. He watched great part of the nights in heavenly contemplation; and sometimes, when the rising sun called him to his daily tasks, he complained that its visible light robbed him of the greater interior light which he enjoyed, and interrupted his close application and solitude. He always rose after a short sleep at midnight, and continued in prayer on his knees with his hands lifted up to heaven till sunrise, and sometimes till three in the afternoon, as Palladius relates in his Lausiac history.

St. Antony, in the year 339, saw in a vision, under the figure of mules kicking down the altar, the havoc which the Arian persecution made two years after in Alexandria, and clearly foretold it, as St. Athanasius, St. Jerom, and St. Chrysostom assure us. He would not speak to a heretic, unless to exhort him to the true faith; and he drove all such from his mountain, calling them venomous serpents. At the request of the bishops, about the year 355, he took a journey to Alexandria, to confound the Arians, preaching aloud in that city that God the Son is not a creature, but of the same substance with the Father; and that the impious Arians, who called him a creature, did not differ from the heathens themselves, *who worshipped and served the creature rather than the Creator.* All the people ran to see him, and rejoiced to hear him: even the pagans, struck with the dignity of his character, flocked to him; saying, "We desire to see the man of God." He converted many, and wrought several miracles: St. Athanasius conducted him back as far as the gates of the city, where he cured a girl possessed by the devil. Being desired by the duke or general of Egypt, to make a longer stay in the city than he had proposed, he answered: "As fish die if they leave the water, so does a monk if he forsakes his solitude."

St. Jerom and Rufin relate, that at Alexandria he met with the famous Didymus, and told him that he ought not to regret much the loss of eyes, which were common to ants and flies, but to rejoice in the treasure of that interior light, which the apostles enjoyed, and by which we see God, and kindle the fire of his love in our souls. Heathen philosophers, and others, often went to dispute with him, and always returned much astonished at his humility, meekness, sanctity, and extraordinary wisdom. He admirably proved to them the truth and security of the Christian religion, and confirmed it by miracles. "We," said he, "only by naming Jesus Christ crucified, put to flight those devils which you adore as gods; and where the sign of the cross is formed, magic and charms lose their power." At the end of this discourse he invoked Christ, and signed with the cross twice or thrice several persons possessed with devils: in the same moment they stood up sound, and in their senses, giving thanks to God for his mercy in their regard. When certain philosophers asked him how he could spend his time in solitude, without the pleasure of reading books, he replied, that nature was his great book, and amply supplied the want of others. When others, despising him as an illiterate man, came with the design to ridicule his ignorance, he asked them with great simplicity, which was first, reason or learning, and which had produced the other? The philosophers answered, "Reason, or good sense." "This, then," said Antony, "suffices." The philosophers went away astonished at the wisdom and dignity with which he prevented their objections. Some others demanding a reason of his faith in Christ, on purpose to insult it, he put them to silence, by showing that they degraded the notion of the divinity, by ascribing to it infamous human passions, but that the humiliation of the cross is the greatest demonstration of infinite goodness, and its ignominy appears the highest glory, by the triumphant resurrection, the miraculous raising of the dead, and curing of the blind and the sick. He then admirably proved, that faith in God and his works is more clear and satisfactory than the sophistry of the Greeks. St. Athanasius mentions, that he disputed with these Greeks by an interpreter. Our holy author assures us, that no one visited St. Antony under any affliction and sadness, who did not return home full of comfort and joy; and he relates many miraculous cures wrought by him, also several heavenly visions and revelations with which he was favoured. Belacius, the duke or general of Egypt, persecuting the catholics with extreme fury; St. Antony, by a letter, exhorted him to leave the servants of Christ in peace. Belacius tore the letter, then spit and trampled upon it, and threatened to make the abbot the next victim of his fury; but five days after, as he was riding with Nestorius, governor of Egypt, their horses began to play and prance, and the governor's horse, though otherwise remarkably tame, by justling, threw Belacius from his horse, and by biting his thigh, tore it in such a manner that the general died miserably on the third day. About the year 337, Constantine the Great and his two sons, Constantius and Constans, wrote a joint letter to the saint, recommending themselves to his prayers, and desiring an answer. St. Antony, seeing his monks surprised, said, without being moved: "Do not wonder that the emperor writes to us, one man to another; rather admire that God should have wrote to us, and that he has spoken to us by his Son." He said he knew not how to answer it: at last, through the importunity of his disciples, he penned a letter to the emperor and his sons, which St. Athanasius has preserved; and in which he exhorts them to the contempt of the world, and the constant remembrance of the judgment to come. St. Jerom mentions seven other letters of St. Antony to divers monasteries, written in the style of the apostles, and filled with their maxims: several monasteries of Egypt possess them in the original Egyptian language. We have them in an obscure, imperfect Latin translation from the Greek. He inculcates perpetual watchfulness against temptations, prayer, mortification, and humility. He observes, that as the devil fell by pride, so he assaults virtue in us principally by that temptation. A maxim which he frequently repeats is, that the knowledge of ourselves is the necessary and only step by which we can ascend to the knowledge and love of God. The Bollandists give us a short letter of St. Antony to St. Theodorus, abbot of Tabenna, in which he says that God had assured him in a revelation that he showed mercy to all true adorers of Jesus Christ, though they should have fallen, if they sincerely repented of their sin. No ancients mention any monastic rule written by St. Antony. His example and instructions have been the most perfect rule for the monastic life to all succeeding ages. It is related that St. Antony, hearing his disciples express their surprise at the great multitudes who embraced a monastic life, and applied themselves with incredible ardour to the most austere practices of virtue, told them with tears, that the time would come when monks would be fond of living in cities and stately buildings, and of eating at dainty tables, and be only distinguished from persons of the world by their habit; but that still, some among them would arise to the spirit of true perfection, whose crown would be so much the greater, as their virtue would be more difficult amid the contagion of bad example. In the discourses which this saint made to his monks, a rigorous self-examination upon all their actions, every evening, was a practice which he strongly inculcated. In an excellent sermon which he made to his disciples, recorded by St. Athanasius, he pathetically exhorts them to contemn the whole world for heaven, to spend every day as if they knew it to be the last of their lives, having death always before their eyes, continually to advance in fervour, and to be always armed against the assaults of Satan, whose weakness he shows at length. He extols the efficacy of the sign of the cross in chasing him and dissipating his illusions, and lays down rules for the discernment of spirits, the first of which is, that the devil leaves in the soul impressions of fear, sadness, confusion, and disturbance.

St. Antony performed the visitation of his monks a little before his death, which he foretold them with his last instructions; but no tears could move him to die among them. It appears from St. Athanasius, that the Christians had learned from the pagans their custom of embalming the bodies of the dead, which abuse, as proceeding from vanity and sometimes superstition, St. Antony had often condemned: this he would prevent, and ordered that his body should be buried in the earth as the patriarchs were, and privately, on his mountain, by his two disciples Macarius and Amathas, who had remained with him the last fifteen years, to serve him in his remote cell in his old age. He hastened back to that solitude, and some time after fell sick: he repeated to these two disciples his orders for their burying his body secretly in that place, adding, "In the day of the resurrection, I shall receive it incorruptible from the hand of Christ." He ordered them to give one of his sheepskins, with a cloak in which he lay, to the bishop Athanasius, as a public testimony of his being united in faith and communion with that holy prelate; to give his other sheepskin to the bishop Serapion; and to keep for themselves his sackcloth. He added, "Farewell, my children: Antony is departing, and will be no longer with you." At these words they embraced him, and he, stretching out his feet, without any other sign, calmly ceased to breathe. His death happened in the year 356, probably on the 17th January, on which the most ancient martyrologies name him, and which the Greek empire kept as a holy day soon after his death. He was one hundred and five years old. From his youth to that extreme old age, he always maintained the same fervour in his holy exercises: age to the last never made him change his diet (except in the use of a little oil) nor his manner of clothing; yet he lived without sickness, his sight was not impaired, his teeth were only worn, and not one was lost or loosened. The two disciples interred him according to his directions. About the year 561 his body[1] was discovered,

---

[1] This translation of his relics to Alexandria, though doubted of by some protestants, is incontestably confirmed by Victor of Tunone, (Chron. p. 11, in Scalig. Thesauro,) who lived then in banishment at Canope, only twelve miles from Alexandria; also, by St. Isidore of Seville, in the same age, Bede, Usuard, &c. They were removed to

in the reign of Justinian, and with great solemnity translated to Alexandria; thence it was removed to Constantinople, and is now at Vienne in France. Bollandus gives us an account of many miracles wrought by his intercession; particularly in what manner the distemper called the Sacred Fire, since that time St. Antony's Fire, miraculously ceased through his patronage, when it raged violently in many parts of Europe, in the eleventh century.

A most sublime gift of heavenly contemplation and prayer was the fruit of this great saint's holy retirement. Whole nights seemed to him short in

---

Constantinople when the Saracens made themselves masters of Egypt, about the year 635. (See Bollandus, p. 162, 1134.) They were brought to Vienne, in Dauphiné, by Joselin, a nobleman of that country, whom the emperor of Constantinople had gratified with that rich present, about the year 1070. These relics were deposited in the church of La Motte S. Didier, not far from Vienne, then a Benedictine priory belonging to the Abbey of Mont-Majour near Arles, but now an independent abbey of regular canons of St. Antony. In 1089, a pestilential erysipelas distemper, called the Sacred Fire, swept off great numbers in most provinces of France; public prayers and processions were ordered against this scourge; at length it pleased God to grant many miraculous cures of this dreadful distemper to those who implored his mercy through the intercession of St. Antony, especially before his relics; the church in which they were deposited was resorted to by great numbers of pilgrims, and his patronage was implored over the whole kingdom against this disease. A nobleman near Vienne, named Gaston, and his son Girond; devoted themselves and their estate to found and serve a hospital near this priory, for the benefit of the poor that were afflicted with this distemper: seven others joined them in their charitable attendance on the sick, whence a confraternity of laymen who served this hospital took its rise, and continued till Boniface VIII. converted the Benedictine priory into an abbey, which he bestowed on these hospitaller brothers, and giving them the religious rule of regular canons of St. Austin, declared the abbot general of this new order, called Regular Canons of St. Antony. An abbey in Paris which belongs to this order, is called Little St. Antony's, by which name it is distinguished from the great Cistercian nunnery of St. Antony. The general or abbot of St. Antony's, in Viennois, enjoys a yearly revenue of about forty thousand livres, according to Piganiol, Descr. de la Fr. t. 4, p. 249, and Dom. Beaunier, Rec. Abbayes de Fr. p. 982. The superiors of other houses of this order retain the name of commanders, and the houses are called commanderies, as when they were hospitallers; so that the general is the only abbot. See Bollandus, Beaunier, F. Longueval, Hist. de l'Eglise de France, l. 22, t. 8, p. 16, and Drouet, in the late edition of Moreri's Hist. Diction. V. Antoine, from memoirs communicated by M. Bordet, superior of the convent of this order at Paris.

those exercises, and when the rising sun in the morning seemed to him too soon to call him from his knees to his manual labour or other employments, he would lament that the incomparable sweetness which he enjoyed, in the more perfect freedom with which his heart was taken up in heavenly contemplation in the silent watching of the night, should be interrupted or abated. But the foundation of his most ardent charity, and that sublime contemplation by which his soul soared in noble and lofty flights above all earthly things, was laid in the purity and disengagement of his affections, the contempt of the world, a most profound humility, and the universal mortification of his senses and of the powers of his soul. Hence flowed that constant tranquillity and serenity of his mind, which was the best proof of a perfect mastery of his passions. St. Athanasius observes of him, that after thirty years spent in the closest solitude, "he appeared not to others with a sullen or savage, but with a most obliging sociable air." A heart that is filled with inward peace, simplicity, goodness, and charity, is a stranger to a lowering or contracted look. The main point in Christian mortification is the humiliation of the heart, one of its principal ends being the subduing of the passions. Hence true virtue always increases the sweetness and gentleness of the mind, though this is attended with an invincible constancy, and an inflexible firmness in every point of duty. That devotion or self-denial is false or defective, which betrays us into pride or uncharitableness; and whatever makes us sour, morose, or peevish, makes us certainly worse, and, instead of begetting in us a nearer resemblance of the divine nature, gives us a strong tincture of the temper of devils.

ST. MACARIUS OF ALEXANDRIA,
ANCHORET.

From Palladius, Bishop of Helenopolis, who had been his disciple.

A. D. 394.

St. Macarius the younger, a citizen of Alexandria, followed the business of a confectioner. Desirous to serve God with his whole heart, he forsook the world in the flower of his age, and spent upward of sixty years in the deserts, in the exercise of fervent penance and contemplation. He first retired into Thebais, or Upper Egypt, about the year 335. Having learned the maxims, and being versed in the practice of the most perfect virtue, under masters renowned for their sanctity; still aiming, if possible, at greater perfection, he quitted the Upper Egypt, and came to the Lower, before the year 373. In this part were three deserts almost adjoining to each other; that of Sceté, so called from a town of the same name on the borders of Lybia; that of the Cells, contiguous to the former, this name being given to it on account of the multitude of hermit-cells with which it abounded; and a third, which reached to the western branch of the Nile, called from a great mountain the desert of Nitria. St. Macarius had a cell in each of these deserts. When he dwelt in that of Nitria, it was his custom to give advice to strangers, but his chief residence was in that of the Cells. Each anchoret had here his separate cell, which he made his continued abode, except on Saturday and Sunday, when all assembled in one church to celebrate the divine mysteries, and partake of the holy communion. If any one was absent he was concluded to be sick, and was visited by the rest. When a stranger came to live among them, every one offered him his cell, and was ready to build another for himself. Their cells were not within sight of each other.

Their manual labour, which was that of making baskets or mats, did not interrupt the prayer of the heart. A profound silence reigned throughout the whole desert. Our saint received here the dignity of priesthood, and shone as a bright sun influencing this holy company, while St. Macarius the elder lived no less eminent in the wilderness of Sceté, forty miles distant. Palladius has recorded a memorable instance of self-denial professed and observed by these holy hermits. A present was made of a newly gathered bunch of grapes to St. Macarius: the holy man carried it to a neighbouring monk who was sick; he sent it to another; it passed in like manner to all the cells in the desert, and was brought back to Macarius, who was exceedingly rejoiced to perceive the abstinence of his brethren, but would not eat of the grapes himself.

The austerities of all the inhabitants of that desert were extraordinary; but St. Macarius in this regard far surpasses the rest. For seven years together he lived only on raw herbs and pulse, and for the three following years contented himself with four or five ounces of bread a day, and consumed only one little vessel of oil in a year; as Palladius assures us. His watchings were not less surprising, as the same author informs us. God had given him a body capable of bearing the greatest rigours; and his fervour was so intense, that whatever spiritual exercise he heard of, or saw practised by others, he resolved to copy the same. The reputation of the monastery of Tabenna, under St. Pachomius, drew him to this place in disguise, some time before the year 349. St. Pachomius told him that he seemed too far advanced in years to begin to accustom himself to their fastings and watchings; but at length admitted him, on condition he would observe all the rules and mortifications of the house. Lent approaching soon after, the monks were assiduous in preparations to pass that holy time in austerities, each according to his strength and fervour; some by fasting one, others two, three, or four days, without any kind of nourishment; some standing all day, others only sitting at their work. Macarius took some palm-tree leaves steeped in water, as materials for his work, and standing in a private corner, passed the whole time without eating, except a few green cabbage-leaves on Sundays. His hands were employed in almost continual labour and his heart conversed with God by prayer. If he left his station on any pressing occasion, he never stayed one moment longer than necessity required. Such a prodigy astonished the monks, who even remonstrated to the abbot at Easter against a singularity of this nature, which, if tolerated, might on several accounts be prejudicial to their community. St. Pachomius entreated God to know who this stranger was; and learning by revelation that he was the great Macarius, embraced him, thanked him for his edifying visit, and desired him to return to his desert, and there offer up his prayers for them. Our saint happened one day inadvertently to kill a gnat that was biting him in his cell; reflecting that he had lost the opportunity of suffering that mortification, he hastened from his cell to the marshes of Sceté, which abound with great flies, whose stings pierce even wild boars. There he continued six months exposed to those ravaging insects; and to such a degree was his whole body disfigured by them with sores and swellings, that when he returned he was only to be known by his voice. Some authors relate that he did this to overcome a temptation of the flesh.

The virtue of this great saint was often exercised with temptations. One was a suggestion to quit his desert and go to Rome, to serve the sick in the hospitals; which, by due reflection, he discovered to be a secret artifice of vain-glory, inciting him to attract the eyes and esteem of the world. True humility alone could discover the snare which lurked under the specious gloss of holy charity. Finding this enemy extremely importunate, he threw himself on the ground in his cell, and cried out to the fiends: "Drag me hence, if you can, by force, for I will not stir." Thus he lay till night, and by this vigorous resistance they were quite disarmed. As soon as he arose they renewed the assault; and he, to stand firm against them, filled two great baskets with sand, and laying them on his shoulders, travelled along the wilderness. A person of his acquaintance meeting him, asked him what he meant, and made an offer of easing him of his burden; but the saint made no other reply than this: "I am tormenting my tormentor." He returned home in the evening, much fatigued in body, but freed from the temptation. Palladius informs us, that St. Macarius, desiring to enjoy more perfectly the sweets of heavenly contemplation, at least for five days without interruption, immured himself within his cell for this purpose, and said to his soul: "Having taken up thy abode in heaven, where thou hast God and his holy angels to converse with, see that thou descend not thence: regard not earthly things." The two first days his heart overflowed with divine delights; but on the third he met with so violent a disturbance from the devil, that he was obliged to stop short of his design, and return to his usual manner of life. Contemplative souls often desire, in times of heavenly consolation, never to be interrupted in the glorious employment of love and praise: but the functions of Martha, the frailty and necessities of the human frame, and the temptations of the devil, force them, though reluctant, from their beloved object. Nay, God oftentimes withdraws himself, as the saint observed on this occasion, to make them sensible of their own weakness, and that this life is a state of trial. St. Macarius once saw in a vision, devils closing the eyes of the monks to drowsiness, and tempting them by diverse methods to distractions, during the time of public prayer. Some, as often as they approached, chased them away by a secret supernatural force, while others were in dalliance with their suggestions.

The saint burst into sighs and tears; and, when prayer was ended, admonished every one of his distractions, and of the snares of the enemy, with an earnest exhortation to employ, in that sacred duty, a more than ordinary watchfulness against his attacks. St. Jerom and others relate, that a certain anchoret in Nitria, having left one hundred crowns at his death, which he had acquired by weaving cloth, the monks of that desert met to deliberate what should be done with that money. Some were for having it given to the poor, others to the church: but Macarius, Pambo, Isidore, and others, who were called the fathers, ordained that the one hundred crowns should be thrown into the grave and buried with the corpse of the deceased, and that at the same time the following words should be pronounced: *May thy money be with thee to perdition.* This example struck such a terror into all the monks, that no one durst lay up any money by him.

Palladius, who, from 391, lived three years under our saint, was eye-witness to several miracles wrought by him. He relates that a certain priest, whose head, in a manner shocking to behold, was consumed by a cancerous sore, came to his cell, but was refused admittance; nay, the saint at first would not even speak to him. Palladius, by earnest entreaties, strove to prevail upon him to give at least some answer to so great an object of compassion. Macarius, on the contrary, urged that he was unworthy, and that God, to punish him for a sin of the flesh he was addicted to, had afflicted him with this disorder: however, that upon his sincere repentance, and promise never more during his life to presume to celebrate the divine mysteries, he would intercede for his cure. The priest confessed his sin, with a promise, pursuant to the ancient canonical discipline, never after to perform any priestly function. The saint thereupon absolved him by the imposition of hands; and a few days after the priest came back perfectly healed, glorifying God, and giving thanks to his servant

Palladius found himself tempted to sadness, on a suggestion from the devil, that he made no progress in virtue, and that it was to no purpose for him to remain in the desert. He consulted his master, who bade him persevere with fervour, never dwell on the temptation, and always answer instantly the fiend: "My love for Jesus Christ will not suffer me to quit my cell, where I am determined to abide in order to please and serve him agreeably to his will."

The two saints of the name of Macarius happened one day to cross the Nile together in a boat, when certain tribunes, or principal officers, who were there with their numerous trains, could not help observing to each other, that those men, from the cheerfulness of their aspect, must be exceeding happy in their poverty. Macarius of Alexandria, alluding to their name, which in Greek signifies *happy*, made this answer: "You have reason to call us happy, for this is our name. But if we are happy in despising the world, are not you miserable who live slaves to it?" These words, uttered with a tone of voice expressive of an interior conviction of their truth, had such an effect on the tribune who first spoke, that, hastening home, he distributed his fortune among the poor, and embraced an eremitical life. In 375, both these saints were banished for the catholic faith, at the instigation of Lucius, the Arian patriarch of Alexandria. Our saint died in the year 394, as Tillemont shows from Palladius. The Latins commemorate him on the second, the Greeks with the elder Macarius, on the nineteenth of January.

In the desert of Nitria there subsists at this day a monastery which bears the name of St. Macarius. The monastic rule, called St. Macarius's, in the code of rules, is ascribed to this of Alexandria. St. Jerom seems to have copied some things from it in his letter to Rusticus. The concord or collection of rules, gives us another, under the names of the two SS. Macariuses, Serapion (of Arsinoe, or the other of Nitria,) Paphnutius (of Becbale, priest of Sceté,) and thirty-four other abbots. It was probably collected from their discipline, or regulations and example. According to this latter, the monks fasted the whole year, except on Sundays, and the time from Easter to Whitsuntide; they observed the strictest poverty, and divided the day between manual labour and hours of prayer; hospitality was much recommended in this rule, but, for the sake of recollection, it was strictly forbid for any monk, except one who was deputed to entertain guests, ever to speak to any stranger without particular leave. The definition of a monk or anchoret, given by the abbot Rancé of La Trappe, is a lively portraiture of the great Macarius in the desert:—When, says he, a soul relishes God in solitude, she thinks no more of any thing but heaven, and forgets the earth, which has nothing in it that can now please her; she burns with the fire of divine love, and sighs only after God, regarding death as her greatest advantage: nevertheless, they will find themselves much mistaken, who, leaving the world, imagine they shall go to God by straight paths, by roads sown with lilies and roses, in which they will have no difficulties to conquer, but that the hand of God will turn aside whatever could raise any in their way, or disturb the tranquillity of their retreat: on the contrary, they must be persuaded that temptations will everywhere follow them, that there is neither state nor place in which they can be exempt, that the peace which God promises is procured amid tribulations, as the rosebuds amid thorns; God has not promised his servants that they shall not meet with trials, but that with the temptation, he will give them grace to be able to bear it: heaven is offered to us on no other conditions; it is a kingdom of conquest, the prize of victory—but, O God, what a prize!

ST. JOHN THE ALMONER, C.
PATRIARCH OF ALEXANDRIA.

HE received his surname from his profuse almsdeeds: was nobly descended, very rich, and a widower, at Amathus, in Cyprus, where, having buried all his children, he employed the whole income of his estate in the relief of the poor, and was no less remarkable for his great piety. The reputation of his sanctity raised him to the patriarchal chair of Alexandria, about the year 608, at which time he was upward of fifty years of age. On his arrival in that city he ordered an exact list to be taken of his masters. Being asked who these were, his answer was, " The Poor:" namely, on account of their great interest in the court of heaven in behalf of their benefactors. Their number amounted to seven thousand five hundred, whom he took under his special protection, and furnished with all necessaries. He prepared himself by this action, to receive the fulness of grace in his consecration. On the same day he published severe ordinances, but in the most humble terms, conjuring and commanding all to use just weights and measures, in order to prevent injustices and oppressions of the poor. He most rigorously forbade all his officers and servants ever to receive the least presents, which are no better than bribes, and bias the most impartial. Every Wednesday and Friday he sat the whole day on a bench before the church, that all might have free access to him to lay their grievances before him, and make known their necessities. He composed all differences, comforted the afflicted, and relieved the distressed. One of his first actions at Alexandria was to distribute the eighty thousand pieces of gold which he found in the treasury of his church among hospitals and monasteries. He consecrated to the service of the poor the great revenues of his see, then the first in all the East, both in riches and rank. Besides these, incredible charities flowed through his hands in continual streams, which his example excited every one to contribute according to their abilities. When his stewards complained that he impoverished his church, his answer was, that God would provide for them. To vindicate his conduct, and silence their complaints, he recounted to them a vision he had in his youth of a beautiful woman, brighter than the sun, with an olive garland on her head, whom he understood to be Charity, or compassion for the miserable; who said to him: "I am the eldest daughter of the great King. If you enjoy my favour, I will introduce you to the great monarch of the universe. No one has so great an interest with him as myself, who was the occasion of his coming down from heaven to become man for the redemption of mankind." When the Persians had plundered the East, and sacked Jerusalem, St. John entertained all that fled from their swords into Egypt; and sent to Jerusalem, for the use of the poor there, besides a large sum of money, one thousand sacks of corn, as many of pulse, one thousand pounds of iron, one thousand loads of fish, one thousand barrels of wine, and one thousand Egyptian workmen to assist in rebuilding the churches: adding in his letter to Modestus the bishop, that he wished it had been in his power to have gone in person, and contributed the labour of his hands toward carrying on that holy work. He also sent two bishops and an abbot to ransom captives. No number of necessitous objects, no losses, no straits to which he saw himself often reduced, discouraged him, or made him lose his confidence in Divine Providence, and resources never failed him in the end. When a certain person, whom he had privately relieved with a most bountiful alms, expressed his gratitude in the strongest terms, the saint cut him short, saying, "Brother, I have not yet spilled my blood for you, as Jesus Christ my master and my God commands me." A certain merchant, who had been thrice ruined by shipwrecks, had as often found relief from the good patriarch, who the third time gave him a ship belonging to the church, laden with twenty thousand measures of corn. This vessel was driven by storm to the British Islands, and a famine raging there, the owners sold their cargo to great advantage, and brought back a considerable value in exchange, one-half in money, the other in pewter.

The patriarch lived himself in the greatest austerity and poverty as to diet, apparel, and furniture. A person of distinction in the city being informed that our saint had but one blanket on his bed, and this a very sorry one, sent him one of value, begging his acceptance of it, and that he would make use of it for the sake of the donor. He accepted of it and put it to the intended use, but it was only for one night, and this he passed in great uneasiness, with severe self-reproaches for being so richly covered, while so many of his masters (his familiar term for the poor) were so ill accommodated. The next morning he sold it and gave the price to the poor. The friend being informed of it, bought it for thirty-six pieces, and gave it him a second, and a third time; for the saint always disposed of it in the same way, saying facetiously: "We shall see who will be tired first." He was very well versed in the Scriptures, though a stranger to the pomp of profane eloquence. The functions of his ministry, prayer, and pious reading employed his whole time. He studied with great circumspection to avoid the least idle word, and never chose to speak about temporal affairs unless compelled by necessity, and then only in very few words. If he heard any detract from the reputation of their neighbour, he was ingenious in turning the discourse to some other subject, and he forbade them his house, to deter others from that vice. Hearing that when an emperor was chosen it was customary for certain carvers to present to him four or five blocks of marble to choose one out of them for his tomb, he caused his grave to be half dug, and appointed a man to come to him on all occasions of pomp, and say: "My lord, your tomb is unfinished: be pleased to give your orders to have it completed, for you know not the hour when death will seize you." The remembrance of the rigorous account which we are to give to God made him often burst into the most pathetic expressions of holy fear. But humility was his distinguishing virtue, and he always expressed, both in words and actions, the deepest sentiments of his own nothingness, sinfulness, miseries, and pride. He often admired how perfectly the saints saw their own imperfections, and that they were dust, worms, and unworthy to be ranked among men.

The saint regarded injuries as his greatest gain and happiness. He always disarmed his enemies of their rancour by meekness, and frequently fell at the feet of those who insulted him, to beg their pardon. Nicetas, the governor, had formed a project of a new tax, very prejudicial to the poor. The patriarch modestly spoke in their defence. The governor in a passion left him abruptly. St. John sent him this message toward evening: "The sun is going to set:" putting him in mind of the advice of the apostle: *Let not the sun go down upon your anger.* This admonition had its intended effect on the governor, and pierced him to the quick. He arose and went to the patriarch, bathed in tears, asked his pardon, and by way of atonement promised never more to give ear to informers and talebearers. St. John confirmed him in that resolution, adding that he never believed any man whatever against another till he himself had examined the party accused; and that he punished all calumniators and talebearers in a manner which might deter others from so fatal a vice. Having in vain exhorted a certain nobleman to forgive one with whom he was at variance, he soon after invited him to his private chapel to assist at his mass, and there desired him to recite with him the Lord's prayer. The saint stopped at that petition: *Forgive us our trespasses as we forgive those that trespass against us.* When the nobleman had recited it alone, he conjured him to reflect on what he had been saying to God at the hour of the tremendous mysteries— begging to be pardoned in the same manner as he forgave others. The other, feeling himself struck to the heart, fell at his feet, and from that moment was sincerely reconciled with his adversary. The saint often exhorted men against rash judgment, saying: "Circumstances easily deceive us: magistrates are bound to examine and judge criminals; but what have private persons to do with others, unless it be to vindicate them?" He used to relate many examples of persons who were found innocent and eminent saints, though they had been condemned by the world upon circumstances; as that of a certain monk, who brought to that city a Jewess whom he had converted, but was accused as guilty of lewdness with her, and cruelly scourged, for he said nothing to justify himself, out of a desire of humiliation and suffering. But his innocence and sanctity were soon after brought to light. St. John employed Sophronius and John Moschus in reducing to the faith the Severians and other heretics. Observing that many amused themselves without the church during part of the divine office, which was then of a very considerable length, he followed them out and seated himself among them, saying: "My children, the shepherd must be with his flock." This action, which covered them with confusion, prevented their being guilty of that irreverence any more. As he was one day going to church, he was accosted on the way by a woman who demanded justice against her son-in-law that had injured her. The woman being ordered by some standers-by to wait the patriarch's return from church, he, overhearing them, said: "How can I hope that God will hear my prayer if I put off the petition of this woman?" Nor did he stir from the place till he had redressed the grievance complained of.

Nicetas, the governor, persuaded the saint to accompany him to Constantinople to pay a visit to the emperor. St. John was admonished from heaven while he was on his way, at Rhodes, that his death drew near, and said to Nicetas: "You invite me to the emperor of the earth, but the king of heaven calls me to himself." He therefore sailed for Cyprus, and soon after died happily at Amathus, about the year of our Lord 619, in the sixty-fourth of his age, and tenth of his patriarchal dignity. His body was afterward carried to Constantinople, where it was kept a long time. The Turkish emperor made a present of it to Matthias, king of Hungary, which he deposited in his chapel at Buda. In 1530 it was translated to Tall, near Presbourg; and in 1632 to the cathedral itself of Presbourg, where, according to Bollandus, it still remains. The Greeks honour this saint on the 11th of November, the day of his death; but the Roman Martyrology on the 23d of January, the day marked for the translation of his relics. His life, written by his two vicars, Sophronius and Moschus, is lost; but we have that by Leontius, bishop of Naplouse in Cyprus, from the relation of the saint's clergy, commended in the seventh general council. It is published more correct by Rosweide and Bollandus. We have another life of this saint, conformable to the former, given us by Metaphrastes. See Le Quien, Oriens Christi, t. 2, p. 446.

ST. FRANCIS OF SALES,
BISHOP AND CONFESSOR.

From his writings, and authentic Lives, chiefly that written by his nephew, Charles Augustus de Sales.

A. D. 1622.

THE parents of this saint were Francis, count of Sales, and Frances of Sionas. The countess being with child, offered her fruit to God with the most fervent prayers, begging he would preserve it from the corruption of the world, and rather deprive her of the comfort of seeing herself a mother, than suffer her to give birth to a child who should ever become his enemy by sin. The saint was born at Sales, three leagues from Annecy, the seat of that noble family; and his mother was delivered of him when she was but seven months advanced in her pregnancy. Hence he was reared with difficulty, and was so weak that his life, during his infancy, was often despaired of by physicians. However, he escaped the danger, and grew robust: he was very beautiful, and the sweetness of his countenance won the affections of all who saw him: but the meekness of his temper, the pregnancy of his wit, his modesty, tractableness, and obedience were far more valuable qualifications. The countess could scarce suffer the child out of her sight, lest any tincture of vice might infect his soul. Her first care was to inspire him with the most profound respect for the church, and all holy things; and she had the comfort to observe in him a recollection and devotion at his prayers far above his age. She read to him the lives of the saints, adding recollections suited to his capacity; and she took care to have him with her when she visited the poor, making him the distributer of her alms, and to do such little offices for them as he was able. He would set by his own meat for their relief, and when he had nothing left to bestow on them, would beg for them of all his relations. His horror of a lie, even in his infancy, made him prefer any disgrace or chastisement to the telling of the least wilful untruth.

His mother's inclination for a domestic preceptor, to prevent his being corrupted by wicked youth in colleges, was overruled by her husband's persuasion of the usefulness of emulation for advancing children in their studies; hoping his son's virtue and modesty would, under God, be a sufficient guard of his innocency. He was accordingly sent to Rocheville, at six years of age, and some time after to Annecy. An excellent memory, a solid judgment, and a good application could not fail of great progress. The young count spent as much of his time as possible in private studies and lectures of piety, especially that of the lives of saints; and by his diligence always doubled or trebled his school tasks. He showed an early inclination for the ecclesiastical state, and obtained his father's consent, though not without some reluctance, for his receiving tonsure in the year 1578, and the eleventh of his age. He was sent afterward, under the care of a virtuous priest, his preceptor, to pursue his studies in Paris; his mother having first instilled into him steady principles of virtue, a love of prayer, and a dread of sin and its occasions. She often repeated to him those words of Queen Blanche to her son St. Lewis, king of France: "I had rather see you dead, than hear you had committed one mortal sin." On his arrival at Paris, he entered the Jesuits' schools, and went through his rhetoric and philosophy with great applause. In pure obedience to his father's orders, he learned in the academy to ride, dance, and fence, whence he acquired that easy behaviour which he retained ever after. But these exercises, as matters of amusement, did not hinder his close application to the study of the Greek and

Hebrew languages, and of positive divinity for six years, under the famous Genebrard and Maldonatus. But his principal concern all this time was a regular course of piety, by which he laboured to sanctify himself and all his actions. Pious meditation and the study of the Holy Scripture were his beloved entertainments: and he never failed to carry about him that excellent book, called the Spiritual Combat. He sought the conversation of the virtuous, particularly of F. Angelus Joyeuse, who, from a duke and marshal of France, was become a Capuchin friar. The frequent discourses of this good man on the necessity of mortification, induced the count to add to his usual austerities the wearing of a hair-shirt three days in the week. His chief resort during his stay at Paris, was to some churches, that especially of St. Stephen des Grez, as being one of the most retired. Here he made a vow of perpetual chastity, putting himself under the special patronage of the Blessed Virgin. God, to purify his heart, permitted a thick darkness insensibly to overspread his mind, and a spiritual dryness and melancholy to overwhelm him. He seemed, from a perfect tranquillity and peace of mind, to be almost brought to the brink of despair. Seized with the greatest terrors, he passed nights and days in tears and lamentations, and suffered more than can be conceived by those who have not felt the severity of such interior conflicts. The bitterness of his grief threw him into a deep jaundice; he could neither eat, drink, nor sleep. His preceptor laboured, but all in vain, to discover the cause of this disorder, and find out a remedy. At last, Francis, being at prayer in the same church of St. Stephen, cast his eyes on a picture of our Lady: this awaking his confidence in her intercession, he prostrated himself on the ground, and, as unworthy to address the Father of all consolation, begged that she would be his advocate, and procure him the grace to love God with his whole heart. That very moment he found himself eased of his grief as of a heavy weight taken off his heart; and his former peace and tranquillity restored, which he ever after enjoyed. He was now eighteen years old, when his father recalled him from Paris, and sent him to Padua, to study the law, where his master was the celebrated Guy Pancirola; this was in the year 1554. He chose the learned and pious Jesuit, Antony Possevin, for his spiritual director; who at the same time explained to him St. Thomas's Sum, and they read together Bellarmin's controversies. His nephew Augustus gives us his written rule of life, which he made at Padua: it chiefly shows his perpetual attention to the presence of God, his care to offer up every action to him, and implore his aid at the beginning of each. Falling sick, he was despaired of by the physicians, and he himself expected with joy his last moment. His preceptor, Deage, who had ever attended him, asked him with tears, what he had to order about his funeral and other matters. "Nothing," answered he cheerfully, "unless it be, that my body be given to the anatomy theatre to be dissected; for it will be a comfort to me if I can be of any advantage when dead, having been of none while alive. Thus I may also prevent some of the disorders and quarrels which happen between the young physicians and the friends of the dead, whose bodies they often dig up." However, he recovered; and, by his father's orders, being twenty years of age, commenced doctor in laws, with great applause and pomp, in presence of forty-eight doctors. After which he travelled through Italy, to see the antiquities and visit the holy places there. He went to Rome by Ferrara, and returned by Loretto and Venice. To any insult offered him on the road he returned only meekness; for which he met with remarkable blessings from heaven. The sight of the pompous remains of ancient Rome gave him a feeling contempt of worldly grandeur: but the tombs of the martyrs drew everywhere tears of devotion from his eyes. Upon his return his father received him with great joy, at his castle of Tuille, where he had prepared for him a good library of books.

All persons were charmed with the young count, but none so much as the great Antony Favre, afterward first president of the parliament of Chamberry, and Claudius Cranier, the learned and truly apostolic bishop of Geneva, who already consulted him as an oracle. His father had a very good match in view for him, and obtained in his behalf, from the duke of Savoy, patents creating him counsellor of the parliament of Chamberry. Francis modestly, but very firmly refused both; yet durst not propose to his parents his design of receiving holy orders; for the tonsure was not an absolute renouncing of the world. At last, he discovered it to his pious preceptor, Deage, and begged of him to mention it to his father; but this he declined, and used his utmost endeavours to dissuade the young count from such a resolution, as he was the eldest son, and destined by the order of nature for another state. Francis answered all his reasonings, but could not prevail on him to charge himself with the commission. He had then recourse to a cousin, Lewis of Sales, a priest and canon of Geneva, who obtained the consent of his parents, but not without the greatest difficulty. His cousin also obtained for him from the pope, without his knowledge, the provostship of the church of Geneva, then vacant: but the young clergyman held out a long time before he would accept of it. At last he yielded, and took possession of that dignity, and was in a short time after promoted to holy orders by his diocesan, who, as soon as he was deacon, employed him in preaching. His first sermons gained him an extraordinary reputation, and were accompanied with incredible success. He delivered the word of God with a mixture of majesty and modesty; had a strong, sweet voice, and an animated manner of gesture, far from any affectation or vanity; but what chiefly affected the hearts of his hearers was the humility and unction with which he spoke from the abundance of his own heart. Before he preached, he always renewed the fervour of his heart before God, by secret sighs and prayers. He studied as much at the foot of the crucifix as in books, being persuaded that the essential quality of a preacher is to be a man of prayer. He received the holy order of priesthood with extraordinary preparation and devotion, and seemed filled by it with an apostolical spirit. He every day began his functions by celebrating the holy mysteries early in the morning, in which, by his eyes and countenance of fire, the inward flames of his soul appeared. He then heard the confessions of all sorts of people, and preached. He was observed to decline with the utmost care whatever might gain him the applause of men, seeking only to please God, and to advance his glory. He chiefly resorted to cottages and country villages, instructing an infinity of poor people. His piety, his charity to the poor, his disinterestedness, his care of the sick and those in prison, endeared him to all: but nothing was so moving as his meekness, which no provocation was ever capable of disturbing. He conversed among all as their father, with a fellow-feeling of all their wants, being all to all. He was indeed naturally of a hasty and passionate temper, as he himself confesses; and we find in his writings a certain fire and impetuosity which renders it unquestionable. On this account, from his youth he made meekness his favourite virtue, and by studying in the school of a God who was meek and humble of heart, he learned that important lesson to such perfection as to convert his predominent passion into his characteristical virtue. The Calvinists ascribed principally to his meekness the wonderful conversions he made among them. They were certainly the most obstinate of people at that time, near Geneva: yet St. Francis converted no less than seventy-two thousand of them.

Before the end of this first year of his ministry, in 1591, he erected at Annecy a confraternity of the Holy Cross, the associates of which were obliged to instruct the ignorant, to comfort and exhort the sick and prisoners, and to beware of all lawsuits, which seldom fail to shipwreck Christian charity. A Calvinistical minister took occasion from this institution to write against the honour paid by catholics to the cross. Francis answered him by his book entitled, The Standard of the Cross. At this time, fresh matter presented itself for the exercise of the saint's zeal. The bishop of Geneva was formerly lord of that city, paying an acknowledgment to the duke of Savoy. While these two were disputing about the sovereignty the Genevans expelled them both, and formed themselves into a republic in alliance with the Switzers; and their city became the centre of Calvinism. Soon after the protestant canton of Bern seized the country of Vaux and the republic of Geneva, the duchy of Chablais, with the bailiwicks of Gex, Terni, and Gaillard; and there by violence established their heresy, which from that time had kept quiet possession for sixty years. The Duke Charles Emmanuel had recovered these territories, and resolving to restore the catholic religion, wrote in 1594 to the bishop of Geneva to recommend that work to him. The wise ones, according to this world, regarded the undertaking as impracticable; and the most resolute, whether ecclesiastics or religious, were terrified at its difficulties and dangers. Francis was the only one that offered himself for the work, and was joined by none but his cousin-german, Lewis de Sales. The tears and remonstrances of his parents and friends to dissuade him from the undertaking made no impression on his courageous soul. He set out with his cousin on the 9th of September, in 1594. Being arrived on the frontiers of Chablais, they sent back their horses, the more perfectly to imitate the apostles. On his arrival at Thonon, the capital of Chablais, situate on the lake of Geneva, he found in it only seven catholics. After having commended their souls to God, and earnestly implored his mercy through the intercession of the guardian angels and tutelar saints of the country, he was obliged to take up his quarters in the castle of Allinges, where the governor and garrison were catholics, two leagues from Thonon, whither he went every day, visiting also the neighbouring country. The Calvinists for a long time shunned him, and some even attempted his life. Two assassins, hired by others, having missed him at Thonon, lay in wait to murder him on his return; but a guard of soldiers had been sent to escort him safe, the conspiracy having taken wind. The saint obtained their pardon, and overcome by his lenity and formed by his holy instructions, they both became very virtuous converts. All our saint's relations, and many friends whom he particularly respected for their great virtue and prudence, solicited him by the most pressing letters to abandon such a dangerous and fruitless enterprise. His father, to the most tender entreaties, added his positive commands to him to return home, telling him that all prudent persons called his resolution to continue his mission a foolish obstinacy and madness; that he had already done more than was needful, and that his mother was dying of grief for his long absence, the fear of losing him entirely, and the hardships, atrocious slanders, and continual alarms and dangers in which he lived. To compel him to abandon this undertaking, the father forbade his friends to write any more to him, or to send him necessary supplies. Nevertheless, St. Francis persevered, and at length his patience, zeal, and eminent virtue wrought upon the most obdurate, and insensibly wore away their prejudices. His first converts were among the soldiers, whom he brought over, not only to the faith, but also to an entire change of manners and strict virtue, from habits of swearing, duelling, and drunkenness. He was near four years, however, without any great fruit among the inhabitants, till the year 1597, when God was pleased to touch several of them with his grace. The harvest daily increased, both in the town and country, so plentifully that a supply of new labourers from Annecy was necessary, and the bishop sent some Jesuits and Capuchins to carry on the good work with Francis and under his direction. In 1598 the public exercise of the catholic religion was restored, and Calvinism banished by the duke's orders over all Chablais and the two bailiwicks of Terni and Gaillard. Though the plague raged violently at Thonon, this did not hinder Francis either by day or night from assisting the sick in their last moments; and God preserved him from the contagion, which seized and swept off several of his fellow-labourers. It is incredible what fatigues and hardships he underwent in the course of this mission: with what devotion and tears he daily recommended the work of God: with what invincible courage he braved the greatest dangers: with what meekness and patience he bore all manner of affronts and calumnies. Baron D'Avuli, a man of quality and of great worth and learning, highly esteemed among the Calvinists, and at Geneva, being converted by him, induced him to go thither to have a conference with the famous minister La Faye. The minister during the whole conference was ever shifting the matter in debate as he found himself embarrassed and pressed by his antagonist. His disadvantage being so evident that he himself could read it in the countenance of every one present, he broke off the conference by throwing out a whole torrent of injurious language on Francis, who bore it with so much meekness as not to return the least sharp answer. During the whole course of his ministry in these parts, the violent measures, base cowardice in declining all dispute, and the shameful conduct of the ministers in other respects, set the saint's behaviour and his holy cause still in a more shining light. In 1597 he was commissioned by Pope Clement VIII. to confer with Theodore Beza at Geneva, the most famous minister of the Calvinist party, in order to win him back to the catholic church. He accordingly paid him four visits in that city, gained a high place in that heresiarch's esteem, and made him often hesitate in deep silence and with distracted looks, whether he should return to the Roman catholic church or not, wherein he owned from the beginning that salvation was attainable. St. Francis had great hopes of bringing him over in a fifth visit, but his private conferences had alarmed the Genevans so much that they guarded Beza too close for him to find admittance to him again, and Beza died soon after. 'Tis said, that a little before his death he lamented very much he could not see Francis. It is certain, from his first conference with him, he had ever felt a violent conflict within himself, between truth and duty on one hand, and on the other the pride of being head of a party, the shame of recanting, inveterate habits, and certain secret engagements in vice, to which he continued enslaved to the last. The invincible firmness and constancy of the saint appeared in the recovery of the revenues of the curacies and other benefices which had been given to the orders of St. Lazarus and St. Maurice; the restoration of which after many difficulties he effected by the joint authority of the pope and the duke of Savoy. In 1596 he celebrated mass on Christmas-day in the church of St. Hippolytus at Thonon, and had then made seven or eight hundred converts. From this time he charged himself with the parish of the town, and established two other catholic parishes in the country. In the beginning of the year 1599 he had settled zealous clergymen in all the parishes of the whole territory.

The honours the saint received from the pope, the duke of Savoy, the cardinal of Medicis, and all the church, and the high reputation which its virtues had acquired him, never made the least impression on his humble mind, dead to all notions of pride and vanity. His delight was with the poor: the most honourable functions he left to others, and chose for himself the meanest and most laborious. Every one desired to have him for director, wherever he went: and his extraordinary sweetness, in conjunction with his eminent piety, reclaimed as many vicious catholics as it converted heretics. In 1599 he went to Annecy to visit his diocesan, Granier, who had procured him to be made his coadjutor. The fear of resisting God, in refusing this charge when pressed upon him by the pope, in conjunction with his bishop and the duke of Savoy, at last extorted his consent; but the apprehension of the obligations annexed to episcopacy was so strong that it threw him into an illness which had like to have cost him his life. On his recovery he set out for Rome to receive his bulls, and to confer with his Holiness on matters relating to the missions of Savoy. He was highly honoured by all the great men at Rome, and received of the pope the bulls for being consecrated bishop of Nicopolis and coadjutor of Geneva. On this occasion he made a visit of devotion to Loretto, and returned to Annecy before the end of the year 1599. Here he preached the Lent the year following, and assisted his father during his last sickness, heard his general confession, and administered to him the rites of the church. An illness he was seized with at Annecy made him defer his consecration.

On his recovery he was obliged to go to Paris on affairs of his diocess, and was received there by all sorts of persons with all the regard due to his extraordinary merit. The king was then at Fontainbleau; but the saint was desired to preach the Lent to the court in the chapel of the Louvre. This he did in a manner that charmed every one, and wrought innumerable wonderful conversions. The duchesses of Mercœur and Longueville sent him thereupon a purse of gold: he admired the embroidery, but gave it back, with thanks to them for honouring his discourses with their presence and good example. He preached a sermon against the pretended reformation, to prove it destitute of a lawful mission; it being begun at Meaux, by Peter Clark, a wool-carder; at Paris, by Masson Riviere, a young man called to the ministry by a company of laymen; and elsewhere after the like manner. This sermon converted many Calvinists; among others the countess of Perdricuville, who was one of the most obstinate learned ladies of the sect; she consulted her ministers, and repaired often to Francis's conferences, till she had openly renounced Calvinism with all her numerous family. The whole illustrious house of Raconis followed her example, and so many others, even of the most inveterate of the sect, that it made Cardinal Perron, a man famous for controversy, say: " I can confute the Calvinists; but to persuade and convert them, you must carry them to the coadjutor of Geneva." Henry IV. was charmed with his preaching, and consulted him several times in matters relating to the direction of his conscience. There was no project of piety going forward about which he was not advised with. He promoted the establishment of the Carmelite nuns in France, and the introduction of F. Berulle's congregation of the oratory. The king himself earnestly endeavoured to detain him in France by promises of twenty thousand livres pension, and the first vacant bishopric; but Francis said God had called him against his will to the bishopric of Geneva, and he thought it his obligation to keep it till his death; that the small revenue he had sufficed for his maintenance, and more would only be an incumbrance. The king was astonished at his disinterestedness, when he understood that the bishopric of Geneva, since the revolt of that city, did not yield the incumbent above four or five thousand livres, that is, not two hundred and fifty-nine pounds a year.

Some envious courtiers endeavoured to give the king a suspicion of his being a spy. The saint heard this accusation just as he was going into the pulpit; yet he preached as usual without the least concern; and that prince was too well convinced of the calumny by his sanctity and candour. After a nine months' stay in Paris, he set out with the king's letters, and heard on the road that Granier, bishop of Geneva, was dead. He hastened to Sales-Castle, and as soon as clear of the first visits, made a twenty days' retreat to prepare himself for his consecration. He made a general confession, and laid down a plan of life, which he ever punctually observed. This was, never to wear any silk or camlets, or any cloths but woollen, as before: to have no paintings in his house but of devotion: no magnificence in furniture: never to use coach or litter, but to make his visits on foot: his family to consist of two priests, one for his chaplain, the other to take care of his temporalities and servants: nothing but common meats to be served at his table: to be always present at all feasts of devotion kept in any church in town: his regulation with respect to alms was incredible for his revenues: to go to the poor and sick in person: to rise every day at four, make an hour's meditation, say lauds and prime, then morning prayers with his family: to read the Scripture till seven, then say mass, which he did every day, afterward to apply to affairs till dinner, which being over, he allowed an hour for conversation, the rest of the afternoon he allotted to business and prayer. After supper he read a pious book to his family for an hour, then night prayers; after which he said matins. He fasted all Fridays and Saturdays, and our Lady's eves: he privately wore a hair-shirt, and used the discipline, but avoided all ostentatious austerities. But his exact regularity and uniformity of life, with a continued practice of interior self-denials, was the best mortification. He redoubled his fasts, austerities, and prayers, as the time of his consecration drew nearer. This was performed on the third of December, 1602. He immediately applied himself to preaching and the other functions of his charge. He was exceeding cautious in conferring holy orders. He ordained but few, neither was it without the strictest scrutiny passed upon all their qualifications for the priesthood. He was very zealous, both by word and example, in promoting the instruction of the ignorant by explanations of the catechism, on Sundays and holydays; and his example had a great influence over the parish priests in this particular, as also over the laity, both young and old. He inculcated to all the making, every hour when the clock struck, the sign of the cross, with a fervent aspiration on the passion of Christ. He severely forbade the custom of Valentines, or giving boys, in writing, the names of girls to be admired and attended on by them: and to abolish it, he changed it into giving billets with the names of certain saints for them to honour and imitate in a particular manner. He performed the visitation of his diocess as soon as possible, published a new ritual, set on foot ecclesiastical conferences, and regulated all things; choosing St. Charles Borromeo for his model.

Above all things he hated lawsuits, and strictly commanded all ecclesiastics to avoid them, and refer all disputes to arbitration. He said they were such occasions of sins against charity, that, if any one during the course of a lawsuit had escaped them, that alone would suffice for his canonization. Toward the close of the visitation of his diocess, he reformed several monasteries. That of Six appealed to the parliament of Chamberry: but our saint was supported there, and carried his point. While Francis was at Six, he heard that a valley, three leagues off, was in the utmost desolation, by the tops of two mountains that had fallen, and buried several villages, with the inhabitants and cattle. He crawled over unpassable ways to comfort and relieve these poor people, who had neither clothes to cover, nor cottages to shelter them, nor bread to stay their hunger; he mingled his tears with theirs, relieved them, and obtained from the duke a remission of their taxes. The city of Dijon having procured leave from the duke of Savoy, the saint preached the Lent there in 1604, with wonderful fruit; but refused the present offered him by the city on that occasion. Being solicited by Henry IV. to accept of a considerable abbey, the saint refused it; alleging that he dreaded riches as much as others could desire them; and that, the less he had of them, the less he would have to answer for. That king offered to name him to the dignity of cardinal at the next promotion; but the saint made answer, that though he did not despise the offered dignity, he was persuaded that great titles would not sit well upon him, and might raise fresh obstacles to his salvation. He was also thought of at Rome as a very fit person to be promoted to that dignity, but was himself the only one who everywhere opposed and crossed the design. Being desired on another occasion by the same king to accept of a pension; the saint begged his majesty to suffer it to remain in the hands of his comptroller till he should call for it; which handsome refusal much astonished that great prince, who could not forbear saying, "That the bishop of Geneva, by the happy independence in which his virtue had placed him, was as far above him as he by his royal dignity was above his subjects." The saint preached the next Lent at Chamberry, at the request of the parliament, which, notwithstanding, at that very time seized his temporalities for refusing to publish a monitory at its request; the saint alleging, that it was too trifling an affair, and that the censures of the church were to be used more reservedly. To the notification of the seizure he only answered obligingly that he thanked God for teaching him by it that a bishop is to be altogether spiritual. He neither desisted from preaching nor complained to the duke, but heaped most favours on such as most insulted him, till the parliament, being ashamed, granted him of their own accord a replevy. But the great prelate found more delight in preaching in small villages than amid such applause, though he everywhere met with the like fruit; and he looked on the poor as the object of his particular care. He took a poor dumb and deaf man into his family, taught him by signs, and by them received his confession. His steward often found it difficult to provide for his family by reason of his great alms, and used to threaten to leave him. The saint would answer:

"You say right; I am an incorrigible creature, and what is worse, I look as if I should long continue so." Or at other times, pointing to the crucifix: "How can we deny any thing to a God who reduced himself to this condition for the love of us!"

Pope Paul V. ordered our saint to be consulted about the school dispute between the Dominicans and Jesuits on the grace of God, or de auxiliis. His opinion appears from his book, On the Love of God: but he answered his Holiness in favour of neutrality, which he ever observed in school opinions; complaining often in how many they occasioned the breach of charity, and spent too much of their precious time, which, by being otherwise employed, might be rendered more conducive to God's honour. In 1609 he went to Bellay, and consecrated bishop John Peter Camus, one of the most illustrious prelates of the church of France, and linked to our saint by the strictest bands of holy friendship. He wrote the book entitled The Spirit of St. Francis of Sales, consisting of many of his ordinary sayings and actions, in which his spirit shines with great advantage, discovering a perpetual recollection always absorbed in God, and a constant overflowing of sweetness and divine love. His writings to this day breathe the same; every word distils that love and meekness with which his heart was filled. It is this which makes his epistles, which we have to the number of five hundred and twenty-nine, in seven books, to be an inestimable treasure of moving instructions, suitable to all sorts of persons and circumstances. His incomparable book, the Introduction to a Devout Life, was originally letters to a lady in the world, which, at the pressing instances of many friends, he formed into a book and finished, to show that devotion suited Christians in a secular life, no less than in cloisters. Villars, the archbishop of Vienna, wrote to him upon it: "Your book charms, inflames, and puts me in raptures, as often as I open any part of it." The author received the like applause and commendations from all parts, and it was immediately translated into all the languages of Europe. Henry IV. of France was extremely pleased with it; his queen, Mary of Medicis, sent it richly bound and adorned with jewels to James I. of England, who was wonderfully taken with. it, and asked his bishops why none of them could write with such feeling and unction. There was however one religious order in which this book was much censured, as if it had allowed of gallantry and scurrilous jests, and approved of balls and comedies, which was very far from the saint's doctrine. A preacher of that order had the rashness and presumption to declaim bitterly against the book in a public sermon, to cut it to pieces, and burn it in the very pulpit. The saint bore this outrage without the least resentment; so perfectly was he dead to self-love. This appears more wonderful to those who know how jealous authors are of their works, as the offspring of their reason and judgment, of which men are of all things the fondest.

His book on the Love of God cost him much more reading, study, and meditation. In it he paints his own soul. He describes the feeling sentiments of divine love, its state of fervour, of dryness, of trials, suffering, and darkness : in explaining which he calls in philosophy to his assistance. He writes on this sublime subject what he had learned by his own experience. Some parts of this book are only to be understood by those souls who have gone through these states; yet the author has been ever justly admired for the performance. The general of the Carthusians had wrote to him upon his Introduction, advising him to write no more, because nothing else could equal that book. But seeing this, he bade him never cease writing, because his latter works always surpassed the former: and James I. was so delighted with the book that he expressed a great desire to see the author. This being told the saint, he cried out: "Ah! who will give me the wings of a dove, and I will fly to the king, into that great island, formerly.

the country of saints, but now overwhelmed with the darkness of error. If the duke will permit me, I will arise and go to that great Ninive: I will speak to the king, and will announce to him, with the hazard of my life, the word of the Lord." In effect, he solicited the duke of Savoy's consent, but could never obtain it. That jealous sovereign feared lest he should be drawn in to serve another state, or sell to some other his right to Geneva; on which account he often refused him leave to go to preach in France, when invited by many cities. His other works are sermons which are not finished as they were preached, except perhaps that on the Invention of the Cross. We have also his Preparation for Mass: his Instructions for Confessors: a collection of his Maxims, pious Breathings, and Sayings, wrote by the bishop of Bellay: some Fragments, nd his Entertainments to his nuns of the Visitation, in which he recommends to them the most perfect interior self-denial, a disengagement of affections from all things temporal, and obedience. The institution of that order may be read in the life of B. Frances Chantal. St. Francis designing his new order to be such that all, even the sickly and weak, might be admitted into it, he chose for it the rule of St. Austin, as commanding few extraordinary bodily austerities, and would have it possess funds and settlements in common, to prevent being carried off from the interior life by anxious cares about necessaries. But then he requires from each person so strict a practice of poverty as to allow no one the propriety or even the long use of any thing; and orders them every year to change chambers, beds, crosses, beads, and books. He will have no manner of account to be made of birth, wit, or talents; but only of humility: he obliges them only to the Little office of our Lady, which all might easily learn to understand; meditations, spiritual reading, recollection, and retreats, abundantly compensating the defect. All his regulations tend to instil a spirit of piety, charity, meekness, and simplicity. He subjects his order to the bishop of each place, without any general. Pope Paul V. approved it, and erected the congregation of the Visitation into a religious order.

St. Francis, finding his health decline, and his affairs to multiply, after having consulted Cardinal Frederic Borromeo, archbishop of Milan, chose for his coadjutor in the bishopric of Geneva, his brother, John Francis of Sales, who was consecrated bishop of Chalcedon at Turin, in 1618. But the saint still applied himself to his functions as much as ever. He preached the Lent at Grenoble, in 1617, and again in 1618, with his usual conquests of souls; converting many Calvinists, and among these the duke of Lesdiguieres. In 1619 he accompanied to Paris the cardinal of Savoy, to demand the sister of King Lewis XIII., Christina of France, in marriage for the prince of Piedmont. He preached the Lent in St. André-des-Arcs, and had always such a numerous audience that cardinals, bishops, and princes could scarce find room. His sermons and conferences, and still more the example of his holy life, and the engaging sweetness of his conversation, most powerfully moved not only the devout, but also heretics, libertines, and atheists; while his eloquence and learning convinced their understandings. The bishop of Bellay tells us that he entreated the saint at Paris not to preach twice every day, morning and evening, for the sake of his health. St. Francis answered him with a smile: "That it cost him much less to preach a sermon than to find an excuse for himself when invited to perform that function." He added: "God has appointed me a pastor and a preacher: and is not every one to follow his profession? But I am surprised that the people in this great city flock so eagerly to my sermons: for my tongue is slow and heavy, my conceptions low, and my discourses flat, as you yourself are witness." "Do you imagine," said the other, "that eloquence is what they seek in your discourses? It is enough for them to see you in the pulpit. Your heart speaks to them by your countenance, and by your eyes, were you only to say the Our Father with them. The most common words in your mouth, burning with the fire of charity, pierce and melt all hearts. There is I know not what so extraordinary in what you say, that every word is of weight, every word strikes deep into the heart. You have said every thing even when you seem to have said nothing. You are possessed of a kind of eloquence which is of heaven: the power of this is astonishing." St. Francis, smiling, turned off the discourse. The match being concluded, the Princess Christina chose Francis for her chief almoner, desiring to live always under his direction: but all her entreaties could neither prevail on him to leave his diocess, though he had a coadjutor, nor to accept of a pension: and it was only on these two conditions he undertook the charge, always urging that nothing could dispense with him from residence. The princess made him a present of a rich diamond, by way of an investiture, desiring him to keep it for her sake. "I will," said he, "unless the poor stand in need of it." She answered, she would then redeem it. He said, "This will happen so often that I shall abuse your bounty." Finding it given to the poor afterward at Turin, she gave him another richer, charging him to keep that at least. He said: "Madam, I cannot promise you: I am very unfit to keep things of value." Inquiring after it one day, she was told it was always in pawn for the poor, and that the diamond belonged not to the bishop, but to all the beggars of Geneva. He had indeed a heart which was not able to refuse any thing to those in want. He often gave to beggars the waistcoat off his own back, and sometimes the cruets of his chapel. The pious cardinal, Henry de Condi, bishop of Paris, used all manner of arguments to obtain his consent to be his coadjutor in the see of Paris; but he was resolved never to quit the church which God had first committed to his charge.

Upon his return to Annecy he would not touch a

farthing of his revenue for the eighteen months he had been absent; but gave it to his cathedral, saying, it could not be his, for he had not earned it. He applied himself to preaching, instructing, and hearing confessions with greater zeal than ever. In a plague which raged there, he daily exposed his own life to assist his flock. The saint often met with injurious treatment, and very reviling words, which he ever repaid with such meekness and beneficence as never failed to gain his very enemies. A lewd wretch, exasperated against him for his zeal against a wicked harlot, forged a letter of intrigue in the holy prelate's name, which made him pass for a profligate and a hypocrite with the duke of Nemours and many others: the calumny reflected also on the nuns of the Visitation. Two years after, the author of it lying on his death-bed, called in witnesses, publicly justified the saint, and made an open confession of the slander and forgery. The saint had ever an entire confidence in the Divine Providence, was ever full of joy, and resigned to all the appointments of heaven, to which he committed all events. He had a sovereign contempt of all earthly things, whether riches, honours, dangers, or sufferings. He considered only God and his honour in all things: his soul perpetually breathed nothing but his love and praises; nor could he contain this fire within his breast, for it discovered itself in his countenance; which, especially while he said mass, or distributed the blessed eucharist, appeared shining, as it were, with rays of glory, and breathing holy fervour. Often he could not contain himself in his conversation, and would thus express himself to his intimate friends: "Did you but know how God treats my heart, you would thank his goodness, and beg for me the strength to execute the inspirations which he communicates to me. My heart is filled with an inexpressible desire to be for ever sacrificed to the pure and holy love of my Saviour. Oh! it is good to live, to labour, to rejoice only in God. By his grace I will for ever more be nothing to any creature; nor shall any creature be any thing to me but in him and for him." At another time he cried out to a devout friend: "Oh! if I knew but one string of my heart which was not all God's, I would instantly tear it out. Yes; if I knew that there was one thread in my heart which was not marked with the crucifix, I would not keep it one moment."

In the year 1622, he received an order from the duke of Savoy to go to Avignon to wait on Lewis XII., who had just finished the civil wars in Languedoc. Finding himself indisposed, he took his last leave of his friends, saying, he should see them no more; which drew from them floods of tears. At Avignon he was at his prayers during the king's triumphant entry, and never went to the window to see any part of that great pomp. He was obliged to attend the king and the cardinal of Savoy to Lyons, where he refused all the grand apartments offered him by the intendant of the province and others, to lodge in the poor chamber of the gardener to the monastery of the Visitation: as he was never better pleased than when he could most imitate the poverty of his Saviour. He received from the king and queen-mother, and from all the princes, the greatest marks of honour and esteem: and though indisposed, continued to preach and perform all his functions, especially on Christmas-day, and St. John's in the morning.

After dinner he began to fall gradually into an apoplexy, was put to bed by his servant, and received extreme unction; but as he had said mass that day, and his vomiting continued, it was thought proper not to give him the viaticum. He repeated with great fervour: "My heart and my flesh rejoice in the living God; I will sing the mercies of the Lord to all eternity. When shall I appear before his face? Show me, my beloved, where thou feedest, where thou restest at noonday. O my God, my desire is before thee, and my sighs are not hidden from thee. My God and my all! my desire is that of the hills eternal." While the physicians applied blistering plasters, and hot irons behind his neck, and a caustic to the crown of his head, which burned him to the bone, he shed abundance of tears under excess of pain, repeating: *"Wash me, O Lord, from my iniquities, and cleanse me from my sin. Still cleanse me more and more.* What do I here, my God, distant from thee, separated from thee?" And to those about him: "Weep not, my children; must not the will of God be done?" One suggesting to him the prayer of St. Martin, "If I am still necessary for thy people, I refuse not to labour:" he seemed troubled at being compared to so great a saint, and said, he was an unprofitable servant, whom neither God nor his people needed. His apoplexy increasing, though slowly, he seemed at last to lose his senses, and happily expired on the feast of Holy Innocents, the 28th December, at eight o'clock at night, in the year 1622, the fifty-sixth of his age, and the twentieth of his episcopacy. His corpse was embalmed, and carried with the greatest pomp to Annecy, where he had directed by will it should be interred. It was laid in a magnificent tomb near the high altar in the church of the first monastery of the Visitation. After his beatification by Alexander VII. in 1661, it was placed upon the altar in a rich silver shrine. He was canonized in 1665 by the same pope, and his feast fixed to the 29th of January, on which day his body was conveyed to Annecy. His heart was kept in a leaden case, in the church of the Visitation at Lyons: it was afterward exposed in a silver one, and lastly in one of gold, given by King Lewis XIII. Many miracles, as the raising to life two persons who were drowned, the curing of the blind, paralytic, and others, were authentically attested to have been wrought by his relics and intercession; not to mention those he had performed in his lifetime, especially during his missions. Pope Alexander VII., then Cardinal Chigi, and plenipotentiary in Germany, Lewis

XIII., XIV., and others, attributed their cures in sickness to this saint's patronage.

Among his ordinary remarkable sayings, we read that he often repeated to Bishop Camus, "That truth must be always charitable; for bitter zeal does harm instead of good. Reprehensions are a food of hard digestion, and ought to be dressed on a fire of burning charity so well that all harshness be taken off; otherwise, like unripe fruit, they will only produce gripings. Charity seeks not itself nor its own interests, but purely the honour and interest of God; pride, vanity, and passion cause bitterness and harshness: a remedy injudiciously applied may be a poison; A judicious silence is always better than a truth spoken without charity." St. Francis, seeing a scandalous priest thrown into prison, fell at his feet, and with tears conjured him to have compassion on him, his pastor, on his religion, which he scandalized, and on his own soul; which sweetness converted the other, so that he became an example of virtue. By his patience and meekness under all injuries, he overcame the most obstinate, and ever after treated them with singular affection, calling them dearer friends, because regained. A great prelate observes from his example that the meek are kings of other hearts, which they powerfully attract, and can turn as they please, and in an express and excellent treatise, proposes him as an accomplished model of all the qualifications requisite in a superior to govern well.

Meekness was the favourite virtue of St. Francis de Sales. He once was heard to say, that he had employed three years in studying it in the school of Jesus Christ, and that his heart was still far from being satisfied with the progress he had made. If he, who was meekness itself, imagined, nevertheless, that he had possessed so little of it; what shall we say of those, who, upon every trifling occasion, betray the bitterness of their hearts in angry words and actions of impatience and outrage? Our saint was often tried in the practice of this virtue, especially when the hurry of business and the crowds that thronged on him for relief in their various necessities, scarce allowed him a moment to breathe. He has left us his thoughts upon this situation, which his extreme affability rendered very frequent to him. "God," says he, "makes use of this occasion to try whether our hearts are sufficiently strengthened to bear every attack. I have myself been sometimes in this situation: but I have made a covenant with my heart and with my tongue, in order to confine them within the bounds of duty. I considered those persons who crowd in one upon the other, as children who run into the embraces of their father: as the hen refuseth not protection to her little ones when they gather around her, but, on the contrary, extendeth her wings so as to cover them all; my heart, I thought, was in like manner expanded, in proportion as the numbers of these poor people increased. The most powerful remedy against sudden starts of impatience is a sweet and amiable silence; however little one speaks, self-love will have a share in it, and some word will escape that may sour the heart, and disturb its peace for a considerable time. When nothing is said, and cheerfulness preserved, the storm subsides, anger and indiscretion are put to flight, and nothing remains but a joy, pure and lasting. The person who possesses Christian meekness is affectionate and tender toward every one; he is disposed to forgive and excuse the frailties of others; the goodness of his heart appears in a sweet affability that influences his words and actions, and presents every object to his view in the most charitable and pleasing light; he never admits in his discourse any harsh expression, much less any term that is haughty or rude. An amiable serenity is always painted on his countenance, which remarkably distinguishes him from those violent characters, who, with looks full of fury, know only how to refuse; or who, when they grant, do it with so bad a grace, that they lose all the merit of the favour they bestow."

Some persons thinking him too indulgent toward sinners, expressed their thoughts one day with freedom to him on this head: he immediately replied: "If there was any thing more excellent than meekness, God would have certainly taught it us; and yet there is nothing to which he so earnestly exhorts us, as to be *meek and humble of heart.* Why would you hinder me to obey the command of my Lord, and follow him in the exercise of that virtue which he so eminently practised and so highly esteems? Are we then better informed in these matters than God himself?" But his tenderness was particularly displayed in the reception of apostates and other abandoned sinners; when these prodigals returned to him, he said, with all the sensibility of a father: "Come, my dear children, come, let me embrace you; ah, let me hide you in the bottom of my heart! God and I will assist you: all I require of you is not to despair: I shall take on myself the labour of the rest." Looks full of compassion and love expressed the sincerity of his feelings: his affectionate and charitable care of them extended even to their bodily wants, and his purse was open to them as well as his heart: he justified this proceeding to some, who, disedified at his extreme indulgence, told him, it served only to encourage the sinner, and harden him still more in his crimes, by observing, "Are they not a part of my flock? Has not our blessed Lord given them his blood, and shall I refuse them my tears? These wolves will be changed into lambs: a day will come when, cleansed from their sins, they will be more precious in the sight of God than we are: if Saul had been cast off, we would never have had a St. Paul."

ST. SYNCLETICA, V.

SHE was born at Alexandria in Egypt, of wealthy Macedonian parents. From her infancy she had imbibed the love of virtue, and in her tender years she consecrated her virginity to God. Her great fortune and beauty induced many young noblemen to become her suitors for marriage, but she had already bestowed her heart on her heavenly spouse. Flight was her refuge against exterior assaults, and, regarding herself as her own most dangerous enemy, she began early to subdue her flesh by austere fasts and other mortifications. She never seemed to suffer more than when obliged to eat oftener than she desired. Her parents, at their death, left her heiress to their opulent estate; for the two brothers she had died before them; and her sister, being blind, was committed entirely to her guardianship. Syncletica, having soon distributed her fortune among the poor, retired with her sister into a lonesome monument, on a relation's estate; where, having sent for a priest, she cut off her hair in his presence, as a sign whereby she renounced the world, and renewed the consecration of herself to God. Mortification and prayer were from that time her principal employment; but her close solitude, by concealing her pious exercises from the eyes of the world, has deprived us in a great measure of the knowledge of them.

The fame of her virtue being spread abroad, many women resorted to her abode to confer with her upon spiritual matters. Her humility made her unwilling to take upon herself the task of instructing, but charity on the other side, opened her mouth. Her pious discourses were inflamed with so much zeal, and accompanied with such an unfeigned humility, and with so many tears, that it cannot be expressed what deep impressions they made on her hearers. "Oh," said the saint, "how happy should we be, did we but take as much pains to gain heaven and please God, as worldlings do to heap up riches and perishable goods! By land they venture among thieves and robbers; at sea they expose themselves to the fury of winds and storms; they suffer shipwrecks, and all perils; they attempt all, try all, hazard all; but we, in serving so great a master, for so immense a good, are afraid of every contradiction." At other times, admonishing them of the dangers of this life, she was accustomed to say, "We must be continually upon our guard, for we are engaged in a perpetual war; unless we take care, the enemy will surprise us, when we are least aware of him. A ship sometimes passes safe through hurricanes and tempests, yet, if the pilot, even in a calm, has not a great care of it, a single wave, raised by a sudden gust, may sink her. It does not signify whether the enemy clambers in by the window, or whether all at once he shakes the foundation, if at last he destroys the house. In this life we sail, as it were, in an unknown sea. We meet with rocks, shelves, and sands; sometimes we are becalmed, and at other times we find ourselves tossed and buffeted by a storm. Thus we are never secure, never out of danger; and if we fall asleep, are sure to perish. We have a most intelligent and experienced pilot at the helm of our vessel, even Jesus Christ himself, who will conduct us safe into the haven of salvation, if, by our supineness, we cause not our own perdition." She frequently inculcated the virtue of humility, in the following words:—"A treasure is secure so long as it remains concealed; but when once disclosed, and laid open to every bold invader, it is presently rifled: so virtue is safe as long as secret, but, if rashly exposed, it but too often evaporates into smoke. By humility, and contempt of the world, the soul, like an eagle, soars on high, above all transitory things, and tramples on the backs of lions and dragons." By these, and the like discourses, did this devout virgin excite others to charity, humility, vigilance, and every other virtue.

The devil, enraged to behold so much good, which all his machinations were not capable to prevent, obtained permission of God, for her trial, to afflict this his faithful servant, like another Job: but even this served only to render her virtue the more illustrious. In the eightieth year of her age she was seized with an inward burning fever, which wasted her insensibly by its intense heat; at the same time an imposthume was formed in her lungs; and a violent and most tormenting scurvy, attended with a corroding, hideous, stinking ulcer, eat away her jaws and mouth, and deprived her of speech. She bore all with incredible patience and resignation to God's holy will; and with such a desire of an addition to her sufferings, that she greatly dreaded the physicians would alleviate her pains. It was with difficulty that she permitted them to pare away or embalm the parts already dead. During the three last months of her life, she found no repose. Though the cancer had robbed her of her speech, her wonderful patience served to preach to others more movingly than words could have done. Three days before her death she foresaw, that on the third day she should be released from the prison of her body; and on it, surrounded by a heavenly light, and ravished by consolatory visions, she surrendered her pure soul into the hands of her Creator, in the eighty-fourth year of her age. The Greeks keep her festival on the 4th, the Roman Martyrology mentions her on the 5th of January. The ancient beautiful life of St. Syncletica is quoted in the old lives of the fathers published by Rosweide, l. 6, and in the ancient notes of St. John Climacus. It appears from the work itself, that the author was personally acquainted with the saint. It has been ascribed to St. Athanasius, but without sufficient grounds. It was translated into French, though not scrupulously, by d'Andilly, Vies des SS. Pêres des Déserts, t. 3, p. 91. The antiquity of this piece is confirmed by Montfaucon, Catal. Bibl. Coislianæ, p. 417.

ST. MARY OF EGYPT.

From her Life commended in the Seventh General Council, and by St Sophonius.

IN the reign of Theodosius the Younger, there lived in Palestine a holy monk and priest named Zosimus, famed for the reputation of his sanctity, and resorted to as an oracle for the direction of souls in the most perfect rules of a religious life. He had served God from his youth with great fervour, in the same house, for the space of three and fifty years, when he was tempted to think that he had attained to a state of perfection, and that no one could teach him any thing more in regard to a monastic life. God, to discover the delusion and danger of this suggestion of the proud spirit, and to convince him that we may always advance in perfection, directed him by revelation to quit his monastery for one near the Jordan, where he might learn lessons of virtue he yet was unacquainted with. Being admitted among them, it was not long before he was undeceived, and convinced from what he saw practised there how much he had been mistaken in the judgment he had formed of himself and his advancement in virtue. The members of this community had no more communication with the rest of mankind than if they had belonged to another world. The whole employment of their lives was manual labour, which they accompanied with prayer, the singing of psalms, (in which heavenly exercise they spent the whole night, relieving each other by turns,) and their chief subsistence was on bread and water. It was their yearly custom, after having assisted at the divine mysteries, and received the blessed Eucharist on the first Sunday in Lent, to cross the river, and disperse themselves over the vast deserts which lie toward Arabia, to pass in perfect solitude the interval between that and Palm-Sunday; against which time they all returned again to the monastery to join in celebrating the passion and resurrection of our Lord. Some subsisted during this time on a small parcel of provision they took with them, while others lived on the herbs which grew wild; but when they came back, they never communicated to each other what they did during that time.

About the year 430, the holy man Zosimus passed over the Jordan with the rest at the usual time, endeavouring to penetrate as far as he could into the wilderness, in hopes of meeting with some hermit of still greater perfection than he had hitherto seen or conversed with, praying with great fervour as he travelled. Having advanced thus for twenty days, as he one day stopped at noon to rest himself and recite a certain number of psalms according to custom, he saw as it were the figure of a human body. He was at first seized with fright and astonishment; and imagining it might be an illusion of the enemy, he armed himself with the sign of the cross and continued in prayer. Having finished his devotions, he plainly perceived, on turning his eyes that way, that it was somebody that appeared naked, extremely sunburnt, and with short white hair, who walked very quick, and fled from him. Zosimus, judging it was some holy anchoret, ran that way with all his speed to overtake him. He drew nearer by degrees, and when he was within hearing, he cried out to the person to stop and bless him; who answered: "Abbot Zosimus, I am a woman; throw me your mantle to cover me, that you may come near me." He, surprised to hear her call him by his name, which he was convinced she could have known only by revelation, readily complied with her request. Having covered herself with his garment, she approached him, and they entered into conversation after mutual prayer: and on the holy man's conjuring her by Jesus Christ to tell him who she was, and how long, and in what manner she had lived in that desert, she said: "I ought to die with confusion and shame in telling you what I am; so horrible is the very mention of it, that you will fly from me as from a serpent: your ears will not be able to bear the recital of the crimes of which I have been guilty. I will, however, relate to you my ignominy, begging of you to pray for me, that God may show me mercy in the day of his terrible judgment.

"My country is Egypt. When my father and mother were still living, at twelve years of age I went without their consent to Alexandria: I cannot think, without trembling, on the first step by which I fell into sin, nor my disorders which followed." She then described how she lived a public prostitute seventeen years, not for interest, but to gratify an unbridled lust; she added: "I continued my wicked course till the twenty-ninth year of my age, when perceiving several persons making towards the sea, I inquired whither they were going, and was told they were about to embark for the holy land, to celebrate at Jerusalem the feast of the Exaltation of the glorious Cross of our Saviour. I embarked with them, looking only for fresh opportunities to continue my debauches, which I repeated both during the voyage and after my arrival at Jerusalem. On the day appointed for the festival, all going to church, I mixed with the crowd to get into the church where the Holy Cross was shown and exposed to the veneration of the faithful; but found myself withheld from entering the place by some secret but invisible force. This happening to me three or four times, I retired into a corner of the court and began to consider with myself what this might proceed from; and seriously reflecting that my criminal life might be the cause, I melted into tears. Beating therefore my sinful breast, with signs and groans, I perceived above me a picture of the Mother of God. Fixing my eyes upon it, I addressed myself to that holy Virgin, begging of her, by her incomparable purity, to succour me, defiled with such a load of abominations, and to render my repentance the more acceptable to God. I besought her I might be suffered to enter the church-doors to behold the sacred wood of my redemption; promising from that moment to consecrate myself to God by a life of penance, taking her for my surety in this change of my heart. After this ardent prayer, I perceived in my soul a secret consolation under my grief; and attempting again to enter the church, I went up with ease into the very middle of it, and had the comfort to venerate the precious wood of the glorious cross which brings life to man. Considering therefore the incomprehensible mercy of God, and his readiness to receive sinners to repentance, I cast myself on the ground, and after having kissed the pavement with tears, I arose and went to the picture of the Mother of God, whom I had made the witness and surety of my engagements and resolutions. Falling there on my knees before her image, I addressed my prayers to her, begging her intercession, and that she would be my guide. After my prayer, I seemed to hear this voice: "If thou goest beyond the Jordan, thou shalt there find rest and comfort." Then weeping and looking on the image, I begged of the holy queen of the world that she would never abandon me. After these words I went out in haste, bought three loaves, and asking the baker which was the gate of the city which led to the Jordan, I immediately took that road, and walked all the rest of the day, and at night arrived at the church of St. John Baptist on the banks of the river. There I paid my devotion to God, and received the precious body of our Saviour Jesus Christ. Having eat the one-half of one of my loaves, I slept all night on the ground. Next morning, recommending myself to the holy Virgin, I passed the Jordan, and from that time I have carefully shunned the meeting of any human creature."

Zosimus asked how long she had lived in that desert. "It is," said she, "as near as I can judge, forty-seven years." "And what have you subsisted upon all that time?" replied Zosimus. "The loaves I took with me," answered she, "lasted me some time: since that I have had no other food but what this wild and uncultivated solitude afforded me. My clothes being worn out, I suffered severely from the heat and the cold, with which I was often so afflicted that I was not able to stand." "And have you passed so many years," said the holy man, "without suffering much in your soul?" She answered: "Your question makes me tremble, by the very remembrance of my past dangers and conflicts, through the perverseness of my heart. Seventeen years I passed in most violent temptations, and almost perpetual conflicts with my inordinate desires. I was tempted to regret the flesh and fish of Egypt, and the wines which I drank in the world to excess; whereas here I often could not come at a drop of water to quench my thirst. Other desires made assaults on my mind; but, weeping and striking my breast on those occasions, I called to mind the vows I had made under the protection of the Blessed Virgin, and begged her to obtain my deliverance from the affliction and danger of such thoughts. After long weeping and bruising my body with blows, I found myself suddenly enlightened, and my mind restored to a perfect calm. Often the tyranny of my old passions seemed ready to drag me out of my desert: at those times I threw myself on the ground and watered it with my tears, raising my heart continually to the Blessed Virgin till she procured me comfort: an she has never failed to show herself my faithful protectress." Zosimus taking notice that in her discourse with him she from time to time made use of Scripture phrases, asked her, if she had ever applied herself to the study of the sacred books. Her answer was that she could not even read, neither had she conversed nor seen any human creature since she came into the desert till that day, that could teach her to read the Holy Scripture or read it to her, but "it is God," said she "that teacheth man knowledge. Thus have I given you a full account of myself: keep what I have told you as an inviolable secret during my life, and allow me, the most miserable of sinners, a share in your prayers." She concluded with desiring him not to pass over the Jordan next Lent, according to the custom of his monastery, but to bring with him on Maunday-Thursday the body and blood of our Lord, and wait for her on the banks of the river on the side which is inhabited. Having spoken thus, and once more entreated him to pray for her, she left him. Zosimus hereupon fell on his knees, thanked God for what he had seen and heard, kissed the ground whereon she stood, and returned by the usual time to his monastery.

The year following, on the first Sunday in Lent, he was detained at home on account of sickness, as indeed she had foretold him. On Maunday-Thursday, taking the sacred body and blood of our Lord in a small chalice, and also a little basket of figs, dates, and lentils, he went to the banks of the Jordan. At night she appeared on the other side, and making the sign of the cross over the river, she went forward, walking upon the surface of the water, as if it had been dry land, till she reached the opposite shore. Being now together, she craved his blessing, and desired him to recite the Creed and the Lord's Prayer. After which she received from his hands the holy sacrament. Then lifting up her hands to heaven, she said aloud with tears: *Now thou dost dismiss thy servant, O Lord, according to thy word, in peace; because my eyes have seen my Saviour.* She begged Zosimus to pardon the trouble she had given him, and desired him to return the following Lent, to the place where he first saw her. He begged of her on his side to accept the sustenance he had brought her. But she took only a few of the lentils; and conjuring him never to forget her miseries, left him, and then went over the river as she came. Zosimus returned home, and at the very time fixed by the saint, set out in quest of her, with the view of being still further edified by her holy conversation, and of learning also her name, which he had forgot to ask. But on his arrival at the place where he had first seen her, he found her corpse stretched out on the ground, with an inscription declaring her name, Mary, and the time of her death. Zosimus, being miraculously assisted by a lion, dug a grave, and buried her. And having recommended both himself and the whole church to the saint's intercession, he returned to his monastery, where he recounted all that he had seen and heard of this holy penitent, and continued there to serve God till his happy death, which happened in the hundredth year of his age: and it is from a relation of the monks of that community, that an author of the same century wrote her life as above related: which history is mentioned soon after by many authors, both of the Eastern and Western Church. Papebroke places her conversion in 383, and her death in 421.

In the example of this holy woman, we admire the wonderful goodness and mercy of God, who raised her from the sink of the most criminal habits and the most abandoned state to the most sublime and heroic virtue. While we consider her severe penance, let us blush at the manner in which we pretend to do penance. Let her example rouse our sloth. The kingdom of heaven is only for those who do violence to themselves. Let us tremble with her at the remembrance of our baseness and sins, as often as we enter the sanctuary of the Lord, or venerate his holy cross, the instrument of our redemption. We insult him, when we pretend exteriorly to pay him our homages, and at the same time dishonour him by our sloth and sinful life. God, by the miraculous visible repulse of this sinner, shows us what he does invisibly with regard to all obstinate and wilful sinners. We join the crowd of adorers at the foot of his altar; but he abhors our treacherous kisses like those of Judas. We honour his cross with our lips; but he sees our heart, and condemns its irregularities and its opposition to his holy spirit of perfect humility, meekness, self-denial, and charity. Shall we then so much fear to provoke his indignation by our unworthiness, as to keep at a distance from his holy places or mysteries? By no means. This would be irrecoverably to perish, by cutting off the most essential means of salvation. Invited by the infinite goodness and mercy of God, and pressed by our own necessities and dangers, the more grievous these are, with so much greater earnestness and assiduity must we sue for pardon and grace, provided we do this in the most profound sentiments of compunction, fear, and confidence. It will be expedient often to pray with the publican at a distance from the altar, in a feeling sentiment that we ought to be treated as persons excommunicate before God and men. Sometimes we may in public prayers pronounce the words with a lower voice, as unworthy to unite our praises with others, as base sinners, whose homages ought rather to be offensive to God, who hates the sight of a heart filled with iniquity and self-love. We must at least never present ourselves before God without purifying our hearts by compunction, and, trembling, to say to ourselves, that God ought to drive us out of his holy presence with a voice of thunder: *Let the wicked man be taken away, and let him not see the glory of God.* But in these dispositions of fear and humility, we must not fail assiduously to pour forth our supplications, and sound the divine praises with our whole hearts.

ST. SISOES OR SISOY,

ANCHORET IN EGYPT.

AFTER the death of St. Antony, St. Sisoes was one of the most shining lights of the Egyptian deserts. He was an Egyptian by birth. Having quitted the world from his youth, he retired to the desert of Sceté, and lived some time under the direction of Abbot Hor. The desire of finding a retreat yet more unfrequented induced him to cross the Nile and hide himself in the mountain where St. Antony died some time before. The memory of that great man's virtues being still fresh, wonderfully supported his fervour. He imagined he saw him, and heard the instructions he was wont to deliver to his disciples: and he strained every nerve to imitate his most heroic exercises, the austerity of his penance, the rigour of his silence, the almost unremitting ardour of his prayer; insomuch that the reputation of his sanctity became so illustrious as to merit the full confidence of all the neighbouring solitaries. Some even came a great distance to be guided in the interior ways of perfection; and, in spite of the pains he took, he was forced to submit his love of silence and retreat to the greater duty of charity. He often passed two days without eating, and was so rapt in God that he forgot his food, so that it was necessary for his disciple Abraham to remind him that it was time to break his fast. He would sometimes be even surprised at the notice, and contend that he had already made his meal; so small was the attention he paid to the wants of his body. His prayer was so fervent that it often passed into ecstasy. At other times his heart was so inflamed with divine love, that, scarce able to support its violence, he only obtained relief from his sighs, which frequently escaped without his knowledge, and even against his will. It was a maxim with him, that a solitary ought not to choose the manual labour which is most pleasing to him. His ordinary work was making baskets. He was tempted, one day, as he was selling them, to anger; instantly he threw the baskets away and ran off. By efforts like these to command his temper he acquired a meekness which nothing could disturb. His zeal against vice was without bitterness; and when his monks fell into faults, far from affecting astonishment or the language of reproach, he helped them to rise again with a tenderness truly paternal. When he once recommended patience and the exact observance of rules, he told the following anecdote: "Twelve monks, benighted on the road, observed that their guide was going astray. This, for fear of breaking their rule of silence, they forbore to notice, thinking within themselves that at daybreak he would see his mistake and put them in the right road. Accordingly, the guide, discovering his error, with much confusion, was making many apologies; when the monks, being now at liberty to speak, only said, with the greatest good humour: 'Friend, we saw very well that you went out of your road; but we were then bound to silence.' The man was struck with astonishment, and very much edified at this answer, expressive of such patience and strictness of observance."

Some Arians had the impudence to come to his mount, and utter their heresy before his disciples. The saint, instead of an answer, desired one of the monks to read St. Athanasius's treatise against Arianism, which at once stopped their mouths and confounded them. He then dismissed them with his usual good temper. Saint Sisoes was singularly devoted to humility; and in all his advices and instructions to others, held constantly before their eyes this most necessary virtue. A recluse saying to him one day, "Father, I always place myself in the presence of God;" he replied: "It would be much more your advantage to place yourself below every creature, in order to be securely humble." Thus, while he never lost sight of the divine presence, it was ever accompanied with the consciousness of his own nothingness and misery. "Make yourself little," said he to a monk, "renounce all sensual satisfactions, disengage yourself from the empty cares of the world, and you will find true peace of mind." To another, who complained that he had not yet arrived at the perfection of St. Antony, he said: "Ah! if I had but one only of that great man's feelings, I would be all one flame of divine love."

Notwithstanding his extraordinary mortifications, they appeared so trifling in his mind, that he called himself a sensual man, and would have every one else to be of the same opinion. If charity for strangers sometimes constrained him to anticipate dinner-hour, at another season, by way of indemnification, he protracted his fast, as if his body were indebted to so laudable a condescension. He dreaded praise so much, that in prayer, as was his custom, with his hands lifted up to heaven, when sometimes he apprehended observation, he would suddenly drop them down. He was always ready to blame himself, and saw nothing praiseworthy in others which did not serve him for an occasion to censure his own lukewarmness. On a visit of three solitaries wanting instruction, one of them said: "Father, what shall I do to shun hell-fire?" He made no reply. "And for my part," added another, "how shall I escape the gnashing of teeth, and the worm that never dies?" "What also will become of me?" concluded the third, "for every time I think on utter darkness I am ready to die with fear." Then the saint breaking silence, answered: "I confess that these are subjects which never employ my thoughts, and as I know that God is merciful, I trust he will have compassion on me. You are happy," he added, "and I envy your virtue. You speak of the torments of hell, and your fears on this account must be powerful guards against the admission of sin. Alas! then, it is I should exclaim, What shall become of me? I, who am so insensible as never even to reflect on the place of torments destined to punish the wicked after death. Undoubtedly this is the reason I am guilty of so much sin." The solitaries retired much edified with this humble reply. The saint said one time: "I am now thirty years praying daily that my Lord Jesus may preserve me from saying an idle word, and yet I am always relapsing." This could only be the language which humility dictates; for he was singularly observant of the times of retirement and silence, and kept his cell constantly locked to avoid interruption, and always gave his answers to those who asked his advice in the fewest words. The servant of God, worn out with sickness and old age, yielded at last to his disciple Abraham's advice, and went to reside a while at Clysma, a town on the border, or at least in the neighbourhood of the Red Sea. Here he received a visit from Ammon, or Amun, abbot of Raithe, who, observing his affliction for being absent from his retreat, endeavoured to comfort him by representing that his present ill state of health wanted the remedies which could not be applied in the desert. "What do you say," returned the saint, with a countenance full of grief, "was not the ease of mind I enjoyed there every thing for my comfort?" He was not at ease till he returned to his retreat, where he finished his holy course. The solitaries of the desert assisting at his agony, heard him, as Rufinus relates, cry out, "Behold, Abbot Antony, the choir of prophets and the angels come to take my soul." At the same time his countenance shone, and being some time interiorly recollected with God, he cried out anew, "Behold! our Lord comes for me." At the instant he expired, his cell was perfumed with a heavenly odour. He died about the year 429, after a retreat of at least sixty-two years in St. Antony's Mount. His feast is inserted in the Greek Menologies on the 6th of July; and in some of the Latin calendars on the 4th of the same month. See Rosweide; Cotelier; Tillemont, t. 12, p. 453; and the Bollandists ad diem 6 Julii, t. 2, p. 280.

This saint must not be confounded with two other Sisoes who lived in the same age. One, surnamed the Theban, lived at Calamon, in the territory of Arsinoe. Another had his cell at Petra. It is of Sisoes the Theban, that the following passage is related, though some authors by mistake have ascribed it to St. Sisoes of Sceté:—A certain recluse having received some offence, went to Sisoes to tell him that he must have revenge. The holy old man conjured him to leave his revenge to God, to pardon his brother, and forget the injury he had received. But seeing that this advice had no weight with him, "At least," said he, "let us both join in an address to God;" then standing up, he prayed thus aloud: "Lord, we no longer want your care of our interests or your protection, since this monk maintains that we can and ought to be our own avengers." This extraordinary petiton exceedingly moved the poor recluse, and throwing himself at the saint's feet, he begged his pardon, protesting from that moment he would forget he had ever been injured. This holy man loved retirement so much that he delayed not a moment even in the church after the mass to hasten to his cell. This was not to indulge self-love or an affected singularity, but to shun the danger of dissipation, and enjoy in silence and prayer the sweet conversation of God. For at proper seasons, especially when charity required it, he was far from being backward in giving himself to the duties of society. Such was his self-denial that he seldom or ever ate bread. However, being invited one time by the neighbouring solitaries to a small repast, in condescension, and to show how little he was guided by selfwill, observing that it would be agreeable, "I will eat," said he, "bread, or any thing you lay before me." See Bulteau, Hist. Mon. d'Orient, l. 1, c. 3, n. 7, p. 56; Tillemont, t. 12; and Pinius, one of the continuators of Bollandus, on the sixth of July.

ST. JOHN THE DWARF,

ANCHORET.

St. John, surnamed, from his low stature, Colobus, that is, the Little, or the Dwarf, was famous among the eminent ancient saints that inhabited the deserts of Egypt. He retired, together with an elder brother, into the vast wilderness of Sceté, and putting himself under the direction of a holy old hermit, he set himself, with his whole heart, and with all his strength, to labour in subduing himself, and in putting on the divine spirit of Christ. The first condition which Christ requires, the preliminary article which he lays down for his service, is a practice of perfect self-denial, by which we learn to die to ourselves and all our vicious inclinations. So long as inordinate self-love and passions reign in the heart, they cannot fail to produce their fruits; we are imperceptibly governed by them in the circle of our ordinary actions, and remain habitually enslaved to pride, anger, impatience, envy, sensuality, and other vices, which often break forth into open transgressions of the divine law; and a lurking inordinate self-love, while it holds the empire in the affections, insinuates itself, under subtle disguises, into all our actions, becomes the mainspring of all the motions of our heart, and debases our virtues themselves with a mixture of vice and imperfection. Virtue is generally defective, even in many who desire to serve God, because very few have the courage perfectly to vanquish themselves. It is strange that men should be so blind, or so cowardly, in a point of such infinite importance, since Christ has laid down the precept of perfect abnegation and humility as the foundation of the empire of his divine grace and love in a soul; upon this all the saints raise the edifice of their virtue. He who builds not upon it, builds upon sand. He who, without this precaution, multiplies his alms, his fasts, and his devotions, takes a great deal of pains to lose, in a great measure, the fruit of his labours.

Our holy anchoret, lest he should be in danger of missing his aim, resolved to neglect no means by which he might obtain the victory over himself. The old hermit who was his director, for his first lesson, bade him plant in the ground a dry walking-stick which he held in his hand, and water it every day till it should bring forth fruit. John did so with great simplicity, though the river was at a considerable distance. It is related that when he had continued his task without speaking one word, in the third year, the stick, which had taken root, pushed forth leaves and buds, and produced fruit; the old hermit, gathering the fruit, carried it to the church, and giving it to some of the brethren, said: "Take and eat the fruit of obedience." Posthumian, who was in Egypt in 402, assured St. Sulpicius Severus that he was shown this tree, which grew in the yard of the monastery, and which he saw covered with boughs and green leaves. St. John used to say, that as a man who sees a wild beast or a serpent coming toward him, climbs up a tree to be out of their reach, so a person who perceives any evil thoughts coming upon him, in order to secure himself against the danger, must ascend up to God by earnest prayer. Being yet a novice in the monastic state, and much taken with the charms of heavenly contemplation, he said one day to his elder brother: "I could wish to live without distraction, or earthly concerns, like the angels, that I might be able to serve and praise God without interruption." Saying this, and leaving his cloak behind him, he went into a more secret part of the wilderness. After being absent a week, he returned, and knocked at the door of his brother's cell. Being asked his name, he said: "I am your brother John." "How can that be?" replied the other; "for my brother John is become an angel, and lives no more among men." St. John begged pardon for his rashness, and acknowledged that this mortal state does not admit such a perfection, but requires that contemplation and manual labour mutually succeed and assist each other, and confessed that man's life on earth is labour and penance, not fruition. It was one of this saint's maxims: "If a general would take a city, he begins the siege by debarring it from supplies of water and provisions; so, by sobriety, fasting, and maceration of the flesh, are our affections and passions to be reduced, and our domestic enemy weakened."

How careful he was to watch against all occasions of danger, appears from the following instances:—As he was praying and plying his work in platting mats, on the road to Sceté, he was one day met by a carrier driving camels, who reviled him in the most injurious terms. The saint, for fear the tranquillity of his soul should be in any way impaired, threw down the work he had in his hands, and ran away. Another time, when he was reaping corn in the harvest, he ran away, because he heard one of the reapers angry with another. Happening, one day as he was going to the church of Sceté, to hear two persons wrangling together, he made haste back to his cell, but walked several times round it, in profound recollection, before he went in, that he might purify his ears from the injurious words he had heard, and bring his mind perfectly calm to converse with God. By this continual watchfulness over himself, he acquired so perfect a habit of meekness, humility, and patience, that nothing was able to cloud or disturb his mind. When one said to him: "Thou hast a heart full of venom," he sweetly answered: "That is true, and much more so than you think." By the following example he inculcated to others the great necessity of overcoming ourselves, if we desire truly to serve God:—A certain young man entreated a celebrated philosopher to permit him to attend his lectures. "Go first," said the philosopher, "to the marble quarries, and carry stones to the river, among the malefactors condemned to the mines, during three years." He did so, and came back at the end of that term. The philosopher bid him go again, and pass three years in receiving all sorts of injuries and affronts, and make no answer, but give money to those who should most bitterly revile him. He complied likewise with this precept, and upon his return, the experienced tutor told him he might now go to Athens, and be initiated in the schools of the philosophers. At the gate of that city sat an old man who made it his pastime to abuse those who came that way. The young novice never justified himself, nor was angry, but laughed to hear himself so outrageously railed at; and being asked the reason, said: "I have given money these three years to all who have treated me as you do; and shall not I laugh, now it costs me nothing to be reviled?" Hereupon the old man replied: "Welcome to the schools of philosophy; you are worthy of a seat in them." The saint added: "Behold the gate of heaven. All the faithful servants of the Lord have entered into this joy by suffering injuries and humiliations with meekness and patience." To recommend tenderness and charity to those who labour in converting others to God, he said: "It is impossible to build a house by beginning at the top in order to build downward. We must first gain the heart of our neighbour before we can be useful to him."

It was a usual saying of this saint: "The safety of a monk consists in his keeping always his cell, watching constantly over himself, and having God continually present to his mind." As for his own part, he never discoursed on worldly affairs, and never spoke of news, the ordinary amusement of the slothful. Some persons, one day, to try him, began a conversation with him, saying: "We ought to thank God for the plentiful rains that are fallen this year. The palm-trees sprout well, and our brethren will easily find leaves and twigs for their work in making mats and baskets." St. John contented himself with answering: In like manner, when the Spirit of God comes down upon the hearts of his servants, they grow green again, as I may say, and are renewed, shooting, as it were, fresh leaves in the fear of God." This reply made them attempt no more any such conversation with him. The saint's mind was so intent on God in holy contemplation, that at his work he sometimes platted in one basket the twigs which should have made two, and often went wrong in his work, forgetting what he was doing. One day, when a driver of camels or a carrier knocked at his door, to carry away his materials and instruments for his work, St. John thrice forgot what he went to fetch in returning from his door, till he continued to repeat to himself, "The camel, my platting instrument." The same happened to him when one came to fetch the baskets he had made, and as often as he came back from his door, he sat down again to his work, till at last he desired the brother to come in, and take them himself.

St. John called humility and compunction the first and most necessary of all virtues. By the fervour and assiduity of his prayer and heavenly contemplation, all his discourse on God was inflamed. A certain brother coming one day to see him, designing to speak to him only for two or three minutes, being in haste to go back to his cell, so ardent and sweet was their conversation on spiritual things that they continued it the whole night till morning. Perceiving it day, they went out of the saint's cell, the one to return home, the other to conduct him some steps, and falling into discourse on heaven, their entertainment lasted till midday. Then St. John took him again into his cell to eat a morsel for his refection; after which they parted. St. John seeing a monk laugh in a conference, sat down, and bursting into tears, said: "What reason can this brother have to laugh, while we have so many to weep?" A certain charitable devout young woman, named Paësia, fell into poverty, and gradually into a disorderly life. The monks of Sceté entreated St. John to endeavour to reclaim her from her evil courses. The saint repaired to her house, but was refused entrance, till persisting a long time, and repeating that she would have no reason to repent that she had spoken to him, he got admittance. Then sitting down by her, he said, with his accustomed sweetness: "What reason can you have to complain of Jesus, that you should thus abandon him, to plunge yourself in so deplorable an abyss!" At these words she was struck to the quick; and seeing the saint melt into tears, she said to him: "Why do you weep so bitterly?" St. John replied: "How can I refrain from weeping, while I see Satan in possession of your heart?" She said: "Is the gate of penitence yet open to me?" The saint having answered that the treasures of the divine mercy are inexhaustible, she replied: "Conduct me whither you please." Hereupon, he rising up, said: "Let us go." The penitent followed him without saying another word, and without giving any orders about her household or servants; a circumstance which he took notice of with joy, as it showed how entirely she was taken up with the thoughts only of saving her soul. She spent the remainder of her life in austere penance, and died happily soon after in the wilderness, having no other pillow than a hillock to lay her head on. John learned by a revelation, that her short but fervent penitence had been perfect before God. When our saint drew near his end, his disciples entreated him to leave them, by way of legacy, some wholesome lesson of Christian perfection. He sighed; and that he might, out of humility, shun the air of a teacher, alleging his own maxim and practice, he said: "I never followed my own will; nor did I ever teach any other what I had not first practised myself." St. John died about the beginning of the fifth century. See Cotelier, Apophth. Patrum. litt. i, p. 468 to 484; Rosweide, l. 5, Vitæ Patrum, translated into Latin by

Pelagius, deacon of Rome, who was chosen pope in 558; Tillemont, t. 10, p. 427.

ST. CATHARINE, V. M.

SAINT CATHARINE, whom the Greeks call Æcatherina, glorified God by an illustrious confession of the faith of Christ, at Alexandria, under Maximinus II. Her Acts are so much adulterated that little use can be made of them. The Emperor Basil, in his Greek Menology, relates with them that this saint, who was of the royal blood, and an excellent scholar, confuted a company of the ablest heathen philosophers, whom Maximinus had commanded to enter into a disputation with her, and that, being converted by her to the faith, they were all burnt in one fire, for confessing the same. He adds, that Catharine was at length beheaded. She is said first to have been put under an engine made of four wheels jointed together, and stuck with sharp-pointed spikes, that, when the wheels were moved, her body might be torn to pieces. The Acts add that at the first stirring of the terrible engine, the cords with which the martyr was tied were broke asunder by the invisible power of an angel, and, the engine falling to pieces by the wheels being separated from one another, she was delivered from that death. Hence the name of Saint Catharine's Wheel.

The learned Joseph Assemani thinks that all the account we have of the particulars relating to this saint upon which we can depend, is what we meet with in Eusebius, though that historian mentions not her name. His relation is as follows:—" There was a certain woman, a Christian, and the richest and most noble of all the ladies of Alexandria, who, when the rest suffered themselves to be defloured by the tyrant, (Maximin,) resisted and vanquished his unbounded and worse than beastly lust. This lady was most illustrious for her high birth and great wealth, and likewise for her singular learning; but she preferred her virtue and her chastity to all worldly advantages. The tyrant, having in vain made several assaults upon her virtue, would not behead her, seeing her ready to die, but stripped her of all her estates and goods, and sent her into banishment." Maximin, not long after, declared war against Licinius, and, after several engagements, was at length defeated by him in 313. Having lost his empire after a reign of five years, he fled to Tarsus, and there died in extreme misery. The body of St. Catharine was discovered by the Christians in Egypt about the eighth century, when they groaned under the yoke of the Saracens. It was soon after translated to the great monastery on the top of Mount Sinai in Arabia, built by St. Helen, and sumptuously enlarged and beautified by the emperor Justinian, as several old inscriptions and pictures in Mosaic work in that place testify. Falconius, archbishop of San-Severino, speaks of this translation as follows:—"As to what is said, that the body of this saint was conveyed by angels to Mount Sinai, the meaning is that it was carried by the monks of Sinai to their monastery, that they might devoutly enrich their dwelling with such a treasure. It is well known that the name of an angelical habit was often used for a monastic habit, and that monks, on account of their heavely purity and functions, were anciently called *Angels.*" From that time we find more frequent mention made of the festival and relics of St. Catharine. St. Paul of Latra kept her feast with extraordinary solemnity and devotion. In the eleventh age, Simeon, a monk of Sinai, coming to Rouen to receive an annual alms of Richard, duke of Normandy, brought with him some of her relics, which he left there. The principal part of the mortal remains of this saint is still kept in a marble chest in the church of this monastery on Mount Sinai, described by Dr. Richard Pocock.

From this martyr's uncommon erudition, and the

extraordinary spirit of piety by which she sanctified her learning, and the use she made of it, she is chosen in the schools the patroness and model of Christian philosophers. Learning is, next to virtue, the most noble ornament and the highest improvement of the human mind, by which all its natural faculties obtain an eminent degree of perfection. The memory is exceedingly improved by exercise: those who complain that in them this faculty is like a sieve, may, especially in youth, render it, by use, retentive of whatever is necessary, and particularly adapted to be a storehouse of names, facts, or entire discourses, according to every one's exigency or purposes. But nothing ought to be learned by heart by children but what is excellent or absolutely necessary. To load a mind with other men's lumber, and to make it a magazine of errors, trumpery, or toys, is to pervert all the purposes of this faculty, and a certain proof of the sloth, ignorance, and stupidity of a master. As the understanding is the light of the soul, so it is plain how exceedingly this is enlarged both by exercise and by the acquisition of solid science and useful knowledge. Judgment, the most valuable of all the properties of the mind, and by which the other faculties are poised, governed, and directed, is formed and perfected by experience and regular, well-digested studies and reflection; and by them it attains to true justness and taste. The mind by the same means acquires a steadiness, and conquers the aversion which sloth raises against the serious employment of its talents. It is doubtless the will of the Creator that all his works be raised to that degree of perfection of which they are capable; and where our industry is required to this, it becomes a duty incumbent upon us. This is in nothing so essential and important as in our own mind, the dignity of our being, and the masterpiece of the visible world. How much its perfection depends upon culture appears in the difference of understanding between the savages (who, except in treachery, cunning, and shape, scarce seem to differ from the apes which inhabit their forests) and the most elegant civilized nations. A piece of ground left wild produces nothing but weeds and briers, which by culture would be covered with corn, flowers, and fruit. The difference is not less between a rough mind and one that is well cultivated. The same culture, indeed, suits not all persons. Geniuses must be explored, and the manner of instructing proportioned to them. Conditions and circumstances must be considered. Generally the more sublime theological studies suit not those who are excluded from teaching, though women, upon whom the domestic instruction of children in their infancy mainly depends, ought to be well instructed in the motives of religion, articles of faith, and all the practical duties and maxims of piety. Then history, geography, and some tincture of works of genius and spirit may be joined with suitable arts and other accomplishments of their sex and condition, provided they be guided by, and referred to religion, and provided books of piety and exercises of devotion always have the first place both in their hearts and in their time.

ST. THAIS THE PENITENT.

ABOUT the middle of the fourth age, there lived in Egypt a famous courtezan named Thaïs, who had been educated a Christian; but the sentiments of grace were stifled in her by an unbridled love of pleasure, and desire of gain. Beauty, wit, and flattering, loose company brought her into the gulf; and she was engaged in the most criminal, infamous habits, out of which only an extraordinary grace can raise a soul. This unhappy, thoughtless sinner was posting to eternal destruction when the divine mercy interposed in her favour. Paphnutius, a holy anchoret of Thebais, wept without intermission for the loss of her soul, the scandal of her vicious courses being public in the whole country. At length, having earnestly recommended the matter to God, he formed a project, or a pious stratagem, in order to have access to her, that he might endeavour to rescue her out of her disorders. He put off his penitential weeds, and dressed himself in such a manner as to disguise his profession. Going to her house, full of an ardent zeal for her conversion, he called for her at the door, and was introduced to her chamber. He told her he desired to converse with her in private, but wished it might be in some more secret apartment. "What is it you fear?" said Thaïs. "If men, no one can see us here; but if you mean God, no place can hide us from his all-piercing eye." "What!" replied Paphnutius, "do you know there is a God?" "Yes," said she, "and I moreover know that a heaven will be the portion of the good, and that everlasting torments are reserved in hell for the punishment of the wicked." "Is it possible," said the venerable old hermit, "you should know these great truths, and yet dare to sin in the eyes of Him who knows and will judge all things?" Thaïs perceived by this stinging reproach, that the person to whom she spoke was a servant of God who came inspired with holy zeal to draw her from her unhappy state of perdition; and, at the same time, the Holy Ghost, who moved Paphnutius to speak, enlightened her understanding to see the baseness of her sins, and softened her heart by the touch of his omnipotent grace. Filled with confusion at the sight of her crimes, and penetrated with bitter sorrow, detesting her baseness and ingratitude against God, she burst into a flood of tears, and throwing herself at the feet of Paphnutius, said to him: "Father, enjoin me what course of penance you think proper; pray for me, that God may vouchsafe to show me mercy. I desire only three hours to settle my affairs, and I am ready to comply with all you shall counsel me to do." Paphnutius appointed a place to which she should repair, and went back to his cell.

Thaïs got together all her jewels, magnificent furniture, rich clothes, and the rest of her ill-gotten wealth, and making a great pile in the street, burnt it all publicly, inviting all who had made her those presents, and been the accomplices of her sins, to join her in her sacrifice and penance. To have kept any of those presents would have been not to cut off all dangerous occasions which might again revive her passions, and call back former temptations. By this action she endeavoured also to repair the scandal she had given, and to show how perfectly she renounced sin, and all the incentives of her passions. This being done, she hastened to Paphnutius, and was by him conducted to a monastery of women. There the holy man shut her up in a cell, putting on the door a seal of lead, as if that place had been made her grave, never more to be opened. He ordered the sisters, as long as she lived, to bring her every day only a little bread and water, and he enjoined her never to cease soliciting heaven for mercy and pardon. She said to the holy man: "Father, teach me how I am to pray." Paphnutius answered: "You are not worthy to call upon God by pronouncing his holy name, because your lips have been filled with iniquity; nor to lift up your hands to heaven, because they are defiled with impurities; but turn yourself to the east and repeat these words: Thou who hast created me, have pity on me." Thus she continued to pray with almost continual tears, not daring to call God *Father*, she having deserved to forfeit the title of his child, by her unnatural ingratitude and treasons; nor *Lord*, she having renounced him to become a slave to the devil; nor *Judge*, which name filled her with terror by the remembrance of his dreadful judgments; nor *God*, which name is most holy and adorable, and comprises in one word his supreme essence and all his attributes: but, howsoever she had by her actions disowned him, she remained the work of his hands; and by this title she conjured him, for the sake of his boundless mercy and goodness, to look upon her with compassion, to raise her from her miseries, restore her to his favour, and inspire her with his pure and most perfect love. In repeating this short prayer, she exercised all acts of devotion in her heart, exciting in her affections not only the most profound sentiments of compunction, humility, and holy fear; but also those of hope, praise, adoration, thanksgiving, love, and all interior virtues; in which her affections most feelingly dilated themselves. When she had persevered thus with great fervour for the space of three years, St. Paphnutius went to St. Antony to ask his advice whether this penitential course did not seem sufficient to prepare her for the benefit of reconciliation, and the holy communion. St. Antony said St. Paul the Simple should be consulted; for God delights to reveal his will to the humble. They passed the night together in prayer. In the morning, St. Paul answered that God had prepared a place in heaven for the penitent. Paphnutius therefore went her cell to release her from penance. The penitent, considering the inscrutable judgments of God, and full of deep sentiments of compunction, and of her absolute unworthiness ever to be admitted to sing the divine praises in the company of the chaste spouses of Christ, earnestly begged she might be permitted to continue in her penitential state to the end of her life; but this Paphnutius would not suffer. She said that from the time of her coming thither she had never ceased bewailing her sins, which she had always before her eyes. "It is on this account," said Paphnutius, "that God has blotted them out." She therefore left her prison, to live with the rest of the sisters. God, satisfied with her sacrifice, withdrew her out of this world fifteen days after her releasement, about the year 348. She is honoured in the Greek Menologies on the 8th of October. See her life, written by an ancient Greek author, in Rosweide, p. 374; D'Andilly; Bulteau; and Villefore.

ST. PELAGIA, PENITENT.

This saint had been a comedian at Antioch, even while she was a catechumen; but afterward renounced that profession, and became a true penitent. The manner of her conversion is thus related in the Greek Menæa, published by the emperor Basil. The patriarch of Antioch having assembled a council of bishops in that city, St. Nonnus, one of the number, was commissioned to announce the word of God to the people. Accordingly he preached before the church of St. Julian Martyr, in the presence of the other bishops. During the sermon, Pelagia passed that way richly adorned with jewels; and her beauty, heightened with all the elegance of dress, drew on her the attention of the whole assembly, except the bishops, who turned away their eyes from so scandalous an object. But Nonnus, looking earnestly at Pelagia, cries out in the middle of his discourse: "The Almighty in his infinite goodness will show mercy even to this woman, the work of his hands." At these words, she stopped suddenly, and, joining the audience, was so touched with remorse for her criminal life, that she shed abundance of tears; and immediately after the sermon she addressed herself to Nonnus, imploring him to instruct her how to expiate her sins, and to prepare her for the grace of baptism. The holy penitent distributed all her goods among the poor, changed her name from Margaret to Pelagia, and resolved to spend the remainder of her life in the exercise of prayer and the austerities of penance. After her baptism, which she received at the hands of Nonnus, she retired to Jerusalem, and having taken the religious vail, shut herself up in a grotto on Mount Olivet, in the fifth age. Phocas, a monk of Crete, in the relation of his voyage from

Palestine in 1185, describes Mount Olivet, and the grotto where the saint completed the martyrdom of her penance, and where her relics were preserved in an urn. St. Pelagia is mentioned on this day in the Roman Martyrology, and in the Greek and Muscovite Calendars; but in an ancient inscription on marble in Naples on the 5th of October. See her life written by James, deacon of Heliopolis in Syria, an eyewitness of her conversion and penance, ap. Rosweide, Vit. Patr. p. 374. The same is found in an ancient MS. in folio, on vellum well preserved, which formerly belonged to the abbey of St. Edmundsbury in England, and is at present in the author's possession. This MS. contains a fine collection in Latin of the lives of the Fathers of the desert, which Rosweide published from MSS. found in different libraries of the Low Countries. It were to be wished that the learned Jesuit had either suppressed, or distinguished by some mark, two or three spurious pieces, which are evidently the work of modern Greeks. See also Theophanes, in his Chronology, under the year 432; Nicephorus Callixtus, &c.

ST. FRANCIS BORGIA, C.

A. D. 1572.

MANY Christians seem afraid of following Jesus Christ with their whole hearts, and live as if they were for compounding with God and the world. These persons have a very false idea of virtue, which they measure only by their want of courage. If they once opened their hearts to the divine grace, and were sincerely resolved to spare nothing that they might learn to die to themselves, and to put on the spirit of Christ, they would find all their pretended difficulties to be only shadows; for, by the omnipotent power of grace, the roughest deserts are changed into smooth and agreeable paths under the feet of the just man. This St. Francis Borgia experienced, both in private life in the world, at court, in a religious retirement, and in the functions of an apostolic life. St. Francis Borgia, fourth duke of Gandia, and third general of the Jesuits, was son to John Borgia, duke of Gandia, and grandee of Spain, and of Joanna of Arragon, daughter of Alphonso, natural son to Ferdinand V. king of Arragon, who was also regent of Castile for his daughter Joanna, and his grandson Charles, afterward emperor. Ferdinand, who, by taking Granada in 1491, had put an end to the reign of the Moors in Spain, and by marrying Isabel, the heiress of Castile, united the whole monarchy in his family, was great-grandfather to our saint. The family of Borgia or Borja, had long flourished in Spain; but received a new lustre by the exaltation of Cardinal Alphonso Borgia to the pontificate, under the name of Calixtus III., in 1455. St. Francis was born in 1510, at Gandia, a town which was the chief seat of the family, in the kingdom of Valencia. His pious mother had a great devotion to St. Francis of Assisum, and, in the pangs of a dangerous labour, made a vow that if she brought forth a son, he should be called Francis. As soon as he began to speak, his parents taught him to pronounce the holy names of Jesus and Mary, which he used often to repeat with wonderful seriousness. At five years of age he recited every day on his knees the chief parts of the catechism. All his diversion was to set up pious pictures, make little altars, imitate the ceremonies of the church, and teach them to the little boys who were his pages. From the cradle he was mild, modest, patient, and affable to all. The noble sentiments of gratitude and generosity which he then began to discover, were certain presages of an innate greatness of soul; the former being inseparable from a goodness of heart, and the latter, when regulated by prudence and charity, being the greatest virtue of a prince, who is raised above others, only that he may govern, and do good to mankind.

Francis, at seven years of age, could read his mother tongue, and the Latin office of the Blessed Virgin very distinctly. His father, therefore, thought it time for him to learn writing and grammar, for which purpose he appointed him a preceptor of known prudence, learning, and piety, who was called Doctor Ferdinand. At the same time he was furnished with a governor, whose business it was at different hours to fashion the young prince to the exercises that were suitable to his birth, in proportion as his age was capable of them. It was the first care of the parents, in the choice of the masters whom they placed about their son, that they were persons of uncommon piety, whose example might be a continual lesson of virtue, and whose instructions should all ultimately tend to the grafting in his mind true sentiments of morality and religion, without which all other accomplishments lose their value. Learning, good breeding, and other such qualifications, are useful and necessary instructions and helps; but these never make the man; every one is properly only such as the principles and maxims are by which he is governed. It is by these that a man's life is guided; if they are false or depraved, his understanding is deprived of the light of truth, his heart is corrupted, and it is impossible he should not go astray, and fall headlong down the precipices which the world and his passions prepare for him. It is therefore the first duty of every parent and master to study, by every means, to cure the passions of a youth, to begin this by repressing their exterior effects, and removing all occasions and incentives, and then to instil into their minds the strongest antidotes, by which he may be enabled and encouraged to expel their poison; and for this task no age is too early or tender; for if the mind has once taken any wrong bent, it becomes infinitely more painful and difficult to redress it. Opportunities are also to be taken in all studies of seasonably and strongly incucating short lessons of religion, and all virtues. By this means their seeds are to be sown in such a manner in a tender heart, that they may shoot deep roots, and gather such strength as to be proof against all storms. Our saint was blessed by God with such dispositions to virtue, and so good a capacity for his studies, that in all these parts of his education his masters found this task both agreeable and easy. Before he was ten years old he began to take wonderful delight in hearing sermons, and spent much time in devotion, being tenderly affected to the Passion of our divine Redeemer, which he honoured with certain daily exercises. In his tenth year, his pious mother fell dangerously ill; on which occasion Francis, shutting himself up in his chamber, prayed for her with abundance of tears, and after his devotions, took a sharp discipline a long time together. This was the first time he used that practice of mortification which he afterward frequently made a part of his penance. It pleased God that the duchess died of that distemper, in 1520. This loss cost Francis many tears, though he moderated his grief by his entire resignation to the divine will. Her pious counsels had always been to him a great spur to virtue; and he took care never to forget them.

At that time Spain was filled with tumults and insurrections of the common people against the regency. The rebels, taking their advantage of the absence of the young king, Charles V., (who was then in Germany, where he had been chosen emperor,) plundered the houses of the nobility in the kingdom of Valencia, and made themselves masters of the town of Gandia. The duke fled with his whole family. Going to Saragossa, he left his son Francis, then twelve years old, under the care of the archbishop, John of Arragon, who was his uncle, being brother to his deceased mother. The archbishop made up a household for his nephew, and provided him with masters in grammar, music, and fencing, which he had begun to learn at Gandia. The young nobleman laboured at the same time to improve daily in grace and in every virtue. Two sermons which he heard a Hieronymite friar, who was his confessarius, and a learned and spiritual man, preach, one on the last judgment, the other on the passion of Christ, made strong impressions on his mind, so that he remained ever after exceedingly terrified at the consideration of the divine judgments, and, on the other side, conceived an ardent desire to lay down his life for the love of his divine Redeemer, who died for him. Going to Baëza to see his great-grandmother, Donna Maria de Luna, wife of Don Henriquez, uncle and master of the household to King Ferdinand, and great commander of Leon, with several other relations, he was confined there six months by a grievous fit of illness; during which time he gave great proofs of admirable patience and humility. From Baëza he was sent to Tordesillas, to be taken into the family and service of the Infanta Catherine, sister to Charles V., who was soon after to be married to John III., king of Portugal. The marriage was accomplished in 1525; but when the infanta went into Portugal, the Duke of Gandia, who had greater views for his son in Spain, recalled him, and engaged the archbishop of Saragossa to reassume the care of his education.

Francis was then fifteen years old, and, after he had finished rhetoric, studied philosophy two years under an excellent master with extraordinary diligence and applause. Many so learn these sciences as to put on in their thoughts and expressions a scholastic garb, which they cannot lay aside, so that their minds may be said to be cast in Gothic moulds. Hence it is become a proverb, that nothing is more horrid than a mere scholar, that is, a pedant, who appears in the world to have reaped from his studies scarce any other advantage than to be rendered by them absolutely unfit for civilized society. Nothing contributes more to improve all the faculties of the human mind than a well-regulated and well-digested course of studies, especially of the polite arts and philosophy; but then these must be polished by a genteel address and expression, by great sentiments of modesty and generosity, by a fine carriage suitable to a person's rank, and by sincere Christian virtue. The prudent archbishop was solicitous to procure his nephew all these advantages. He was particularly careful to make his pupil active and laborious, by seeing that he went from one employment to another, without leaving any void or unprofitable time between them; nor did his masters fix the end of their instructions in the letter of his studies; but made use of every thing in them to frame his judgment, and form in him true taste; and they taught him to refer every thing to virtue. This seemed the natural bent of the young nobleman's soul, and in the eighteenth year of his age he had strong inclinations to a religious state. The devil raised up instruments to second his attack, and assailed the servant of God with most violent temptations of impurity, in order to profane that pure soul which God had consecrated to himself. Francis opposed to this dangerous enemy very frequent confession, fervent prayer, reading pious books, mortification, humility, distrust in himself, and a firm confidence in God, whose mercy alone bestows the inestimable gift of chastity, and to whom this glorious victory belongs. By these means the saint triumphed over this passion, and had preserved his virginal purity unspotted, when providence fixed him in the holy state of marriage. His father and uncle, to divert his thoughts from a religious life, removed him from Saragossa to the court of Charles V. in 1528, where they hoped his thoughts would take a different turn. The ripeness of his judgment and prudence were such as seldom appear in a more advanced age; and by his virtue, and his unaffected obsequiousness and assiduity in serving his prince, he could not fail of gaining a high place in his favour. Francis had a heart not insensible to the motives of gratitude and generosity, but still more of those of religion. He considered his duty to his prince as his duty to God;

and though he willingly accepted of every mark of his prince's regard for him, he was very solicitous in all things to refer himself, his actions, and whatever he received from God, purely to the divine honour. The perfect sanctification of his own soul was his great and constant aim in all he did. As religious exercises themselves, without regularity, can never be steady, and without this advantage lose a considerable part of their lustre and merit, Francis was extremely exact in regulating both his personal devoirs, and the principal duties of his family. In it hours were appointed for every one to go every day to mass, for pious reading, and meals. He heard sermons as often as possible, and conversed much with pious persons, went to confession almost every Sunday, and on all great festivals. It was also a part of his care that his whole family should spend well those days which are particularly set apart for the divine service. It is indeed from the manner in which a Christian employs them, that we may form an idea of his conduct with regard to his general practice and sense of religion.

St. Francis, though he delighted chiefly in the company of the most virtuous, was courteous and obliging to all, never spoke ill of any one, nor ever suffered others to do it in his presence. He was a stranger to envy, ambition, gallantry, luxury, and gaming; vices which are often too fashionable in courts, and against which he armed himself with the utmost precaution. He not only never played, but would never see others play, saying that a man commonly loses by it four things—his money, his time, the devotion of his heart to God, and his conscience. One of his servants discovered, that on the days on which he was obliged to visit company in which ladies made a part, he wore a hair-shirt. In him it appeared that there is no readier way to gain the esteem of men, though without seeking it, than by the heroic practice of Christian virtue. Nothing is so contemptible, even among men of the world, as insolence, pride, injustice, or anger; nothing so hateful as one who loves nobody but himself, refers every thing to himself, and makes himself the centre of all his desires and actions. Nor is there any thing more amiable than a man who seeks not himself, but refers himself to God, and seeks and does all things for God and the service of others; in which Christian piety consists. The wicked themselves find no more solid comfort or protection in affliction than the friendship of such a person; even those who persecute him, because his virtue is a censure of their irregularities, nevertheless admire in their breasts the sincere piety which condemns them. This is more conspicuous when such a virtue shines forth in an exalted station. It is not therefore to be wondered that Francis was honoured and beloved by all the court, particularly by the emperor, who called him the miracle of princes.

The empress had so great an esteem for him, and so high an idea of his merit, that she fixed her eye on him to marry Eleanor de Castro, a Portuguese lady of the first rank, a person of great piety and accomplishments, her principal favourite, who had been educated with her, and whom she had brought with her out of Portugal. The emperor was well pleased with the proposal, and concluded a treaty with the duke of Gandia for his son's marriage. The great qualities and virtue of the lady, and his deference for the emperor and his father, did not allow Francis long to deliberate upon so advantageous an offer, which opened to him a road to the highest favours of the court. The marriage was solemnized in the most Christian manner; to which state the saint brought the best preparation, innocence of life with unsullied purity, and an ardent spirit of religion and devotion. The emperor on that occasion created him marquis of Lombay, and master of the horse to the empress; and having had experience of his wisdom, secrecy, and fidelity, not only admitted him into his privy-council, but took great delight in conferring often privately with him upon his most difficult undertakings, and communicated to him his most important designs. The marquis, to rid himself of the importunities of those who followed more dangerous diversions, spent some of his time in music, played on several instruments, and sang very well; he also set poetical pieces to music, and composed cantatas wh.ch were sung in some churches in Spain, and called the compositions of the duke of Gandia. But he never could bear any profane songs. It was to please the emperor, who was fond of hawking, that he first followed the diversion, always in his majesty's company; he was afterward very expert, and took much delight in it. He sometimes mentioned the aspirations with which he entertained his soul on those occasions, sometimes admiring and adoring the Creator in the instinct of a bird or beast, or in the beauty of the fields and heavens; sometimes considering the obedience and docility of a bird, and the disobedience of man to God; the gratitude of a wild and fierce beast or bird, which, being furnished with a little food, forgets its natural ferocity, and is made tame; yet man is ungrateful to God from whom he receives all things; the hawk soars to heaven as soon as its pinion is at liberty; yet man's soul grovels on the earth. In such like reflections and self-reproaches the pious marquis was often much affected and confounded within himself, and to pursue his pious meditations he often left the company to hide himself in some thicket. The emperor studied mathematics, and Francis made use of the same master to learn those sciences, especially the branches which are most useful for fortifying towns, and the whole military art, on which subjects his majesty frequently conversed with him. The emperor made him his companion in his expedition into Africa against Barbarossa in 1535, and in another which he undertook against France into Provence in 1536, whence he despatched him to the empress to carry her news of his health and affairs.

Under a violent fever with which the marquis was

seized in 1535, he made a resolution to employ for his ordinary reading no other books but those of piety, especially devout instructions, the Lives of Saints, and the Holy Scripture, particularly the New Testament, with a good commentator; in reading which, he often shut his book, to meditate on what he had read. In 1537, being at the court, which was then at Segovia, he fell sick of a dangerous quinsy, in which he never ceased praying in his heart, though he was not able to pronounce the words. These accidents were divine grace, which weaned Francis daily more and more from the world; though, while it smiled upon him, he saw the treachery, the shortness, and the dangers of its flattering enjoyments, through that gaudy flash in which it danced before his eyes. Others receive the like frequent admonitions, but soon drown them in the hurry of pleasures or temporal affairs in which they plunge their hearts. But none of those calls were lost on Francis. His life at court had always appeared a model of virtue. But as he had not yet learned perfectly to die to himself, a mixture of the world found still a place in his heart, and his virtues were very imperfect. He even feared and bitterly accused himself that he had some time in his life been betrayed into mortal sin. But God was pleased to call him perfectly to his service.

In 1537 died his grandmother, Donna Maria Henriquez, called in religion Mary Gabriel. She was cousin-german to King Ferdinand, and married John Borgia, the second duke of Gandia. By his sudden death she remained a widow at nineteen years of age, having had by him two children, John, our saint's father, and Isabel, who became a Poor Clare at Gandia, who was afterward chosen abbess of that house, and was eminent for her extraordinary devotion, and love of extreme poverty and penance. Mary, her mother, after having brought up and married her son, and seen the birth of our saint, entered the same austere order, in the thirty-fourth year of her age.

The physicians declared, that if she embraced so severe a manner of life, she could not live one year; nevertheless, she survived in it thirty-three years, living the most perfect model of humility, poverty, recollection, and penance, under obedience to her own daughter, who was abbess of that monastery. She met death with so much joy, that in her agony she desired a *Te Deum* might be sung as soon as she should have expired, in thanksgiving for her happy passage from this world to God. The marquis used afterward to say, that from the time that his grandmother went to heaven he found his soul animated with new strength and courage to devote himself most perfectly to the divine service. God blessed his marriage with a numerous and happy offspring, five boys and three girls; Charles, the eldest, who was duke of Gandia when Ribadeneira wrote the life of our saint; Isabel, John, Alvarez, Johanna, Fernandez, Dorothy, and Alphonsus. Dorothy died young a Poor Clare at Gandia; the rest all married, enjoyed different titles and posts of honour, and left families behind them.

St. Francis was much affected at the death of his intimate friend, the famous poet, Garcilaso de Vega, who was killed at the siege of a castle in Provence, in 1537. The death of the pious Empress Isabel happened two years after, on the first of May, 1539, while the emperor was holding the states of Castile at Toledo with the utmost pomp and magnificence. His majesty was much afflicted for the loss of so virtuous a consort. The marquis and marchioness of Lombay were commissioned by him to attend her corpse to Granada, where she was to be buried. When the funeral convoy arrived at Granada, and the marquis delivered the corpse into the hands of the magistrates of that city, they were on both sides to make oath that it was the body of the late empress. The coffin of lead was therefore opened, and her face was uncovered, but appeared so hideous and so much disfigured that no one knew it, and the stench was so loathsome that everybody made what haste he could away. Francis, not knowing the face, would only swear it was the body of the empress, because, from the care he had taken, he was sure nobody could have changed it upon the road. Being exceedingly struck at this spectacle, he repeated to himself: "What is now become of those eyes, once so sparkling? Where is now the beauty and graceful air of that countenance, which we so lately beheld? Are you her sacred majesty, Donna Isabel? Are you my empress, my lady, my mistress?" The impression which this spectacle made on his soul remained strong and lively during the thirty-three years that he survived it, to his last breath. Returning that evening from the royal chapel to his lodgings, he locked himself up in his chamber, and passed the whole night without a wink of sleep. Prostrate on the floor, shedding a torrent of tears, he said to himself: "What is it, my soul, that I seek in the world? How long shall I pursue and grasp at shadows? What is she already become, who was lately so beautiful, so great, so much revered? This death, which has thus treated the imperial diadem, has already levelled his bow to strike me. Is it not prudent to prevent its stroke, by dying now to the world, that at my death I may live to God?" He earnestly conjured his Divine Redeemer to enlighten his soul, to draw him out of the abyss of his miseries, and to assist him by his all-powerful grace, that with his whole heart he might serve that Master whom death could not rob him of. The next day, after the divine office and mass in the great church, the celebrated and holy preacher, John of Avila, made the funeral sermon, in which, with a divine unction and energy, he set forth the vanity and deceitfulness of all the short-lived enjoyments of this world, false and empty in themselves, and which entirely vanish when death cuts the thread of our life, and overturns at once all those castles which our foolish imagination has raised in the air. He then spoke of the eternal glory or misery which follows death, and of the astonishing madness of those who in this moment of life neglect to secure what is to them of such infinite importance. This discourse completed the entire conversion of the marquis, who, that afternoon, sent for the preacher, laid open to him the situation of his soul, and his desire of bidding adieu to the world. The holy director confirmed him in his resolution of quitting the court, where a soul is always exposed to many snares, and of entering upon a new course of serving God with the utmost fervour. Francis determined upon the spot to forsake the court, and soon after made a vow to embrace a religious state of life if he should survive his consort.

At his return to Toledo, the emperor made him viceroy of Catalonia, and created him knight and commander of the order of St. James, or of the Red Cross, the most honourable in Spain. Barcelona was the residence of his government; and no sooner had he taken possession of his post, but he changed the whole face of the province. The highways were cleared of robbers: against their bands the viceroy marched in person, and caused the criminals to be rigorously executed, having first provided them with the best spiritual assistance to prepare them for their punishment and death. He carefully watched the judges, obliging them to administer justice impartially, and to despatch lawsuits with all reasonable expedition. He set up, in all parts of the province, schools and seminaries for youth, and assisted debtors and all distressed persons with extraordinary charities. The great duties of his charge, to which he applied himself with unwearied diligence, and which made him at once the judge, the father, and the protector of a numerous people, were no impediments to his exercises of religion. Four or five hours together were devoted by him to mental and vocal prayer every morning as soon as he rose, without any prejudice to public affairs or neglect of his family. He added to every hour of the divine office, which he said every day, a meditation on a station of our Saviour's passion, so as to accompany him every day through all its parts, from the garden to the sepulchre. He performed daily devotions to our Lady, in which he meditated on the principal mysteries and virtues of her life. At the times in which he gave audience or applied himself to business, he had God always present to his mind. When he was obliged to assist at public entertainments or diversions, his mind was usually so absorbed in God that if he was afterward asked about them, he could give no account of what had passed or been said at them. Tears of devotion often gushed from his eyes, even in the midst of business, and he would sometimes thus address himself to God: "Who could ever soften this heart of mine, which is harder than flint or adamant, but thou alone, O Lord! Thou, O God of mercies, who couldst draw fountains of water from a rock, and raise up sons of Abraham out of stones, couldst change a stony heart into one of flesh." His austerities were excessive. He entirely laid aside suppers, that he might employ that time in prayer. Having passed two lents without taking any other sustenance than once a day a mess of leeks, or some pulse with a piece of bread, and a cup of water to drink, he was desirous to fast in that manner a whole year. At the same time he kept a table, suitable to his rank, for the lords who visited him, and the officers that attended him; dining with his company, he ate his leeks or pulse very slow, and conversed facetiously with them, that no one might observe him, if possible, though at table his discourse generally turned on piety. His watchings, disciplines, and other austerities were very severe. By this rigorous way of living, he, who was before very fat, became so lean that his servant found his clothes grown about half a yard too big for him within the space of a year. He used often to say: "We must take our way toward eternity, never regarding what men think of us or our actions, studying only to please God." Knowing the obligation of dying perfectly to ourselves, this he endeavoured to effect from the beginning of his conversion, by humiliations and a sovereign contempt of himself. He had formerly been accustomed to communicate only once a month. Since he had altered his manner of living, he confessed his sins once every week, communicated in public on all great festivals, and privately every Sunday, generally with wonderful spiritual consolations and delights. He sometimes considered the peace, serenity, and solid joy with which divine love fills a soul whose affections are disentangled from earthly things, and the inexpressible pure delights and sweetness, which the presence of the Holy Ghost infuses into hearts which he prepares by his grace to receive his communications; and comparing these with the foolish, empty, and base satisfactions of worldlings, he was not able to suppress his astonishment, but cried out: "O sensual, base, miserable, and blind life! is it possible that men should be such strangers to their own happiness, such enemies to themselves, to be fond of thy false enjoyments, and for their sake to deprive themselves of those that are pure, permanent, and solid!" This was the life of the devout viceroy when F. Antony Aroaz, the first professed Jesuit after the ten that were concerned in the foundation of that order, came to preach at Barcelona. By his means Francis became acquainted with this new institute, and the character of its holy founder, to whom he wrote to consult him whether so frequent a communion as once a week was to be commended in persons engaged in the world. St. Ignatius, who was then at Rome, answered him that frequent communion is the best means to cure the disorders of our souls, and to raise them to perfect virtue; but advised him to make choice of a prudent and pious director, and to follow his advice. Pursuant to this direction, Francis continued his weekly communion, employing three days before it in preparatory exercises, and three days after it in acts of thanksgiving. From that time he began frequently to make use of Jesuits for his directors, and to promote the Society of Jesus in Spain, which had been approved by Paul III. two years before.

During this interval died John duke of Gandia, his father, a nobleman of singular virtue. When a person complained that his alms exceeded his estate, his answer was: "If I had thrown away a larger sum on my pleasures, no one would have found fault with me. But I had rather incur your censure, and deprive myself of necessaries, than that Christ's members should be left in distress." Francis was much affected at the news of his death, by which the title and honours of duke of Gandia devolved upon him. Shortly after, he obtained of the emperor, as he passed through Barcelona on his road to Italy, leave to quit his government; but his majesty insisted that he should repair to court, and accept of the office of master of the household to the infanta, Maria of Portugal, daughter to King John III., then upon the point of being married to Philip, the emperor's son; but the death of that princess before the intended marriage, set our saint at liberty to follow his own inclinations to a retired life. He therefore returned to Gandia, in 1543, which town he fortified, that it might not be exposed to the plunders of the Moors and pirates from Barbary. He built a convent for the Dominicans at Lombay, repaired the hospital, and founded a college of Jesuits at Gandia. His duchess Eleanor, who concurred with him in all his pious views, fell sick of a lingering distemper, during which Francis continued to fast, pray, and give large alms for her recovery. One day as he was praying for her, prostrate in his closet, with great earnestness, he was on a sudden visited with an extraordinary interior light in his soul, and heard, as it were, a voice saying distinctly within him: "If thou wouldst have the life of the duchess prolonged, it shall be granted; but it is not expedient for thee." This he heard so clearly and evidently that, as he assured others, he could not doubt, either then or afterward, but that it was a divine admonition. He remained exceedingly confounded; and penetrated with a most sweet and tender love of God, and bursting into a flood of tears he addressed himself to God as follows: "O my Lord and my God, leave not this, which is only in thy power, to my will. Who art thou but my Creator and sovereign good? and who am I but a miserable creature? I am bound in all things to conform my will to thine. Thou alone knowest what is best, and what is for my good. As I am not my own, but altogether thine, so neither do I desire that my will be done, but thine, nor will I have any other will but thine. Do what thou pleasest with the life of my wife, that of my children, and my own, and with all things thou hast given me." Thus, in all our prayers which we put up to God for health, life, or any temporal blessings, we only ask that he grant them in mercy, and so far only as he sees expedient for our spiritual good. The duke made this oblation of himself and all things that he possessed with extraordinary fervour and resignation. From that day the duchess grew every day sensibly much worse, and died on the 27th of March, 1546, leaving the duke a widower in the thirty-sixth year of his age. Her great piety, and the heroic practices of all Christian virtues by which she prepared herself for her passage, gave him the greatest comfort under his loss, by an assured hope of her eternal happiness. A few days after her death, F. Peter Le Fevre or Faber, St. Ignatius's first associate in founding his Order, came to Gandia. He was then leaving Spain to go into Italy, and was ordered by St. Ignatius to call upon the duke of Gandia in his way. Our saint made a retreat under his direction according to the spiritual exercises of St. Ignatius, and rejoiced exceedingly that he had found in this experienced director such a spiritual master and guide as he wished. With him the saint agreed upon the execution of a design he had formed of founding a college of Jesuits at Gandia, and F. Le Fevre, after having said mass, laid the first stone, the duke the second, and his sons each another, on the 5th of May, 1546. In favour of this college the duke procured that Gandia should be honoured by the pope and emperor with the privileges of a university. F. Le Fevre died on the first of August the same year, 1546, soon after his arrival at Rome. After his departure from Gandia, St. Francis, from the conferences he had with him, composed several small treatises of piety, which show by what exercises he began to lay the foundation of a spiritual life. The two first of these books treat of the method of acquiring a true knowledge of ourselves, and sincere humility.

In the mean time, the good duke took a resolution to consecrate himself to God in some religious order, and having long recommended the affair to God, and taken the advice of learned and pious men, deliberating with himself whether to prefer an active or a contemplative state, he made choice of the active, and determined to embrace the society of Jesus, then lately founded, in which he was much delighted with the zealous views of that holy order, and with that rule by which all preferment to ecclesiastical dignities is cut off. He sent his petition for admittance to St. Ignatius at Rome by a servant. The holy founder received his request with great joy; but, in his answer, advised the duke to defer the execution of his design till he had settled his children, and finished the foundations he had begun, advising him in the mean time to study a regular course of theology at Gandia, and to take the degree of doctor in that faculty. The duke punctually obeyed his directions, but was obliged to assist, in 1547, at the cortes or general states of three kingdoms, of which that of Arragon was then compounded, and which were assembled at Monson. The reconciliation of the nobility, both among themselves and with their sovereign, was the important and delicate affair which was to be there settled. The emperor, who by former experience was well acquainted with the extraordinary integrity and abilities of the duke of

Gandia, had enjoined his son, Prince Philip, who held the states, to take care that he should be appointed tratador or president. By his dexterity and steady virtue, matters were settled to the satisfaction of all parties, and the saint delivered himself this last time in which he spoke on the public affairs of state, in such a manner as to move exceedingly all who heard him. In the same year he made the first vows of the society before private witnesses in the chapel of the college he had founded at Gandia. For St. Ignatius, knowing the earnestness of his desire to complete his intended sacrifice, and considering by how many ties he was held, which it was difficult for him to break at once, obtained a brief of the pope, by which he was allowed to spend four years in the world after he should have made his first vows. By them the saint consecrated himself with his whole heart as a holocaust to God; and, leaving his castle to his eldest son, retired into a private house, where he studied the positive and scholastic theology under the learned Doctor Perez, whom he invited from Valencia to settle in his new college at Gandia. The rule of life which he prescribed himself was as follows:—He rose every morning at two o'clock, spent six hours in private prayers till eight, and then went to confession, heard mass, and received every day the holy communion; which he did in the great church on Sundays and holydays; on other days, in his own private chapel or that of the nunnery of St. Clare. At nine o'clock he received his theological lesson, and studied till almost dinner-time, when he took some moments to give audience to his officers of justice, and despatch business; he dined at twelve very temperately; after which he spent an hour in giving useful directions to his children, servants, or others; the afternoons he gave to his studies, and the evenings to his devotions, without ever taking any supper or collation. In his night examination he was remarkably rigorous in calling himself to account, and punishing himself for the least failings that he apprehended. He married his eldest son Charles to Donna Maria Centellas, the daughter of Francis Centellas, count of Oliva, and Donna Maria Cardona, daughter to the duke of that name. The saint also made a provision for all his other children, took the degree of doctor at Gandia, and made his will, which was no difficult task, as, by his prudence and economy he was his own executor, and left no obligations undischarged; only he recommended to his heirs the protection of his three convents, of the Jesuits, Dominicans, and Poor Clares.

Having finished his affairs, though the four years which were granted him were not expired, he set out for Rome in 1549, being accompanied by his second son John, thirty servants, and some Jesuits who went from their convent at Gandia to a general chapter which was then held at Rome. In going out of the town of Gandia he sang those two verses: *When Israel went out of Egypt;* and, *Our soul is escaped as a bird out of the snare of the fowler: the snare is broken, and we are escaped.* In his journey he observed the same rule of life which he had followed the three last years, spending as much time in prayer, and going to confession, and receiving the communion every day. Notwithstanding his repugnance, he was obliged to submit to the magnificent receptions he met with at Ferrara, that of the duke of Florence, and at Rome, where he arrived on the 31st of August, 1550. He refused to lodge in the pope's palace, or any other, which he was earnestly pressed to do, and chose a mean cell in the convent of the Jesuits. St. Ignatius waited to receive him at the door, and the duke, throwing himself at his feet, begged his blessing, and honoured him as his father and superior. After paying his obeisance to the pope, and receiving and returning the visits of all the great men at Rome, he performed his devotions for the Jubilee. With a considerable sum of money which he brought from Spain he built a church for the use of the Professed House, and laid the foundation of a great college of

Jesuits, called the Roman College; but refused the title and honour of founder. Pope Gregory XIII. finished it in the most magnificent and complete manner. From Rome he sent a gentleman, who was a domestic client, to the emperor in Germany, to beg his license to resign his duchy to his eldest son. He laments, in his letter to that prince, and accuses himself that by the scandalous life he had led in his court, he had deserved hell, and even the lowest place in hell; earnestly thanks the divine mercy for having borne with him with infinite goodness and patience; he expresses an humble and tender gratitude to the fathers of the society, who, out of compassion for his soul, had admitted him among them to spend the remaining part of his life in penance and in the divine service. He promises his imperial majesty to pray that God who had made him victorious over his enemies, would give him the more important victory over his passions and himself, and enkindle his pure love in his soul, with an ardent devotion to the passion of Jesus Christ, so that the cross should become his delight and his glory. This letter was dated at Rome, the 15th of January, 1551.

Upon a rumour that Pope Julius III. was resolved to promote our saint to the dignity of cardinal, he obtained the leave of St. Ignatius, after having stayed four months at Rome, to withdraw privately into Spain, where he lived some time concealed in Guipuscoa, (a small province in Biscay,) at the castle of Loyola—then retired to a small convent of his order at Ognata, a town about four leagues from Loyola. In this place the emperor's obliging answer was brought him, in which his majesty expressed how much he was edified at the exchange he had made of the world for heaven, and how much he was afflicted to lose him; but ratified his request, and promised to take his children under his special protection. The duke having read this letter, retired into an oratory, and, prostrate on the ground, made the most perfect consecration of himself to God; and desiring no other riches or possession but him alone, and renouncing in his heart the whole world, he earnestly begged the grace perfectly to die to himself, that God alone, or his love, might live and reign in his soul, and that he might deserve to carry the cross of his Redeemer by the practice of mortification and poverty. Coming out of his closet, he made a solemn renunciation of all his worldly dignities and possessions, according to the legal forms, in favour of his eldest son, who was absent; then cut his hair, put off his ducal robes, and put on the Jesuit's habit. This being done, he went again into the oratory to renew his offering of himself to God, and to beg his grace that his sacrifice might be made entire, and he sang with great joy those words of the psalmist: *I am thy servant.* This passed in 1551. After the most devout preparation, he was ordained priest on the first of August the same year, and said his first mass in the chapel of Loyola.

The saint begged of the magistrates of Ognata a small hermitage dedicated in honour of St. Mary Magdalen, a mile from that town, and with the leave of his superior retired thither with certain fathers of the society, that he might more heartily devote himself to the practices of humility, penance, and prayer. With great importunity he obtained leave to serve the cook, fetch water, and carry wood; he made the fire and swept the kitchen; and when he waited at table, he often fell on his knees to beg pardon of the fathers and lay-brothers for having served them ill; and he frequently kissed their feet with extraordinary affection and humility. He loved and coveted the meanest employs with a sincere affection of humility, and was delighted to carry a wallet on his shoulders to beg, especially where he was not known. He often went through the villages with a bell, calling the children to catechism, and diligently teaching them their prayers and the Christian doctrine, and instructing and preaching to all ranks, especially the poor. At the earnest request of the viceroy of Navarre, Don Bernardin of Cardenas, duke of Marquede, the saint preached in that country with incredible fruit, and the duke regulated his whole conduct and all his affairs by the saint's direction. The emperor and Pope Julius III. concurred in the design of adopting St. Francis into the college of cardinals. St. Ignatius fell at the feet of his Holiness, begging he would not inflict such a wound on his society, by which its fences would be broken down, and one of its most express rules rendered useless. St. Francis had recourse to tears, prayer, and extraordinary mortifications, to avert the danger. When the storm was blown over, St. Ignatius sent St. Francis an order to preach in other parts of Spain, to which he was invited with great importunity. The success which everywhere attended his labours is not to be conceived; and many persons of the first quality desired to regulate their families and their consciences entirely by his advice. After doing wonders in Castile and Andalusia, he seemed to surpass himself in Portugal, especially at Evora and Lisbon. King John III. had been the warmest protector of the society from its infancy. His brother, the Infant Don Lewis, desired to make himself a Jesuit; but Saint Francis and Saint Ignatius, thinking his assistance necessary to the king in the administration of the public affairs, persuaded him to satisfy himself with following a plan of life which St. Francis drew up for him in the world. The most learned doctors acknowledge that the spiritual wisdom of this saint was not learned from the books which he was accustomed to read, but from secret humble prayer, and a close communication with the divine wisdom. Saint Ignatius, augmenting the provinces of the society in Spain to the number of five, besides the Indies, appointed St. Francis commissary-general of the Order in Spain, Portugal, and the Indies, in 1554; but obliged him in the practice of particular austerities to obey another; for such had always been the fervour of our saint in his severe penitential exercises, that the holy general had found it necessary from the beginning of his conversion to mitigate them by strict injunctions. Amid the numerous conversions of souls, and the foundations of new houses, St. Francis found time and opportunities for his accustomed devotions and humiliations in serving his brethren and the poor in hospitals and prisons. When any one was fallen into any fault, he would say to him: "Through my unworthiness God has permitted such a misfortune to befall you. We will join our endeavours to doing penance. For my part, I will fast, or pray, or take a discipline so and so; what will you do?" On the like occasions, such was his patience and humility, it seemed impossible for any one to resist the force of his example and charity. Saint Ignatius dying in 1556, F. Laynez was chosen second general of the society, St. Francis being at that time detained in Spain by a fit of the gout.

The Emperor Charles V., sated with the emptiness of worldly grandeur, and wearied with the dissipation, fatigues, and weight of government, forsook the world, abdicated the empire by a solemn act which he signed at Zuytburg in Zell, on the 7th of September, 1556, and chose for the place of his retirement a great monastery of Hieronymites, called of St. Justus, in the most agreeable plains of Placentia, in Spanish Estramadura, not far from Portugal. Antonio de Vera, De Thou, Surius, Sleidan, and many other historians give us an edifying account of the life he led in this solitude, applying himself much to pious reading, (in which the works of St. Bernard were his chiefest delight,) to the practice of devotion, and to frequent meditation on death. That this might make the stronger impression on his mind, he caused his own funeral office to be celebrated before he died, and assisted himself at the ceremony, dressed in black. He worked in his garden, and at making clocks, assisted at all the divine offices, communicated very often at mass, and took the discipline with the monks every Friday. As he travelled through Spain to the place of his retirement, from Biscay, where he landed, he saw himself neglected by the president of Castile and others who had the greatest obligations to him; and he found the payments slack of the small pension which was all he had reserved out of so many kingdoms. Hereupon he let drop some words of complaint; but desiring to see F. Francis Borgia, the saint waited upon him, and the emperor was wonderfully comforted by his discourses. This prince had been prepossessed against the society, and expressed his surprise that F. Francis should have preferred it to so many ancient orders. The saint removed his prejudices, and for the motives which had determined him in his choice, he alleged that God had called him to a state in which the active and contemplative life are joined together, and in which he was freed from the danger of being raised to dignities, to shun which he had fled from the world. He added that if the society was a new order, the fervour of those who are engaged in it answered that objection. After staying three days with the emperor, he took leave, and continued his visitation of the colleges and new foundations erected in favour of his order in Spain.

The society sustained a great loss by the death of John III., the most valiant and pious king of Portugal, who was carried off by an apoplexy in the year 1557. This great and religious prince, who had succeeded his father Emmanuel the Great in 1521, during a reign of thirty-six years had laboured with great zeal to propagate the faith in Asia and Africa, and had founded many colleges and convents. The crown devolved upon his grandson Sebastian, then only three years old, his father, the Infant John, son to the late king, and his mother Joanna, daughter to Charles V., being both dead. His grandmother, Queen Catharine, was regent of the kingdom, to whom St. Francis wrote a letter of condolence and consolation, tenderly exhorting her to praise God for all his mercies, to be resigned to his holy will, and to have no other view than to advance in his grace and love.

Afterward the emperor deputed St. Francis to make his compliments of condolence to the queen-regent, and treat with her about certain affairs of great importance. A dangerous pestilential fever and her majesty's great respect for his person detained him a considerable time in Portugal; but before the end of the year he went back to the emperor to inform him of the result of his commission. His majesty soon after sent for him again, and discoursed with him on spiritual things, especially prayer, works of satisfaction, and penance, and the making the best preparation for death. The emperor told St. Francis that since he had been twenty-one years of age he had never passed a day without mental prayer, and he asked, among other scruples, whether it was a sign of vanity in him to have committed to writing several actions of his life, seeing he had done it for the sake, not of human applause, but of truth, and merely because he had found them misrepresented in other histories he had read. St. Francis left him, to go to Valladolid, but had not been there many days before news was brought of the emperor's death. That prince, after devoutly confessing his sins, and receiving the viaticum and the extreme unction, holding a crucifix in his hands, and repeating the holy name of Jesus, expired on the 21st of September, 1558. St. Francis made his funeral panegyric at Valladolid, insisting on his happiness in having forsaken the world before it forsook him, in order to complete his victory over himself.

The true greatness of our saint appeared not in the honours and applause which he often received, but in the sincere humility which he took care constantly to nourish and improve in his heart. In these dispositions he looked upon humiliations as his greatest gain and honour. From the time that he began to give himself totally to the divine service, he learned the infinite importance and difficulty of attaining to perfect humility. The most profound interior exercise of that virtue was the constant employment of his soul. At all times he studied most perfectly to confound and humble himself in the divine presence beneath all creatures, and within himself. Amid the greatest honours and respect that was shown him at Valladolid, his companion, F. Bustamanti, took notice that he was not only mortified and afflicted, but more than ordinarily confounded; of which he asked the reason. "I considered," said the saint, "in my morning meditation, that hell is my due; and I think that all men, even children, and all dumb creatures, ought to cry out to me, Away; hell is thy place; or, Thou art one whose soul ought to be in hell." From this reflection he humbled his soul, and raised himself to the most ardent love of God, and tender affection toward the divine mercy. He one day told the novices that, in meditating on the actions of Christ, he had for six years always placed himself in spirit at the feet of Judas; but that, considering that Christ had washed the feet of that traitor, he durst not approach, and from that time looked upon himself as excluded from all places, and unworthy to hold any in the world, and looked upon all other creatures with a degree of respect, and at a distance. When the mules and equipages of many cardinals and princes preceded him, to show him honour in the entry he made at Rome in 1550, before he had laid aside his titles and rank in the world, he said: "Nothing is more just than that brute beasts should be the companions of one who resembles them." At all commendations or applause he always shuddered, calling to mind the dreadful account he must one day give to God, how far he was from the least degree of virtue, and how base and execrable hypocrisy will appear at the last day. Upon his renouncing the world, in his letters he subscribed himself *Francis the sinner*, calling this his only title, till St. Ignatius ordered him to omit it, as a singularity. In this interior spirit of humility he laid hold of every opportunity of practising exterior humiliations, as the means perfectly to extinguish all pride in his heart, and to ground himself in the most sincere contempt of himself. He pressed with the utmost importunity Don Philip, while that prince was regent of Spain for his father, to extort from him a promise that he would never concur to his being nominated bishop, or raised to any other ecclesiastical dignity; adding, that this would be the highest favour he could receive from him. Others, he said, could live humble in spirit amid honours, and in high posts, which the established subordination of the world makes necessary; but, for his part, it was his earnest desire and ambition to leave the world in embracing the state of a poor religious man. When a gentleman, whom John, king of Portugal, sent to compliment him upon his first coming to Lisbon, used the title of his lordship, the saint was uneasy, and said, he was indeed tired with his journey, but much more with that word. He used to say that he had reaped this only advantage from having been duke, that he was on that account admitted into the society; for he should otherwise have been rejected as unfit and incapable. His greatest delight was to instruct the poor in places where he was unknown, or to perform the meanest offices in the convents where he came. It was his ambition at college to teach the lowest class of grammer, and only dropped that request upon being told he was not qualified for the task. At Evora, when the whole country assembled to receive from him some instructions, he threw himself on his knees, and kissed the feet of all the fathers and lay-brothers; with which act of humility they were more affected than they could have been by any sermon. At Porto, though commissary of his order, he took the keys of the gate, and served as porter. A certain postulant, who was sent thither to him from Seville at that time, in order to be admitted to the novitiate, found him at the gate among the poor. St. Francis told him there was a great heap of filth near them, which he was to carry away, and asked if he would help him. The postulant readily assented, and they cleansed the place. When he had eaten something very bitter and very ill dressed, on a journey, his companion, F. Bustamanti, asked him how he could eat it. His answer was: "It would seem delicious to one who had tasted of the gall with which the damned are tormented in hell." In travelling, he generally lay on straw, in winter, in barns. A nobleman, who had been his friend in the world, asked him how he could rest so ill accommodated, and entreated him to accept of better lodgings, and, in journeys, to send a messenger to prepare necessaries before he arrived. The saint replied: "I always send a faithful messenger before me to do all that." "Who is that?" said the other. "It is," replied the saint, "the consideration of what I deserve for my sins. Any lodging appears too good for one whose dwelling ought to be in hell." Being once on a journey with F. Bustamanti, they lay all night together in a cottage upon straw, and F. Bustamanti, who was very old and asthmatical, coughed and spit all night; and, thinking that he spit upon the wall, frequently disgorged a great quantity of phlegm on his face, which the saint never turned from him. Next morning, F. Bustamanti, finding what he had done, was in great confusion, and begged his pardon. Francis answered: "You have no reason; for you could not have found a fouler place, or fitter to be spit upon." Trials which are involuntary are much more profitable than humiliations of choice, in which self-love easily insinuates itself. Such, therefore, as Providence sent, the saint most cheerfully embraced. Among others, while he was employed at Porto in the foundation of a convent, he heard that the Inquisition had forbid the reading of some of the little tracts he had written while he was duke of Gandia, upon a groundless suspicion of errors. His silence and modesty on that occasion seemed at first to embolden his adversaries; but these works were at last cleared of all suspicions of error, and the censure taken off. Some raised a clamour against him on account of his former intimacy with the learned Dominican, Bartholomew Caranza, archbishop of Toledo, whom, at the instigation of King Philip II., the Inquisition in Spain cast into prison, upon false surmises; but that prelate was protected by the pope, and at last died at Rome in peace. Many slanders were raised against the society in Spain, which Melchior Cano, the learned bishop of the Canaries, author of the excellent book on Theological Commonplaces, suffered himself to be too much carried away by. But the pious Lewis of Granada and our saint, after some time, dispersed them.

By the extraordinary humility of St. Francis we may form some idea how much he excelled in all other virtues. No one could be a greater lover of holy poverty than our saint. This he showed in all his actions. From the day of his profession he never intermedled in money concerns, thinking it his happiness that he was never employed as procurator or dispenser in any house of his order. How sparing he was in fire, paper, and clothes is altogether incredible. One pair of shoes often lasted him two years. The same cassock served him in journeys and at home, in all seasons; only in travelling he turned the wrong side out, that it might be kept neater, and last better. No one could ever prevail upon him to use boots, or any additional clothing, in travelling in sharp or rainy weather; and he never seemed better pleased than when he came in wet and fatigued to a place where neither fire nor any refreshment was to be had. The marchioness of Pliego having sent him a present of a pair of warm stockings, they were laid by his bedside in the night, and the old ones taken away, in hopes he would not have perceived the change; but in the morning he was not to be satisfied till the brother had brought him his old darned stockings. The oldest habit and the meanest cell he sought. The Spanish ambassador's sister at Rome once said to him at table: "Your condition, Francis, is wretched, if, after exchanging your riches for so great poverty, you should not gain heaven in the end." "I should be miserable indeed," said the saint; "but as for the exchange, I have been already a great gainer by it."

A perfect spirit of obedience made him always respect exceedingly all his superiors; the least intimation of their will he received as if it had been a voice from heaven. When letters from St. Ignatius were delivered to him in Spain, he received them on his knees, and prayed, before he opened them, that God would give him grace punctually to obey whatever orders they contained. When he served in the kitchen, he would never stir without the leave of the brother who was the cook; and when for a long time he was ordered to obey a lay-brother, called Mark, in all things that regarded his health and diet, he would neither eat nor drink the least thing without his direction. He used to say that he hoped the society would flourish to the divine honour by three things: first, the spirit of prayer, and frequent use of the sacraments; secondly, by the opposition of the world, and by persecutions; thirdly, by the practice of perfect obedience. Penance is the means by which every Christian hopes to attain to salvation. St. Francis usually called it the high road to heaven; and sometimes he said he trembled lest he should be summoned before the tribunal of Christ before he had learned to conquer himself. For this grace he prayed daily with many tears. His hair-shirts and disciplines, with the cloths with which he wiped off the blood, he kept under lock and key while he was viceroy of Catalonia, and while he was general of the society. Sometimes he put gravel in his shoes when he walked; and daily, by many little artifices, he studied to complete the sacrifice of his penance, and to overcome himself. When the cook had one day, by mistake, made his broth with wormwood, which he had gathered instead of other herbs, the saint ate it cheerfully without saying a word. Being asked how he liked it, he said: "I never ate any thing fitter for me."

When others found out the mistake, and the cook in great confusion asked his pardon: "May God bless and reward you!" said he. "You are the only person among all my brethren that knows what suits me best." To his daughter, the countess of Lerma, when she complained of pain in a fit of illness, he said: "God sends pain to those that are unwilling to bear it; and refuses it to those who desire to suffer something for the exercise of patience and penance." Such desires in certain fervent penitents, arising from a great zeal to punish sin in themselves, and subdue sensuality and self-love, ought to confound our sloth, and love of softness and ease. But it is lawful and expedient with humility and charity to deprecate pain, if it may please God to remove or mitigate it; Though to bear it, when sent by God, with patience and resignation, is a duty and precept; as it also is so far to practise mortification, as to endeavour by it to fulfil our penance and gain the victory over ourselves. St. Francis once said to his sister, the Poor Clare at Gandia: "It is our duty in a religious state to die to ourselves twenty-four times a day, that we may be able to say with the apostle, *I die daily*, and be of the number of those of whom he says, *You are dead*." In sickness he chewed bitter pills, and swallowed the most nauseous potions slowly; and being asked the reason, he said: "This beast (so he often called his body) must suffer, to expiate the delight it formerly took in immoderately flattering its palate. And can I forget that Christ drank gall for me on his cross?"

Much might be said on this saint's singular prudence, on his candour and simplicity in all his words and actions, and on his tender charity and humanity toward all men. Though all virtues were eminent in him, none appeared more remarkable than his spirit of prayer. Dead to the world and to himself, and deeply penetrated with a sense of his own weakness and spiritual wants on one hand, and of the divine goodness and love on the other, he raised his pure affections to God with unabated ardour. His prayer, even before he left the world, seemed perpetual; but much more so afterward. Amid the greatest hurry of business he kept himself in the actual presence of God, and often in company appeared quite absorbed in him. Five or six hours which he dedicated together to prayer in the morning seemed to him scarce a quarter of an hour; and when he came from that heavenly exercise, his countenance seemed to shine with a dazzling light. His preparation for mass often held him some hours; and in his thanksgiving after offering that adorable sacrifice, he sometimes so much forgot himself, being transported in God, that it was necessary to force him from church, almost by violence, to dinner. Such were the devotion and modesty which appeared in his face, that many, whenever they found their souls spiritually dry, were excited to devotion by seeing and conversing a little with him. In order to attain the greatest purity of soul possible, he went twice a day to confession, with great compunction, for the smallest imperfections in his actions, before mass, and again in the evening; a practice not to be advised to those who are in danger of doing it negligently, or without sufficient contrition, and endeavour perfectly to purge their hearts. From the heavenly sweetness which he tasted in the communication of his soul with God, he used to express his astonishment at, and compassion for, the blindness of worldlings, who know not the happiness of a spiritual life, and delight themselves in the brutal gratifications of sense. The news of the sudden death of the saint's dearest daughter, Isabel of Arragon, countess of Lerma, a lady of singular piety, and of the greatest endowments, was brought him while he was in the streets of Valladolid, going to court. He stopped, shut his eyes, prayed secretly for about the space of four minutes, and then went on. At court he conversed with the princess as usual. In taking leave, he recommended to her prayers the soul of her late servant Isabel. "What!"

said the princess, "has a father no more feeling for the death of such a daughter?" "Madam," he replied, "she was only lent me. The Master has called her hence. Ought I not to thank him for having given her me so long, and for having now called her to his glory, as I hope in his mercy?" On the same occasion he said to the constable of Castile: "Since the Lord hath called me to his service, and hath required of me to give him my heart, I have endeavoured to resign it to him so entirely, that no creature, living or dead, should ever disturb it."

F. Laynez, second general of the Jesuits, dying in 1565, St. Francis, notwithstanding all the precautions he could take to prevent it, was chosen to succeed him, on the 2d of July. He made tender exhortations to the fathers who composed the general assembly of the society, and kissed the feet of every one among them before they departed. His first care in this new charge was to found a house for the novitiate in Rome. He promoted the interest of the society in all parts of the world with such success that he might be called a second founder; and the zeal with which he propagated the missions, and instructed and animated the labourers in planting the gospel in the most remote countries of the eastern and western hemisphere, entitles him to a great share in the conversion of those countries to the faith. He was not less active in directing his religious brethren in Europe, and in animating them with the zealous spirit of their institute for the reformation of the manners of Christians. Preaching being the principal means instituted by God for the conversion of souls, this holy instructer of preachers, not content most earnestly to recommend this sacred pastoral function, laid down excellent rules for duly performing the same. In 1566, a pestilence broke out, and made great havoc in Rome; upon which occasion St. Francis procured both from the pope and magistrates plentiful alms for the relief of the poor, and commissioned the fathers of his order, two and two, to attend the sick in all parts of the city, with imminent danger of their own lives. In 1570, the year before the victory of Lepanto, Pope Pius V. sent St. Francis, with his nephew, the Cardinal Alexandrin, on an embassy into France, Spain, and Portugal, to engage the Christian princes to send succours for the defence of Christendom against the Mohammedans. The saint had been for some time in a bad state of health; his infirmities, inclination to retirement, and a deep sense of the weight of his post, which he had filled five years, put him upon a design to procure a discharge from that burden in 1570; but this his brethren would by no means listen to. During this legation, his distempers increased upon him, insomuch, that when he arrived at Ferrara in his return, the duke, who was his cousin, sent him from thence to Rome in a litter. During this state of his illness he would admit no visits but from persons whose entertainment turned on spiritual matters, except physicians. The fathers of the society begged he would name his successor, and allow them the satisfaction of taking his picture; but he would do neither. When he had lost his speech in his agony, a painter was introduced to his bedside. The saint, perceiving him, expressed his extreme displeasure with his dying hands and eyes, and turned away his face, so that nothing could be done. F. Condren, the pious general of the French Oratorians, and other holy men, have from a sincere humility shown a like reluctance, while others have been inclined by charity to condescend to such requests of friends. St. Francis closed a holy life by a more holy and edifying death, and a little before midnight, between the last of September and 1st of October, in 1572, having lived sixty-two years, wanting twenty-eight days; Cardinal Buoncompagno, under the name of Gregory XIII., being pope, having lately succeeded Saint Pius V., who died on the 1st of May the same year. F. Verjus gives a history of several miracles, predictions, and raptures of Saint Francis Borgia. His body, which was buried in the old church of the professed house, was afterward, in 1617, by the care of the cardinal and duke of Lerma, the saint's grandson, first minister of state to Philip III., king of Spain, removed to Madrid, where it is honoured at this day in the church of the professed house of the Jesuits. St. Francis was beatified by Urban VIII., in 1624, and canonized by Clement IX., in 1671, and his festival fixed on the 10th of October, by Innocent XI., in 1683.

The active and contemplative life in an ecclesiastical person are two individual sisters, which must always go together, and mutually assist each other. Every pastor owes to God the homage of continual praise, and to his people the suffrages of his sacrifices and supplications in their behalf. How diligently soever he acquits himself of his external duties toward them, he fails essentially if he ceases to recommend earnestly to God their public and private spiritual necessities, being appointed the mediator betwixt them and God. Moreover, recollection and assiduous pious meditation are the very soul of an ecclesiastical spirit. A life of habitual dissipation strikes not at particular duties only, but destroys the very essence and spirit of this state, disqualifies a person for all its functions, and leaves him a stranger to the spirit of all its sacred employments and obligations. The most essential preparation, and the very soul of this state, is a spirit of prayer; without this, a person is no more than the shadow of a pastor, or a body without a soul to animate it, and can never deserve the name of a clergyman, or a religious man.

ST. PHOCAS, GARDENER, M.

A. D. 303.

St. Phocas dwelt near the gate of Sinope, a city of Pontus, and lived by cultivating a garden, which yielded him a handsome subsistence, and wherewith plentifully to relieve the indigent. In his humble profession he imitated the virtue of the most holy anchorets, and seemed in part restored to the happy condition of our first parents in Eden. To prune the garden without labour and toil was their sweet employment and pleasure. Since their sin, the earth yields not its fruit but by the sweat of our brow. But still, no labour is more useful or necessary, or more natural to man, and better adapted to maintain in him vigour of mind or health of body, than that of tillage; nor does any other part of the universe rival the innocent charms which a garden presents to all our senses, by the fragrancy of its flowers, by the riches of its produce, and the sweetness and variety of its fruits; by the melodious concert of its musicians, by the worlds of wonders which every stem, leaf, and fibre exhibit to the contemplation of the inquisitive philosopher, and by that beauty and variegated lustre of colours which clothe the numberless tribes of its smallest inhabitants, and adorn its shining landscapes, vying with the brightest splendour of the heavens, and in a single lily surpassing the dazzling lustre with which Solomon was surrounded on his throne in the midst of all his glory. And what a field for contemplation does a garden offer to our view in every part, raising our souls to God in raptures of love and praise, stimulating us to fervour by the fruitfulness with which it repays our labour, and multiplies the seed it receives; and exciting us to tears of compunction for our insensibility to God by the barrenness with which it is changed into a frightful desert, unless subdued by assiduous toil! Our saint, joining prayer with his labour, found in his garden itself an instructive book, and an inexhausted fund of holy meditation. His house was open to all strangers and travellers who had no lodging in the place; and after having for many years most liberally bestowed the fruit of his labour on the poor, he was found worthy also to give his life for Christ. Though his profession was obscure, he was well known over the whole country by the reputation of his charity and virtue.

When a cruel persecution, probably that of Dioclesian in 303, was suddenly raised in the church, Phocas was immediately impeached as a Christian, and such was the notoriety of his pretended crime, that the formality of a trial was superseded by the persecutors, and executioners were despatched with an order to kill him on the spot wherever they should find him. Arriving near Sinope, they would not enter the town, but stopping at his house without knowing it, at his kind invitation they took up their lodging with him. Being charmed with his courteous entertainment, they at supper disclosed to him the errand upon which they were sent, and desired him to inform them where this Phocas could be most easily met with. The servant of God, without the least surprise, told them he was well acquainted with the man, and would give them certain intelligence of him next morning. After they were retired to bed, he dug a grave, prepared every thing for his burial, and spent the night in disposing his soul for his last hour. When it was day he went to his guests, and told them Phocas was found, and in their power whenever they pleased to apprehend him. Glad at this news, they inquired where he was. "He is here present," said the martyr,—"I myself am the man." Struck at his undaunted resolution, and at the composure of his mind, they stood a considerable time as if they had been motionless; nor could they at first think of imbruing their hands in the blood of a person in whom they discovered so heroic a virtue, and by whom they had been so courteously entertained. He indirectly encouraged them, saying, that as for himself, he looked upon such a death as the greatest of favours, and his highest advantage. At length, recovering themselves from their surprise, they struck off his head. The Christians of that city, after peace was restored to the church, built a stately church which bore his name, and was famous over all the East. In it were deposited the sacred relics, though some portions of them were dispersed in other churches.

St. Asterius, bishop of Amasea about the year 400, pronounced the panegyric of this martyr, on his festival, in a church, probably near Amasea, which possessed a small part of his remains. In this discourse he says, "that Phocas from the time of his death was become a pillar and support of the churches on earth; he draws all men to his house; the highways are filled with persons resorting from every country to this place of prayer. The magnificent church which (at Sinope) is possessed of his body, is the comfort and ease of the afflicted, the health of the sick, the magazine plentifully supplying the wants of the poor. If in any other place, as in this, some small portion of his relics be found, it also becomes admirable, and most desired by all Christians." He adds, that the head of St. Phocas was kept in his beautiful church in Rome, and says: "The Romans honour him by the concourse of the whole people in the same manner they do Peter and Paul. He bears testimony that the sailors in the Euxine, Ægean, and Adriatic seas, and in the ocean, sing hymns in his honour, and that the martyr has often succoured and preserved them; and that the portion of gain which they in every voyage set apart for the poor is called Phocas's part. He mentions that a certain king of barbarians had sent his royal diadem set with jewels and his rich helmet a present to the church of St. Phocas, praying the martyr to offer it to the Lord in thanksgiving for the kingdom which his divine majesty had bestowed upon him. St. Chrysostom received a portion of the relics of St. Phocas, not at Antioch, as Baronius thought, and as Fronto le Duc and Baillet doubt, but at Constantinople, as Montfaucon demonstrates. On that solemn occasion the city kept a great festival two days, and St. Chrysostom preached two sermons, only one of which is extant. In this he says that the emperors left their palaces to reverence these relics, and strove to share with the rest in the blessings which they procure men. The Emperor Phocas built afterward another great church at Constantinople in honour of this martyr, and caused a considerable part of his relics to be translated thither. The Greeks often style St. Phocas hiero-martyr, or sacred martyr, which epithet they sometimes give to eminent martyrs who were not bishops, as Ruinart demonstrates against Baronius.

SAINT ELIZABETH,

QUEEN OF PORTUGAL.

A. D. 1336.

St. Elizabeth was daughter of Peter III., king of Arragon, and grand-daughter of James I., who had been educated under the care of St. Peter Nolasco, and was surnamed the Saint, and, from the taking of Majorca and Valentia, Expugnator or the Conqueror. Her mother, Constantia, was daughter of Manfred, king of Sicily, and grandchild to the Emperor Frederic II. Our saint was born in 1271, and received at the baptismal font by the name of Elizabeth, from her aunt, St. Elizabeth of Hungary, who had been canonized by Gregory IX., in 1235. Her birth established a good understanding between her grandfather James, who was then on the throne, and her father, whose quarrel had divided the whole kingdom. The former took upon himself the care of her education, and inspired her with an ardour for piety above her age, though he died in 1276, (having reigned sixty-three years,) before she had completed the sixth year of her age.

Her father succeeded to the crown, and was careful to place most virtuous persons about his daughter, whose example might be to her a constant spur to all virtue. The young princess was of a most sweet and mild disposition, and from her tender years had no relish for any thing but what was conducive to piety and devotion. It was doing her the most sensible pleasure, if any one promised to lead her to some chapel to say a prayer. At eight years of age she began to fast on vigils, and to practise great self-denials; nor could she bear to hear the tenderness of her years and constitution alleged as a reason that she ought not to fast or macerate her tender body. Her fervour made her eagerly desire that she might have a share in every exercise of virtue which she saw practised by others, and she had been already taught that the frequent mortification of the senses, and still more of the will, is to be joined with prayer to obtain the grace which restrains the passions and prevents their revolt. How little is this most important maxim considered by those parents who excite and fortify the passions of children, by teaching them a love of vanities, and indulging them in gratifications of sense! If rigorous fasts suit not their tender age, a submission of the will, perfect obedience, and humble modesty are in no time of life more indispensably to be inculcated; nor is any abstinence more necessary than that by which children are taught never to drink or eat out of meals, to bear several little denials in them without uneasiness, and never eagerly to crave any thing. The easy and happy victory of Elizabeth over herself was owing to this early and perfect temperance, submissiveness, and sincere humility. Esteeming virtue her only advantage and delight, she abhorred romances and idle entertainments, shunned the usual amusements of children, and was an enemy to all the vanities of the world. She could bear no other songs than sacred hymns and psalms; and from her childhood said every day the whole office of the breviary, in which no priest could be more scrupulously exact. Her tenderness and compassion for the poor, made her even in that tender age to be styled their mother.

At twelve years of age she was given in marriage to Dionysius, king of Portugal. That prince had considered in her, birth, beauty, riches, and sprightliness of genius more than virtue; yet he allowed her an entire liberty in her devotions, and exceedingly esteemed and admired her extraordinary piety. She found no temptation to pride in the dazzling splendour of a crown, and could say with Esther that her heart never found any delight in the glory, riches, and grandeur with which she was surrounded. She was sensible that regularity in our actions is necessary to virtue, this being in itself most agreeable to God, who shows in all his works how much he is the lover of order; also, a prudent distribution of time fixes the fickleness of the human mind, hinders frequent omissions of pious exercises, and is a means to prevent our being ever idle, being governed by humour and caprice in what we do, by which motives a disguised self-love easily insinuates itself into our ordinary actions. Our saint therefore planned for herself a regular distribution of her whole time, and of her religious exercises, which she never interrupted, unless extraordinary occasions of duty or charity obliged her to change the order of her daily practices. She rose very early every morning, and after a long exercise and a pious meditation, she recited matins, lauds, and prime of the church office. Then she heard mass, at which she communicated frequently every week. She said every day also the little office of our Lady, and that of the dead; and in the afternoon had other regular devotions after evensong or vespers. She retired often into her oratory to her pious books, and allotted certain hours to attend her domestic affairs, public business, or what she owed to others. All her spare time she employed in pious reading, or in working for the altar, or the poor, and she made her ladies of honour do the like. She found no time to spend in vain sports and recreations, or in idle discourse or entertainments. She was most abstemious in her diet, mean in her attire, humble, meek, and affable in conversation, and wholly bent upon the service of God in all her actions. Admirable was her spirit of compunction, and of holy prayer; and she poured forth her heart before God with most feeling sentiments of divine love, and often watered her cheeks and the very ground with abundant tears of sweet devotion. Frequent attempts were made to prevail with her to moderate her austerities, but she always answered, that if Christ assures as that his spirit cannot find place in a life of softness and pleasure, mortification is nowhere more necessary than on the throne, where the passions find more dangerous incentives. She fasted three days a week; many vigils, besides those prescribed by the church; all Advent; a Lent of devotion, from the feast of St. John Baptist to the feast of the Assumption; and soon after this she began another Lent, which she continued to St. Michael's day. On all Fridays and Saturdays, on the eves of all festivals of the Blessed Virgin and the apostles, and on many other days, her fast was on bread and water. She often visited churches and places of devotion on foot.

Charity to the poor was a distinguishing part of her character. She gave constant orders to have all pilgrims and poor strangers provided for with lodging and necessaries. She made it her business to seek out and secretly relieve persons of good condition who were reduced to necessity, yet out of shame durst not make known their wants. She was very liberal in furnishing fortunes to poor young women, that they might marry according to their condition, and not be exposed to the danger of losing their virtue. She visited the sick, served them, and dressed and kissed their most loathsome sores. She founded in different parts of the kingdom many pious establishments, particularly a hospital near her own palace at Coïmbra, a house for penitent women who had been seduced into evil courses, at Torres-Novas, and an hospital for foundlings, or those children who, for want of due provision, are exposed to the danger of perishing by poverty, or the neglect and cruelty of unnatural parents. She was utterly regardless of her own conveniences, and so attentive to the poor and afflicted persons of the whole kingdom, that she seemed almost wholly to belong to them; not that she neglected any other duties which she owed to her neighbour, for she made it her principal study to pay to her husband the most dutiful respect, love, and obedience, and bore his injuries with invincible meekness and patience. Though King Dionysius was a friend of justice, and a valiant, bountiful, and compassionate prince, yet he was, in his youth, a worldly man, and defiled the sanctity of the nuptial state with abomininable lusts. The good queen used all her endeavours to reclaim him, grieving most sensibly for the offence of God, and the scandal given to the people; and she never ceased to weep herself, and to procure the prayers of others for his conversion. She strove to gain him only by courtesy, and with constant sweetness and cheerfulness cherished his natural children, and took great care of their education. By these means she softened the heart of the king, who, by the succour of a powerful grace, rose out of the filthy puddle in which he had wallowed for a long time, and kept ever after the fidelity that was due to his virtuous consort. He instituted the order of Christ in 1318; founded, with a truly royal magnificence, the university of Coïmbra, and adorned his kingdom with public buildings. His extraordinary virtues, particularly his liberality, justice, and constancy, are highly extolled by the Portuguese, and after his entire conversion, he was the idol and glory

ST. ELIZABETH, QUEEN.

of his people. A little time before his conversion there happened an extraordinary accident.

The queen had a very pious, faithful page, whom she employed in the distribution of her secret alms. A wicked fellow-page, envying him on account of this favour, to which his virtue and services entitled him, treacherously suggested to his majesty that the queen showed a fondness for that page. The prince, who by his own sensual heart was easily inclined to judge ill of others, gave credit to the slander, and resolved to take away the life of the innocent youth. For this purpose he gave order to a limeburner, that if on such a day he sent to him a page with this errand, to inquire "Whether he had fulfilled the king's commands?" he should take him and cast him into the limekiln, there to be burnt; for that death he had justly incurred, and the execution was expedient for the king's service. On the day appointed he despatched the page with this message to the limekiln; but the devout youth on the road passing by a church, heard the bell ring at the elevation at mass, went in, and prayed there devoutly; for it was his pious custom, if ever he heard the sign given by the bell for the elevation, always to go thither, and not depart until mass was ended. It happened, on that occasion, that as the first was not a whole mass, and it was with him a constant rule to hear mass every day, he stayed in the church, and heard successively two other masses. In the mean time, the king, who was impatient to know if his orders had been executed, sent the informer to the limekiln, to inquire whether his commands had been obeyed; but as soon as he was come to that kiln, and had asked the question, the man supposing him to be the messenger meant by the king's order, seized him, and threw him into the burning lime, where he was soon consumed. Thus was the innocent protected by his devotion, and the slanderer was overtaken by divine justice. The page who had heard the masses went afterward to the limekiln, and having asked whether his majesty's commands had been yet executed, brought him word back that they were. The king was almost out of himself with surprise when he saw him come back with this message, and being soon informed of the particulars, he easily discovered the innocence of the pious youth, adored the divine judgment, and ever after respected the great virtue and sanctity of his queen.

St. Elizabeth had by the king two children, Alphonsus, who afterward succeeded his father, and Constantia, who was married to Ferdinand IV., king of Castille. This son, when grown up, married the infanta of Castille, and soon after revolting against his own father, put himself at the head of an army of malecontents. St. Elizabeth had recourse to weeping, prayer, fasting, and almsdeeds, and exhorted her son in the strongest terms to return to his duty, conjuring her husband at the same time to forgive him. Pope John XXII. wrote to her, commending her religious and prudent conduct; but certain court-flatterers whispering to the king that she was suspected of favouring her son, he, whom jealousy made credulous, banished her to the city of Alanquer. The queen received this disgrace with admirable patience and peace of mind, and made use of the opportunity which her retirement afforded, to redouble her austerities and devotions. She never would entertain any correspondence with the malecontents, nor listen to any suggestions from them. The king himself admired her goodness, meekness, and humility under her disgrace; and shortly after called her back to court, and showed her greater love and respect than ever. In all her troubles she committed herself to the sweet disposal of divine providence, considering that she was always under the protection of God, her merciful Father.

Being herself of the most sweet and peaceable disposition, she was always most active and industrious in composing all differences between neighbours, especially in averting war, with the train of all the most terrible evils which attend it. She reconciled her husband and son, when their armies were marching one against the other; and she reduced all the subjects to duty and obedience. She made peace between Ferdinand IV., king of Castille, and Alphonsus de la Cerda, his cousin-german, who disputed the crown; likewise between James II., king of Arragon, her own brother, and Ferdinand IV., the king of Castille, her son-in-law. In order to effect this last, she took a journey with her husband into both those kingdoms, and, to the great satisfaction of the Christian world, put a happy period to all dissensions and debates between those states. After this charitable work, King Dionysius, having reigned forty-five years, fell sick. St. Elizabeth gave him most signal testimonies of her love and affection, scarce ever leaving his chamber during his illness, unless to go to the church, and taking infinite pains to serve and attend him. But her main care and solicitude was to secure his eternal happiness, and to procure that he might depart this life in sentiments of perfect repentance and piety. For this purpose she gave bountiful alms, and caused many prayers and masses to be said. During his long and tedious illness he gave great marks of sincere compunction, and died at Santaren, on the 6th of January, 1325. As soon as he had expired, the queen retired into her oratory, commended his soul to God, and consecrating herself to the divine service, put on the habit of the third order of St. Francis. She attended the funeral procession, with her husband's corpse, to Odiveras, where he had chosen his burying-place in a famous church of Cistercian monks. After a considerable stay there, she made a pilgrimage to Compostella, and returning to Odiveras, celebrated there her husband's anniversary with great solemnity; after which she retired to a convent of Clares, which she had begun to rebuild before the death of her husband. She was desirous to make her religious profession, but was diverted from that design for some time upon a motive of charity, that she might continue to support an infinity of poor people by her alms and protection. She therefore contented herself at first with wearing the habit of the third order, living in a house which she built contiguous to her great nunnery, in which she assembled ninety devout nuns. She often visited them, and served them at table, having for her companion in this practice of charity and humility her daughter-in-law, Beatrix, the queen then reigning. However, by authentic historical proofs it is evinced that before her death she made her religious profession in the aforesaid third order, as Pope Urban VIII., after mature discussion of those monuments, has declared.

A war being lighted up between her son, Alphonsus IV., surnamed the brave, king of Portugal, and her grandson, Aphonsus XI., king of Castille, the armies being set on foot, she was startled at the news, and resolved to set out to reconcile them, and extinguish the fire that was kindling. Her servants endeavoured to persuade her to defer her journey, on account of the excessive heats, but she made answer that she could not better expend her health and her life than by seeking to prevent the miseries and calamities of a war. The very news of her journey disposed both parties to peace. She went to Estremoz, upon the frontiers of Portugal and Castille, where her son was; but she arrived ill of a violent fever, which she looked upon as a messenger sent by God to warn her that the time was at hand wherein he called her to himself. She strongly exhorted her son to the love of peace and to a holy life; she confessed several times, received the holy viaticum on her knees at the foot of the altar, and shortly after, extreme unction; from which time she continued in fervent prayer, often invoking the Blessed Virgin, and repeating these words: "Mary, mother of grace, mother of mercy, defend us from the wicked enemy, and receive us at the hour of our death." She appeared overflowing with heavenly joys and with those consolations of the Holy Ghost which make death so sweet to the saints; and in the presence of her son, the king, and of her daughter-in-law, she gave up her happy soul to God on the 4th of July, in the year 1336, of her age sixty-five. She was buried with royal pomp in the church of her monastery of Poor Clares, at Coïmbra, and honoured by miracles. Leo X. and Paul IV. granted an office on her festival; and in 1612 her body was taken up and found entire. It is now richly enshrined in a magnificent chapel, built on purpose. She was canonized by Urban VIII., in 1625, and the 8th of July appointed for her festival.

The characteristical virtue of St. Elizabeth was a love of peace. Christ, the prince of peace, declares his spirit to be the spirit of humility and meekness; consequently the spirit of peace. Variance, wrath, and strife are the works of the flesh, of envy, and pride, which he condemns, and which exclude from the kingdom of heaven. Bitterness and contention shut out reason, make the soul deaf to the motives of religion, and open the understanding to nothing but what is sinful. To find the way of peace we must be meek and patient, even under the most violent provocations; we must never resent any wrong, nor return railing for railing, but good for evil; we must regard passion as the worst of monsters, and must judge it as unreasonable to hearken to its suggestions as to choose a madman for our counsellor in matters of concern and difficulty; above all, we must abhor it not only as a sin, but as leading to a numberless variety of other grievous sins and spiritual evils. *Blessed are the peacemakers,* and all who love and cultivate this virtue among men; *they shall be called the children of God,* whose badge and image they bear.

ST. EULOGIUS, C.

PATRIARCH OF ALEXANDRIA.

A. D. 1622.

St. Eulogius was a Syrian by birth, and embraced young the monastic state in that country. The Eutychian heresy was then split into various sects, as it usually happens among such as have left the centre of union. These, by their tyranny and the fury of their contests, had thrown the churches of Syria and Egypt into much confusion, and a great part of the monks of Syria were at that time become remarkable for their loose morals and errors against faith. Eulogius learned from the fall of others to stand more watchfully and firmly upon his guard, and was not less distinguished by the innocence and sanctity of his manners than by the purity of his doctrine. Having, by an enlarged pursuit of learning, attained to a great variety of useful knowledge in the different branches of literature, he set himself to the study of divinity in the sacred sources of that science, which are the Holy Scriptures, and the tradition of the church explained in its councils and the approved writings of its eminent pastors. From the time of his retreat he made this his chief study, to which he directed every thing else; and, as his industry was indefatigable, his parts quick, his apprehensions lively, and his judgment solid, his progress was such as to qualify him to be an illustrious champion for the truth, worthy to be ranked with St. Gregory the Great and St. Eutychius as one of the greatest lights of the church in the age wherein he lived. His character received still a brighter lustre from his sincere humility and spirit of holy compunction and prayer. In the great dangers and necessities of the church he was drawn out of his solitude, and made priest of Antioch by the Patriarch St. Anastasius, who was promoted to that dignity in 561, and, dying in 598, was succeeded by Anastasius the Younger. St. Eulogius, while he lived at Antioch, entered into the strictest connections with St. Eutychius, patriarch of Constantinople, and joined his forces with that holy prelate against the enemies of the truth.

The Emperor Justinian and his nephew and successor, Justin the Younger, had been the plunderers of their empire and the grievous oppressors of their subjects; the former to support his extravagance and vanity, the latter to gratify his insatiable avarice and scandalous lusts. Justin II. dying in 576, after a reign of ten years and ten months, Tiberius Constantine, a Thracian, and a virtuous prince, was raised to the throne. He applied himself to heal the wounds caused during the former reigns, both in the church and state. His charities in all parts of the empire were boundless, and all his treasuries were open to the poor. Among the evils with which the church was then afflicted, the disorders and confusion into which the tyranny of the Eutychians had thrown the church of Alexandria called aloud for powerful remedies, and an able and zealous pastor, endued with prudence and vigour to apply them. Upon the death of the patriarch John, St. Eulogius was raised to that patriarchal dignity toward the close of the year 583, at the earnest desire of the emperor, who, having reigned only six years and ten months, died the same year, leaving his son-in-law, Mauritius, his successor in the imperial throne. Our saint was obliged to make a journey to Constantinople, about two years after his promotion, in order to concert measures concerning certain affairs of his church. He met at court St. Gregory the Great, and contracted with him a holy friendship, so that, from that time, they seemed to be one heart and one soul. Among the letters of St. Gregory, we have several extant which he wrote to our saint. St. Eulogius composed many excellent works against the Acephali and other sects of Eutychians. Photius has preserved us valuable fragments of some of these treatises; also of eleven discourses of our saint, the ninth of which is a commendation of a monastic life; likewise of his six books against the Novatians of Alexandria, in the fifth of which he expressly sets himself to prove that the martyrs are to be honoured. Photius makes no mention of the treatise of St. Eulogius against the Agnoëtæ, a sect of Eutychians, who ascribed to Christ, as man, ignorance of the day of judgment and of many other things. St. Gregory the Great, to whose censure the author submitted it, sent him his approbation with high commendations, saying: "I have not found any thing but what is admirable in your writings," &c. St. Eulogius did not long survive St. Gregory, for he died in the year 606, or, according to others, in 608.

We admire the great actions and the glorious triumphs of the saints; yet it is not so much in these that their sanctity consisted, as in the constant, habitual, heroic disposition of their souls. There is no one who does not sometimes do good actions; but he can never be called virtuous who does well only by humour, or by fits and starts, not by steady habits. It is an habitual poverty of spirit, humility, meekness, patience, purity, piety, and charity, which our divine Master recommends to us. We must take due pains to plant the seeds of virtues in our souls, must watch and labour continually to improve and strengthen them, that they may be converted into nature, and be the principle by which all the affections of our souls, and all the actions of our lives are governed. If these pure heroic sentiments perfectly possess and fill our hearts, the whole tenour of our conduct, whether in private or in public life, will be a uniform train of virtuous actions, which will derive their perfection from the degree of fervour and purity from which they spring, and which, according to the essential property of virtue, is always improving, and always improvable.

ST. MARTIN BISHOP OF TOURS, C.

A. D. 397.

THE great Saint Martin, the glory of Gaul, and the light of the Western Church in the fourth age, was a native of Sabaria, a town of Upper Pannonia, the ruins of which appear upon the river Gunez, in Lower Hungary, two leagues from Sarwar, upon the Raab, near the confines of Austria and Styria. St. Gregory of Tours places his birth in the year 316, or before Easter in 317, the eleventh of Constantine the Great. His parents carried him with them in his infancy to Pavia in Italy, whither they removed, and the saint had his education in that city. His father was an officer in the army, and rose to the commission of a military tribune, not much different from that of a colonel, or rather of a brigadier, among us. Our saint from his infancy seemed animated with the spirit of God, and to have no relish for any thing but for his service, though his parents were idolaters. At ten years of age he made his way to the church against the will of his parents, and desired to be enrolled among the catechumens. His request was granted, and he assisted as often as possible at the instructions that were given to such at the church; by which he conceived so ardent a love of God, that, at twelve years of age, he was for retiring into the desert, and would have done it, had not the tenderness of his age hindered him. His heart, however, was always set upon the church and monasteries. An imperial order being issued, to oblige the sons of veteran officers and soldiers to bear arms, the saint's own father, who very much desired that his son should follow that profession, discovered him, and at fifteen years of age he was compelled to take the military oath, and was entered in the cavalry. He contented himself with one servant, and him he treated as if he were his equal; they ate together, and the master frequently performed for him the lowest offices. All the time he remained in the army, he kept himself free from those vices which too frequently sully and degrade that profession, and by his virtue, goodness, and charity, gained the love and esteem of all his companions. He was humble and patient above what human nature seemed capable of, though he was not yet baptized. He comforted all those that suffered affliction, and relieved the distressed, reserving to himself out of his pay only what was sufficient for his daily support.

Of his compassion and charity St. Sulpicius has recorded the following illustrious example:—One day, in the midst of a very hard winter and severe frost, when many perished with cold, as he was marching with other officers and soldiers, he met at the gate of the city of Amiens a poor man, almost naked, trembling and shaking for cold, and begging alms of those that passed by. Martin, seeing those that went before him take no notice of this miserable object, thought he was reserved for himself; by his charities to others he had nothing left but his arms and the clothes upon his back; when, drawing his sword, he cut his cloak into two pieces, gave one to the beggar, and wrapped himself in the other. Some of the bystanders laughed at the figure he made in that dress, while others were ashamed not to have relieved the poor man. In the following night St. Martin saw in his sleep Jesus Christ dressed in that half of the garment which he had given away, and was bid to look at it well, and asked whether he knew it. He then heard Jesus say to a troop of angels that surrounded him: "Martin, yet a catechumen, has clothed me with this garment." This vision inspired the saint with fresh ardour, and determined him speedily to receive baptism, which he did in the eighteenth year of his age, but still continued almost two years in the army, at the request of his tribune, with whom he lived in the most intimate friendship, and who promised to renounce the world when the term of the service and commission in which he was then employed should be elapsed. During the interval Martin was so entirely taken up with the obligations of his baptism, that he had little more than the name of a soldier, and expressed much impatience at being detained one moment from devoting himself solely to the divine service. Upon an irruption which the Germans made into Gaul, the troops were assembled to march against them, and a donative was distributed among the soldiers. Martin thought it would be ungenerous and unjust to receive the donative when he had thoughts of quitting the service. He therefore begged that the donative might be bestowed on some other person, and asked his dismission, that he might give himself up totally to the service of Christ. He was told that it was for fear of the battle that was expected next day, that he desired his dismission. Martin, with surprising intrepidity, offered to be placed in the front without arms, saying: "In the name of the Lord Jesus, and protected, not by a helmet and buckler, but by the sign of the cross, I will thrust myself into the thickest squadrons of the enemy without fear." That night the barbarians demanded and obtained peace; upon which Martin easily procured leave to retire, after having served in the army about five years, according to the most probable account.

St. Martin having quitted the camp, went to St. Hilary, who had been made bishop of Poitiers in the year 353 or 354. That great prelate soon became acquainted with the saint's extraordinary merit, and, in order to fix him in his diocess, would fain have ordained him deacon, but was not able to overcome his humility, and was obliged to be content only to make him exorcist. Martin was very desirous to pay his parents a visit in Pannonia; for which he obtained the leave of St. Hilary, who made him promise he would return to him again. In crossing the Alps, he fell into the hands of a company of robbers, and one of them lifted up his sword over his head to kill him; but another held his arm. They admired his modesty and intrepidity, and asked him who he was, and whether he was not struck with fear at the sight of a sword lifted up to kill him. He answered that he was a Christian, and that he had never been more calm and secure than under that danger, because he certainly knew that the divine goodness is always most ready to protect us in life or in death, and is never more present to us than in the greatest dangers; but said he was only grieved that they, by the lives which they led, deprived themselves of the mercy of Christ. The robbers listened to him, admired the courage and confidence in God which virtue inspires, and he who had attempted to kill the saint put him in his road, became a Christian, led a penitential religious life in a monastery, and himself afterward related this circumstance. Martin continued his journey through Milan into Pannonia, and converted his mother and many others; but his father remained in his infidelity. In Illyricum he with so much zeal opposed the Arians, who prevailed there without control, that he was publicly scourged by them and banished the country. In Italy he heard that the Church of Gaul was sorely oppressed by those heretics, and St. Hilary banished; upon which melancholy news he chose a retreat near the walls of Milan, where he entered upon a monastic life. Auxentius, the Arian invader of the see of Milan, soon became acquainted with his zeal for the orthodox faith and the council of Nice, and drove him out of that diocess. The saint in this distress fell into the company of a very virtuous priest, with whom he agreed to retire to the little desert island of Gallinaria, upon the coast of Liguria, near Albenga. Here, while he lived in great abstinence on roots and wild herbs, he happened unawares to eat a considerable quantity of hellebore, enough to have caused his death, if he had not been restored to his health, when brought to the last extremity, by having recourse to prayer. Understanding, in 360, that Saint Hilary was returning to his bishopric, he went to Rome to meet him on his road, and finding there that he was already gone by, speedily followed and overtook him, and being most affectionately received by him, accompanied him to Poitiers. It being Martin's earnest desire to pursue his vocation in holy solitude, St. Hilary gave him a little spot of land, called Locociagum, now Lugugé, two leagues from the city, where our saint built a monastery, which was standing in the eighth century, and seems to have been the first that was erected in Gaul. Among others who were received by the saint in this house, was a certain catechumen, who, shortly after, while St. Martin was absent for three days upon business relating to the divine service, fell ill of a fever, and died suddenly, beyond all expectation, and without baptism. The saint returning home, found his monks in great affliction, and the corpse laid out in order to be buried. Bursting into a flood of tears, he fixed his eyes on the corpse; and feeling in himself a divine impulse to work a miracle, he ordered the rest to go out of the chamber, and, like another Eliseus, stretched himself upon the dead body, and prayed for some time with great earnestness, till, perceiving that it began to revive, he rose up and stood by it, while, in less than two hours, the deceased person began to move his limbs, and at last opened his eyes. Being restored to life, he related how, after his departure, his soul seemed to be presented before the divine tribunal, and sentenced to a dark dungeon, but that two angels represented to the Judge that Saint Martin poured forth his prayers in her behalf; and that the Judge ordered them to restore her to the body, and raise it to life. The person was immediately baptized, and lived many years. Another time, the saint restored to life, in the same manner, a slave of a neighbouring rich man, who had hanged himself. These two miracles exceedingly spread his reputation; and in the year 371 he was chosen the third bishop of Tours, and consecrated on the 3d of July. Saint Gatian, who came from Rome about the same time with St. Dionysius of Paris, in 250, had first preached the faith there, founded that see, and governed it fifty years, as St. Gregory of Tours affirms. His successor, after the see had been several years vacant, was St. Litorius, upon whose death the people demanded St. Martin for their bishop. A stratagem was made use of to call him to the door of his monastery to give his blessing to a sick person, and he was forcibly conveyed to Tours under a strong guard. Some of the neighbouring bishops, who were called to assist at the election, urged that the meanness of his dress and appearance, and his slovenly air, showed him to be unfit for such a dignity. But such objections were commendations of the servant of God, who was installed in the episcopal chair.

St. Martin in this new dignity continued the same manner of life, retaining the same humility of mind, austerity of life, and meanness of dress. He lived at first in a little cell near the church, but, not being able to endure the interruption which he met with from the many visits he there received, he retired to a monastery which he built two miles from the city, which is the famous abbey of Marmoutier, the most ancient that now subsists in France, and belongs to the congregation of St. Maur. The place was then a desert, enclosed by a high steep rock on one side, and by the river Loire on the other, and the entrance into it was only by one very narrow passage. The holy bishop had a cell built of wood; several of his monks had cells made in the same manner, but the greater part took up their dwellings in narrow holes, which they dug in the side of the rock; one is still shown in which St. Martin is said to have lodged for some time. He had here in a short time about fourscore monks; among them no one had any distinct property; no one was allowed to buy or sell, as was the practice of the greater part of the monks with regard to their work and sustenance. No art or business was permitted among them, except that of writing, to which only the younger were deputed; the more ancient attended to nothing else but to prayer and spiritual functions. Very rarely any went out of his cell, except to the oratory where they assembled at the hours of public prayer; and they ate altogether in the evening after the hour of the fast. Wine was never afforded to any one, unless sickness required it. Most of them had garments of camel's hair, that is, of coarse camlet, and it was esteemed a crime to wear any soft clothing. There were, nevertheless, many persons of quality among them, who had been educated in a tender and delicate manner. Many bishops were chosen out of this monastery; for there was not a city which did not desire to have a pastor who had been bred under the discipline of St. Martin. The bishop himself was frequently employed in visiting all the parts of his diocess.

Not far from this monastery stood a chapel and an altar, erected by the concession of his predecessors, over the tomb of a pretended martyr. The place was much reverenced by the people; but St. Martin, who was not over credulous, would not go thither to pray, not hearing any assured account of the relics. He asked the eldest of the clergy what they knew of them, and not receiving satisfaction, he went one day to the place with some of his brethren, and, standing over the tomb, besought God to show him who was buried there. Then turning to the left, he saw near him a pale ghost, of a fierce aspect, whom he commanded to speak. The ghost told his name; and it appeared that he had been a robber, was executed for his crimes, whom the people had honoured as a martyr. None but St. Martin saw him; the rest only heard his voice. He thereupon caused the altar to be removed, and freed the people from this superstition. Formerly bishops canonized saints, or declared them such; but, to prevent the danger of abuses, this has been long since reserved to the most mature discussion and solemn approbation of the apostolic see of Rome. To honour relics without a prudent or moral assurance of their authenticity, or without the due authority of pastors as the canons require, is to fall into superstition. Where these rules of prudence are observed, even though a mistake should happen, it is of the same nature as if a person, by inculpable inadvertence, kissed some other book instead of the Bible; and the primary object of such religious actions, which is to glorify God in his saints, is always certain, whatever mistakes may happen in facts, or suchlike human means which excite our devotion. But the example of St. Martin, St. Gregory the Great, St. Charles Borromeo, and all other holy prelates, ought to excite all pastors to be diligent and severe in examining and removing relics which are not sufficiently warranted.

The utter extirpation of idolatry out of the diocess of Tours and all that part of Gaul, was the fruit of the edifying piety, miracles, and zealous labours and instructions of St. Martin. Soon after he had entered upon his episcopal charge, he was obliged (probably on account of the heathenish temples, or some such affairs) to repair to the court of Valentinian I., who generally resided in Gaul. That prince, who was a good soldier, was a most passionate, rough, and proud man, and, though he had been remarkable for his zeal in the reign of Julian the Apostate, seemed on certain occasions afterward too favourable to idolatry, or too indifferent about religion, as appears, among other instances, from the following:—The church never admitted comedians to baptism till they had quitted that profession, so that the pagans dreaded lest any of their comedians should turn Christians, as a prejudice to their public diversions. Valentinian therefore decreed that if any comedians in sickness desired baptism, the magistrates should be informed that they might cause them to be visited, and see if they were really in danger, before they were allowed to be baptized. This prince, knowing that St. Martin was come to beg of him something in favour of the Christian religion which he had no mind to grant, gave orders that he should not be admitted into the palace. Also his wife Justina, who was a furious Arian, endeavoured to prepossess him against the holy bishop. St. Martin, having attempted in vain twice or thrice to get access, had recourse to his ordinary weapons. He put on hair-cloth, covered his head with ashes, abstained from eating and drinking, and prayed day and night. On the seventh day, he was ordered by an angel to go boldly to the palace. Accordingly he went thither, found the doors open, and nobody stopping him, he went to the emperor, who, seeing him at a distance, asked in a passion why they had let him in, and would not vouchsafe to rise; but the place where he sat was suddenly all in a flame; which soon forced him to get up, says Sulpicius Severus. Then finding that he had felt the divine power, he embraced the saint several times, and granted him all that he desired, even before he had time to mention his requests. After this he gave him audience several times, often made him eat at his table, and, at his departure, offered him great presents, which the saint modestly refused, out of love to the poverty he professed. This must have happened before the year 375, in which this emperor died.

St. Martin destroyed many temples of idols, and felled several trees that were held as sacred by the pagans. Having demolished a very ancient temple, he would also have cut down a pine that stood near it. The chief priest and other pagans opposed; but at length agreed that they themselves would fell it, upon condition that he who trusted so strongly in the God whom he preached would stand under it where they should place him. The saint, who was directed in these extraordinary events by a divine inspiration, consented, and suffered himself to be tied to that side of the tree on which it leaned. When it seemed just ready to fall upon him he made the sign of the cross, and it fell on the contrary side. There was not one in a prodigious multitude of pagans that were present, who did not upon the spot demand the imposition of hands in order to be received among the catechumens. Another time, as he was pulling down a temple in the country of Ædui, that is, in the territory of Autun, a great number of pagans fell upon him with great fury, and one attacked him sword in hand. The saint took away his mantle, and presented his bare neck to him; but the pagan, being miraculously terrified, fell backward, and begged he would forgive him. His zeal exposed him on many occasions to the hazard of his life. Wherever he destroyed temples, he immediately built churches or monasteries; and continued frequently to perform great miracles. At Triers, he cured a maid who was sick of a palsy, and just ready to expire, by putting some oil that was blessed into her mouth. He restored to health a slave who belonged to Tetradius, formerly proconsul, that was possessed with a devil. At Paris, as he entered the gate of the city, followed by a great crowd, he kissed a most loathsome leper, and gave him his blessing, and he was forthwith healed. Small threads of the clothes or hair-shirt of St. Martin often cured the sick when applied to them. One time the saint, as he was going to Chartres, passed through a village, the inhabitants of which were all idolaters, yet they all came out to see him pass by. The holy prelate, seeing this multitude of infidels, was moved with extreme compassion, and with earnest affection lifted up his eyes to heaven. Then he began to preach to them the word of God in the manner that he was accustomed, and sweetly to invite them to eternal salvation, with such pathetic words, voice, and energy, that it appeared plainly that it was not he spoke, but God in him. A woman brought to him at that very time her only son, a child who was dead, and besought him, as the friend of God, to restore him to life. The saint, judging that this miracle might occasion the conversion of many, made his prayer, and, in the presence of all the people, restored the child alive to the mother, who was amazed and out of herself for joy. The people who had seen this miracle cried out aloud to heaven, ran to the saint, and cast themselves at his feet, beseeching him to make them catechumens, and to prepare them for baptism. St. Martin rejoiced at the conversion of so many souls to God, much more than any one could have done for the conquest of a kingdom, or all temporal advantages. Paulinus, who flourished with so great reputation for sanctity at Nola, being seized with a violent pain in his eye, where a cataract was beginning to be formed, St. Martin touched him with a pencil, and he was immediately cured. Many other miracles wrought by St. Martin are related by St. Sulpicius Severus, especially in casting out devils, whom he did not expel with threats and terrors, as other exorcists were accustomed to do; but clothed with rough hair-cloth, and covered with ashes, he prostrated himself upon the ground, and, with the arms of holy prayer, subdued them, and forced them at length to yield. The same venerable author recounts several instances of revelations, visions, and the spirit of prophecy with which the saint was favoured by God. An extraordinary prudence, particularly in the discernment of spirits, was the fruit of his profound humility, perfect purity of heart, spirit of prayer, and contemplation. By this he discovered various subtle illusions and snares of the spirit of darkness. One day, when St. Martin was praying in his cell, the devil came to him environed with light, clothed in royal robes, with a crown of gold and precious stones upon his head, and, with a gracious and pleasant countenance, told him twice that he was Christ. Humility is the touchstone which discovers the devil's artifices, in all which a spirit of pride reigns. By this the saint, after some pause, discerned the evident marks of the angel of darkness, and said to him: " The Lord Jesus said not that he was to come clothed with purple, and crowned and adorned with a diadem. Nor will I ever believe him to be Christ who shall not come in the habit and figure in which Christ suffered, and who shall not bear the marks of the cross in his body." At these words the fiend vanished, and left the cell filled with an intolerable stench.

While St. Martin was employed in making spiritual conquests, and in peaceably propagating the kingdom of Jesus Christ, the western empire was shaken with horrible convulsions. Maximus was proclaimed emperor by the Roman legions in Britain in 383, and, passing into Gaul, was acknowledged by the mutinous soldiers there, made Triers the seat of his empire, and defeated Gratian near Paris, who was betrayed by his own forces, and assassinated by Andragathius at Lyons, on the 25th of August, in 383. The churches in Spain and Gaul were at that time disturbed by the Priscillianists, who renewed many errors of Simon Magus, the Gnostics, and the Manichees, to which they added their favourite tenet of dissimulation and lying, it being an avowed principle among them, "Swear, forswear thyself; betray not the secret." Maximus found Ithacius, a Spanish bishop, the warmest accuser of the Priscillianists, waiting for him at Triers. Idacius his colleague joined him there. The new emperor received them favourably, and commanded the ringleaders of the heretics to be conducted thither from Spain, and confronted with their two accusers. St. Martin happened to go to Triers, to intercede with the tyrant in favour of certain persons who were condemned to death for adhering to their late master, Gratian. Many at the same time came from different parts to pay their court to Maximus with the most fawning adulation. But our saint always maintained his apostolical authority, imitating herein St. Ambrose, who had been there before him upon an embassy from Valentinian II., Gratian's younger brother, who remained in possession of Italy. Though St. Martin was Maximus's subject, which the other was not, he discovered the utmost reluctance to communicate with Maximus; and, when he was invited to dine at the emperor's table, he refused a long while, saying boldly that he could not eat at the same table with a man who had deprived one emperor of his dominions, and another of his life. Maximus protested that he had not accepted of the empire voluntarily, but that it had been forced upon him by the soldiery; that his incredible success seemed to testify the will of God, and that not one of his enemies had perished, except those who lost their lives in the battle. St. Martin at length was prevailed upon to accept the invitation, which gave the emperor the utmost satisfaction, who ordered a great entertainment to be made, and invited the most considerable persons of his court, and, among others, his uncle and brother, both counts, and the prefect of the prætorium. The priest who accompanied St. Martin was seated in a most honourable place between two counts, and on the same couch; and St. Martin on a low seat near the emperor. In the midst of the entertainment, an officer presented the cup as usual to Maximus, who ordered it to be given to St. Martin, expecting to receive it from his hand; but, when the bishop had drunk, he gave it to his priest, as the most worthy person in the company; which action was exceedingly applauded by the emperor and the whole court. The empress, who attended night and day to the bishop's discourses, sat always at his feet upon the ground, and would needs give him an entertainment in her turn, to which she invited the emperor. St. Martin consented with the utmost reluctance; for, though he was above seventy years old, he never conversed with women except on necessary spiritual affairs. But he found it unavoidable, as he had several things to petition for, such as the delivery of prisoners, the recalling several that were in banishment, and restoring estates that had been confiscated. The empress herself waited upon him at table in the humble posture of a servant.

Neither St. Ambrose nor St. Martin would communicate with Ithacius, or those bishops who held communion with him, because they sought to put heretics to death. We cannot wonder at the offence these saints took at their prosecuting Priscillian in such a manner, when we consider how much the church abhorred the shedding of the blood even of criminals, and never suffered any of her clergy to have any share in such causes. St. Martin continually reproved Ithacius for his conduct, and pressed him to desist from his accusation. He also besought Maximus not to spill the blood of the guilty, saying, it was sufficient that they had been declared heretics, and excommunicated by the bishops, and that there was no precedent of an ecclesiastical cause being brought before a secular judge. Ithacius, far from hearkening to his advice, presumed to accuse him of this heresy, as he usually did those whose manner of life seemed to him too rigid. But Maximus, out of regard to St. Martin's remonstrances, caused the trial to be deferred all the while he stayed at Triers, and even promised him that the blood of the persons accused should not be spilled. But after the saint had left Triers, he suffered himself to be prevailed upon, and committed the cause of the Priscillianists to Evodius, whom he had made prefect of the prætorium. This severe judge convicted Priscillian of several crimes by his own confession, as of holding nocturnal assemblies with lewd women, of praying naked, and other such things. Ithacius was the accuser, and was even present when Priscillian was put to the torture— though after this he withdrew, and did not assist at their condemnation to death. Evodius laid the whole proceeding before Maximus, who declared Priscillian and his accomplices worthy of death. Evodius therefore pronounced sentence. Priscillian, his two clerks named Felicissimus and Armenius, Latrocinius a layman, and Euchrocia were beheaded. The Bishop Instantius, who had been condemned by the council of Bourdeaux, was banished to the islands of Sylina, or the isles of Scilly, beyond Britain. Soon after, Afarinus and Aurelius, two deacons, were condemned to death; Tiberian was sent to the same islands, and his estate confiscated, and others were punished for the same cause. Ithacius and his associate bishops were supported by the emperor, so that several who disapproved their conduct, durst not condemn them. Only one bishop, named Theognostus, publicly declared against them.

The Ithacians prevailed upon the emperor to send tribunes into Spain with a sovereign power to search out heretics, and deprive them of their lives and possessions. No one doubted but many innocent persons would fall undistinguished in this search; for the paleness of a man's countenance, or his dress, was enough to bring him into suspicion with those people. The day after they had obtained this order, they heard, when they least expected it, that St. Martin was almost got to Triers; for he was obliged to go there very often about affairs of charity. The Ithacians were greatly alarmed at his coming, and when they found that he abstained from their communion, they told the emperor that, if the obstinacy of Theognostus was supported by Martin's authority, their reputation would be entirely ruined. Maximus therefore represented mildly to the holy man that the heretics had been justly condemned for their crimes by the imperial judges, not by the bishops. But perceiving that St. Martin was not moved, but urged that the bishops had carried on the prosecutions, Maximus fell into a passion, and, going away, gave immediate orders that the persons for whom he came to intercede should be put to death. These were Count Narses, and the Governor Leucadius, who were obnoxious to Maximus for having adhered to Gratian's party. The holy man had still more at heart to prevent the tribunes being sent into Spain, and this not only for the sake of many catholics, but also for the heretics, whose lives he was extremely desirous to save. His not communicating with the Ithacians was only meant by him to prevent the mischiefs which might arise from the scandal of their unjust deportment; but, as they were not excommunicated, it was no violation of any canon to communicate with them. St. Martin therefore in this extremity ran to the palace again, and promised the emperor to communicate with Ithacius, provided he would pardon those unfortunate persons, and recall the tribunes who had been sent into Spain. Maximus immediately complied with his demands. The next day being pitched upon by the Ithacians for the ordination of Felix, the newly elected bishop of Triers, St. Martin communicated with them upon that occasion, that so many people might be rescued from slaughter. The day following, he left Triers with some remorse, or a grief for his condescension. But he was comforted by an angel at prayer in the wood near Andethanna, now Echternach, five miles from Triers, who said to him that he had reason to grieve for a condescension which was a misery, but charity rendered it necessary and excusable. St. Sulpicius adds, that St. Martin used to tell them with tears in his eyes, that, from this time, it cost him more difficulty and longer prayers to cast out devils than formerly. Some weakness, imperfection, or venial sin is often an occasion of a subtraction of sensible devotion or grace, till it be recovered by greater humility and compunction; though such subtractions are frequently sent merely for trials.

St. Martin continued his journey to Tours, where he was received as the tutelar angel of his people. In his great age, he relaxed nothing of his austerities, or of his zealous labours for the salvation of others; and he continued to the end of his life to confirm his doctrine by frequent and wonderful miracles, as we are assured by St. Sulpicius Severus. This great man, renouncing the world, chose for his first retreat a little cottage upon an estate which he had at a village upon the borders of Aquitain, now in Languedoc, called Primuliac, and afterward Mount Primlau, a place not now known. He made several visits to St. Martin, and squared his life by his direction. Upon his arrival, the blessed man presented water to him and his companions to wash their hands before eating, ordered them to be served with a moderate corporal refection, then fed them with the spiritual food of his heavenly discourses, strongly exhorting them to renounce sensuality, and the pleasures and distraction of the world, that, without hinderance, they might follow the Lord Jesus with their whole hearts. In the evening he washed their feet with his own hands. St. Sulpicius assures us, that though a stranger to secular learning, he was in his discourses clear, methodical, pathetically vehement, and powerfully eloquent; that he was very ready in solving intricate difficulties of holy writ, in answering questions upon spiritual matters, and in giving to every one suitable advice; that no one confuted errors and infidelity, or set off the truth of the Christian religion with greater perspicuity or force. This illustrious author adds, that he never heard any man speak with so much good sense, with so much knowledge and penetration, or with purer language; and the gravity, dignity, and humility with which he delivered himself, were not to be expressed. Nevertheless, his strongest exhortation to perfect virtue was the almost irresistible influence of his example and wonderful sanctity. No one ever saw him angry, disturbed, sad, or vainly laughing; the same tranquillity of mind, the same serenity of countenance appeared in him in prosperity and adversity, and, under all the vicissitudes of human accidents, even beyond what seemed possible in this mortal life. Christ was always in his mouth and in his heart. Nothing reigned there but sincere humility, piety, peace, mercy, and goodness. He was very cautious never to judge others, and to interpret every one's actions, if it was possible, in the best part. Injuries, slanders, envy, and the jealousy of persecutors, which, in the whole course of his life were never wanting, he recompensed by weeping bitterly for their sins, and by seeking every opportunity of serving them, and of heaping benefits upon them, never excluding any one from his holy friendship. He would never lose any time in the day, and often passed whole nights in labours and watchings. To his body he allowed only that refreshment and repose which extreme necessity required, lying on the bare ground, covered with a coarse sackcloth. Amid his exterior employments his heart was always closely united to God, and he seemed never to lose sight of his presence, either in words or actions. And as smiths, when they have no iron bar before them to work on, strike sometimes on the anvil through use, so St. Martin, whether he read, or wrote, or treated with men, through habit was continually recollected in the interior man, and conversed sweetly with the heavenly Spouse, and with the Giver of all graces. He was accustomed to gather profitable spiritual lessons and thoughts, and to kindle holy affections from all things which occurred. Once, when he saw a sheep newly shorn, he pleasantly said to those that were with him: "This sheep hath fulfilled the precept of the gospel, because, having enough for two coats, it hath parted with one to such as have need; so should you likewise do." Seeing a man keeping swine, very cold, and but half covered with a poor scanty coat of skins, he said: "Behold Adam driven out of Paradise; but let us, leaving the old Adam, clothe ourselves with the new." In visiting his diocess, arriving once at a river, he saw a great quantity of fowl very busy in gorging up the fish; whereupon he said: "These ravenous birds resemble much our infernal enemies, which lie always in wait to catch unwary souls, and suddenly make them their prey." But he commanded the fowls to leave the waters, and betake themselves to the hills and moors; which they instantly did. In this manner every creature served the saint's purified eyes as a lively glass of truth; and, from all things, he gathered, without study or labour, and even with delight, wholesome lessons, to maintain his heart always in pure and heavenly thoughts. In like manner he endeavoured that his subjects should exercise their souls constantly in prayer, that they might be disposed to afford a clean and agreeable lodging to the heavenly Spouse. It was by keeping his mind ever fixed on God, and by the excellent purity of his heart, much more than by the natural vivacity of his wit, and by his reading, that he attained to so high a degree of true science and heavenly eloquence, and acquired that strength with which, as a great captain of the spiritual warfare, he by all means continually waged war against the prince of this world, and, wherever he went, dispossessed him of his ancient tyranny.

St. Martin was above fourscore years old when God was pleased to put a happy end to his labours. Long before his departure, he had knowledge of his approaching death, which he clearly foretold to his disciples. Being informed that a scandalous difference had arisen among the clergy at Cande, a parish at the extremity of his diocess, at the confluence of the Loire and the Vienne in Touraine, upon the borders of Poitou and Anjou, he went thither to compose the disturbance, attended as usual by a great number of his disciples. Having remained there some time, and settled all things to his satisfaction, he was preparing for his return, when he was seized with his last sickness, and found, on a sudden, his strength fail him. As soon as he was taken ill, he called his religious brethren about him, and told them that the time of his departure was come. At this news they all with tears and with one voice said to him: "Father, why do you forsake us? or to whom do you recommend us? The ravening wolves will fall upon your flock. We know you desire to be with Jesus Christ; but your reward is secure, nor will be a whit diminished by being deferred a while. Have pity on our necessity, who are left amid great dangers." The servant of God, moved with their tears, wept also, and prayed thus: "Lord, if I am still necessary to thy people, I refuse no labour. Thy holy will be done." "As if he had said," says St. Sulpicius, "My soul is unconquered by old age, weakness, or fatigues, and ready so sustain new conflicts, if thou callest me to them. But if thou spare my age, and take me to thyself, be the guardian and protector of those souls for which I fear." By these words he showed that he knew not which was dearest to him, either to remain on earth for Christ, or to leave the earth for Christ; and has taught us in prayer for temporal things, to remit ourselves with perfect resignation and indifference to the divine will, begging that God may direct all things in us and through us to his greater glory. The saint had a fever which lasted some days; notwithstanding which he spent the night in prayer, lying on ashes and haircloth. His disciples earnestly entreated him that he would suffer them at least to put a little straw under him. But he replied: "It becomes not a Christian to die otherwise than upon ashes. I shall have sinned if I leave you any other example." He continually held up his eyes and hands to heaven, never interrupting his prayer, so that the priests that stood about him begged he would turn himself on one side, to afford his body a little rest. He answered: "Allow me, my brethren, to look rather toward heaven than upon the earth, that my soul may be directed to take its flight to the Lord to whom it is going." Afterward, seeing the devil near him, he said: "What dost thou here, cruel beast? Thou shalt find nothing in me. Abraham's bosom is open to receive me." Saying these words, he expired on the 8th of November, probably in 397. He died seventeen months after St. Ambrose, as St. Gregory of Tours assures us. They who were present wondered at the brightness of his face and whole body, which seemed to them as if it were already glorified. The inhabitants of Poitiers warmly disputed the possession of his body; but the people of Tours carried it off. The whole city came out to meet it; all the country-people, and many from neighbouring cities flocked thither, with about two thousand monks, and a great company of virgins. They all melted into tears, though no one doubted of his glory. He was carried with hymns to the place of his interment, which was in a little grove at some distance from the monastery, where certain monks lived in separate cells. The place was then five hundred and thirty paces from the city, as St. Gregory of Tours informs us, though at present it is part of it, and the walls were carried so far as to encompass it in the beginning of the inroads of the Normans. Saint Brice, St. Martin's successor, built a chapel over his tomb, and St. Perpetuus, the sixth bishop of Tours, about the year 470, founded upon that spot the great church and monastery, the saint's sumptuous tomb being placed behind the high altar. These monks secularized themselves in the seventh century. Toward the close of the eighth, Pope Adrian I., at the request of Charlemagne, placed there regular canons, and Alcuin was shortly after appointed their abbot. These canons were secularized in the reign of Charles the Bald, in 849, and have continued so ever since. The king of France, from the time of Hugh Capet, is the abbot and first canon. Besides eleven dignitaries, and fifty-one canons, &c., there are ecclesiastical honorary canons, namely, the patriarch of Jerusalem, the archbishops of Mentz, Cologne, Compostella, Sens, and Bourges; the bishops of Liege, Strasbourg, Angers, Auxerre, and Quebec; and the abbots of Marmontier, and Saint Julian's at Tours; and lay honorary canons, the dauphin, the dukes of Burgundy, Anjou, Brittany, Bourbon, Vendôme, and Nevers; the counts of Flanders, Dunois, and Angoulême; also the earl of Douglas, in Scotland, before that family had changed its religion. The extraordinary devotion which the French and all Europe have expressed to St. Martin, and to this church for the sake of his precious tomb, would furnish matter for a large history. The Huguenots rifled the shrine and scattered the relics of this saint. But this church recovered a bone of his arm, and part of his skull. Before this dispersion, certain churches had obtained small portions, which they still preserve. The priory of St. Martin's-in-the-Fields at Paris is possessed of a part; two of his teeth are shown in St. Martin's at Tournay. The cathedral at Tours was built by St. Martin in honour of St. Maurice; but, since the year 1096, bears the title of St. Gatian's. Its chapter is one of the most illustrious in France; the bishop of Tours was suffragan to Rouen till he was made a metropolitan. A vial of sacred oil is kept at St. Martin's, with which Henry IV. was anointed king instead of that from Rheims. St. Sulpicius relates that St. Martin sometimes cured distempers by oil which he had blessed, and that this oil sometimes miraculously increased.

Many miracles wrought at the shrine of St. Martin, or through his intercession, immediately after his happy death, some of which are recounted by St. Gregory of Tours, Fortunatus, and others, excited exceedingly the devotion of the people. Some have imagined that he was the first saint publicly honoured by the church as a confessor; but this is not so much as insinuated by any ancient author; and St. John the Evangelist, St. Thecla, and many others were not properly martyrs, not to mention St. Petronilla, St. Praxedes, and St. Pudentiana. The principal feast of Saint Martin is kept on the 11th of November; that of his ordination and the translation of his relics on the 4th of July; that of bringing them back from Auxerre to Tours, called Relatio, on the 13th of December.

The virtue of St. Martin, which was the miracle of the world, was founded in the most profound humility, perfect meekness and self-denial, by which he was dead to himself, in his continual meditation on religious truths, in his love of heavenly things, and contempt of the world, to which his heart was crucified; lastly, in the constant union of his soul to God, by the exercise of holy prayer, and by the entire resignation of himself to the divine will in all things without reserve. Such a disposition could not but be accompanied with the most ardent fraternal charity, zeal for the divine honour, and all other virtues. Whatever our state and circumstances may be in the world, unless, by learning the same virtues, and studying daily to improve them in our hearts, we put on the spirit of Christ, bear his image in our souls, and wear his livery, we cannot hope to be owned by him at the last day, or to find admittance into the company of his elect; but shall be cast forth with the reprobate into outer darkness.

ST. WILLIAM, CONFESSOR.

ARCHBISHOP OF BOURGES.

A. D. 1209.

WILLIAM BERRUYER, of the illustrious family of the ancient counts of Nevers, was educated by Peter the Hermit, archdeacon of Soissons, his uncle by the mother's side. He learned from his infancy to despise the folly and emptiness of the riches and grandeur of the world, to abhor its pleasures, and to tremble at its dangers. His only delight was in exercises of piety and in his studies, in which he employed his whole time with indefatigable application. He was made canon, first of Soissons, and afterward of Paris: but he soon took the resolution of abandoning all commerce with the world; and retired into the solitude of Grandmont, where he lived with great regularity in that austere order, till seeing its peace disturbed by a contest which arose between the fathers and lay brothers, he passed into the Cistercian, then in wonderful odour of sanctity. He took the habit in the abbey of Pontigny, and, shining as a perfect model of monastic perfection, was after some time chosen prior of that house, and afterward abbot, first of Fontaine-Jean, in the diocess of Sens, (a filiation of Pontigny, founded in 1124, by Peter de Courtenay, son of King Lewis the Fat,) and some time after, of Chaalis, near Senlis, a much more numerous monastery, also a filiation of Pontigny, built by Louis the Fat in 1136, a little before his death. St. William always reputed himself the last among his brethren. The universal mortification of his senses and passions, laid in him the foundation of an admirable purity of heart, and an extraordinary gift of prayer; in which he received great heavenly lights, and tasted of the sweets which God has reserved for those to whom he is pleased to communicate himself. The sweetness and cheerfulness of his countenance testified the uninterrupted joy and peace that overflowed his soul, and made virtue appear with the most engaging charms in the midst of austeries.

On the death of Henry de Sully, archbishop of Bourges, the clergy of that church requested his brother Eudo, bishop of Paris, to come and assist them in the election of a pastor. Desirous to choose some abbot of the Cistercian order, then renowned for holy men, they put on the altar the names of three, written on as many billets. This manner of election by lots would have been superstitious, and a tempting of God, had it been done relying on a miracle without the warrant of divine inspiration. But it deserved not this censure, when all the persons proposed seemed equally worthy and fit, as the choice was only recommended to God, and left to this issue by following the rules of his ordinary providence, and imploring his light without rashness, or a neglect of the usual means of scrutiny: prudence might sometimes even recommend such a method, in order to terminate a debate, when the candidates seemed equally qualified. God, in such cases, is said sometimes to have miraculously interposed.

Eudo, accordingly, having written three billets, laid them on the altar; and having made his prayer, drew first the name of the Abbot William, on whom, at the same time, the majority of the votes of the clergy had made the election fall, the 23d of November, 1200. This news overwhelmed William with grief. He never would have acquiesced, had he not received a double command in virtue of obedience, from the pope, and from his general, the abbot of Citeaux. He left his dear solitude with many tears, and was received at Bourges as one sent by heaven, and soon after was consecrated. In this new dignity his first care was to conform both his exterior and interior to the most perfect rules of sanctity; being very sensible that a man's first task is to honour God perfectly in his own soul. He redoubled all his austerities, saying, it was now incumbent on him to do penance for others, as well as for himself. He always wore a hair-shirt under his religious habit, and never added, nor diminished, any thing in his clothes either winter or summer. He never eat any flesh-meat, though he had it at his table for strangers. His attention to feed his flock was no less remarkable, especially in assisting the poor both spiritually and corporally, saying, that he was chiefly sent for them. He was most mild to penitent sinners; but inflexible toward the impenitent, though he refused to have recourse to the civil power against them, the usual remedy of that age. Many such he at last reclaimed by his sweetness and charity. Certain great men abusing his lenity, usurped the rights of his church; but the saint strenuously defended them even against the king himself, notwithstanding his threat to confiscate his lands. By humility and resolution he overcame several contradictions of his chapter and other clergy. By his zeal he converted many of the Albigenses, contemporary heretics, and was preparing himself for a mission among them at the time he was seized with his last illness. He would, notwithstanding, preach a farewell sermon to his people, which increased his fever to such a degree, that he was obliged to set aside his journey and take to his bed. Drawing near his end, he received first extreme unction, according to the discipline of that age; then, in order to receive the viaticum, he rose out of bed, fell on his knees melting in tears, and prayed long prostrate with his arms stretched out in the form of a cross. The night following, perceiving his last hour approach, he desired to anticipate the nocturns, which are said at midnight; but having made the sign of the cross on his lips and breast, was able to pronounce no more than the two first words. Then, according to a sign made by him, he was laid on ashes in the hair-cloth which he always privately wore. In this posture he soon after expired, a little past midnight, on the morning of the 10th of January, in 1209. His body was interred in his cathedral; and being honoured by many miracles, was taken up in 1217; and in the year following he was canonized by Pope Honorius III. His relics were kept with great veneration till 1562, when they were burnt, and scattered in the winds by the Huguenots, on occasion of their plundering the cathedral of Bourges, as Baillet and Bollandus mention. A bone of his arm is shown with veneration at Chaalis, whither it had been sent soon after the saint's body was taken up; and a rib is preserved in the church of the college of Navarre, at Paris, on which the canons of St. Bourges bestowed it in 1399. His festival is kept in that church with great solemnity, and a great concourse of devout persons; St. William being regarded in several parts of France as one of the patrons of the nation, though his name is not mentioned in the Roman Martyrology. The celebrated Countess Maud, his niece, out of veneration for his memory, bestowed certain lands in the Nivernois on the church of Bourges. B. Philip Berruyer, a nephew of St. William, was archbishop of Bourges from the year 1236 to 1260, in which he died in the odour of sanctity. Nangi ascribes to him many miracles, and other historians bear testimony to his eminent virtue. Dom Martenne has published his edifying original life.

If we look into the lives of all the saints, we shall find that it was by a spirit and gift of prayer that the Holy Ghost formed in their hearts the most perfect sentiments of all virtues. It is this which enlightens the understanding, and infuses a spiritual knowledge and a heavenly wisdom which is incomparably more excellent than that in which philosophers pride themselves. The same purifies the affections, sanctifies the soul, adorns it with virtues, and enriches it with every gift of heaven. Christ, who is the eternal wisdom, came down among us on earth to teach us more perfectly this heavenly language, and he alone is our master in it. He vouchsafed also to be our model. In the first moment in which his holy soul began to exist, it exerted all its powers in contemplating and adoring the divine Trinity, and employed his affections in the most ardent acts of praise, love, thanksgiving, oblation, and the like. His whole mortal life was an uninterrupted prayer; more freely to apply himself to this exercise, and to set us an example, he often retired into mountains and deserts, and spent whole nights in prayer; and to this employment he consecrated his last breath upon the cross. By him the saints were inspired to conceive an infinite esteem for holy prayer, and such a wonderful assiduity and ardour in this exercise, that many renounced altogether the commerce of men for only that of God and his angels; and the rest learned the art of conversing secretly with heaven even amid their exterior employments, which they only undertook for God. Holy pastors have always made retirement and a life of prayer their apprenticeship or preparation for the ministry, and afterward, amid its functions, were still men of prayer in them, having God always present to their mind, and setting apart intervals in the day, and a considerable part of the nights, to apply themselves with their whole attention to this exercise, in the silence of all creatures.

ST. VERONICA, OF MILAN.

From her Life, in Bollandus, t. 1, p. 890.

A. D. 1497.

ALL states furnish abundant means for attaining to sanctity and Christian perfection, and it is only owing to our sloth and tepidity that we neglect to make use of them. This saint could boast of no worldly advantages either by birth or fortune. Her parents maintained their family by hard labour in a village near Milan, and were both very pious; her father never sold a horse, or any thing else he dealt in, without being more careful to acquaint the purchaser with all that was secretly faulty in it than to recommend its good qualities. His narrow circumstances prevented his giving his daughter any schooling, so that she never learned to read; but his own, and his devout wife's example, and fervent though simple instructions, filled her tender heart from the cradle with lively sentiments of virtue. The pious maid from her infancy applied herself to continual prayer, was very attentive to the instructions given in the catechism; and the uninterrupted consideration of the holy mysteries and the important truths of religion, engrossed her whole soul to themselves. She was, notwithstanding, of all others, the most diligent and indefatigable in labour; and so obedient to her parents and masters, even in the smallest trifles, so humble and submissive to her equals, that she seemed to have no will of her own. Her food was coarse and very sparing, and her drink the same which the poorer sort of people used in that country—water, except sometimes whey or a little milk. At her work she continually conversed in her heart with God: insomuch that in company she seemed deaf to their discourses, mirth, and music. When she was weeding, reaping, or at any other labour in the fields, she strove to work at a distance from her companions, to entertain herself the more freely with her heavenly spouse. The rest admired her love of solitude, and, on coming to her, always found her countenance cheerful, yet often bathed in tears, which they sometimes perceived to flow in great abundance; though they did not know the source to be devotion: so carefully did Veronica conceal what passed in her soul between her and God.

Through a divine call to a religious and conventual state of life, she conceived a great desire to become a nun, in the poor, austere, and edifying convent of St. Martha, of the order of St. Austin, in Milan. To qualify herself for this state, being busied the whole day at work, she sat up at night to learn to read and write, which the want of an instructor made a great fatigue to her. One day being in great anxiety about her learning, the Mother of God, to whom she had always recommended herself, in a comfortable vision bade her banish that anxiety; for it was enough if she knew three letters: the first, purity of the affections, by placing her whole heart on God alone, loving no creature but in him and for him; the second, never to murmur, or be impatient at the sins, or any behaviour of others, but to bear them with interior peace and patience, and humbly to pray for them; the third, to set apart some time every day to meditate on the passion of Christ. After three years' preparation, she was admitted to the religious habit in St. Martha's. Her life was entirely uniform, perfect, and fervent in every action—no other than a living copy of her rule, which consisted in the practice of evangelical perfection reduced to certain holy exercises. Every moment of her life she studied to accomplish it to the least tittle, and was no less exact in obeying the order or direction of any superior's will. When she could not obtain leave to watch in the church so long as she desired, by readily complying, she deserved to hear from Christ that obedience was a sacrifice the most dear to him, who, to obey his Father's will, came down from heaven, *becoming obedient even unto death.*

She lay three years under a lingering illness, all which time she would never be exempted from any duty of the house, or part of her work, or make use of the least indulgence, though she had leave: her answer always was, "I must work while I can, while I have time." It was her delight to help and serve every one. She always sought with admirable humility the last place and the greatest drudgery. It was her desire to live always on bread and water. Her silence was a sign of her recollection and continual prayer, in which her gift of abundant and almost continual tears was most wonderful. She nourished them by constant meditation on her own miseries, on the love of God, the joys of heaven, and the sacred passion of Christ. She always spoke of her own sinful life, as she called it, though it was most innocent, with the most feeling sentiments of compunction. She was favoured by God with many extraordinary visits and comforts. By moving exhortations to virtue, she softened and converted several obdurate sinners. She died at the hour which she had foretold, in the year 1497, and the fifty-second of her age. Her sancity was confirmed by miracles. Pope Leo X., by a bull in 1517, permitted her to be honoured in her monastery in the same manner as if she had been beatified according to the usual form. The bull may be seen in Bollandus. Her name is inserted on the 13th of January, in the Roman Martyrology, published by Benedict XIV. in the year 1749; but on the 28th of that month, in that of the Austin friars, approved by the same pope.

Christian perfection consists very much in the performance of our ordinary actions and the particular duties of our respective stations. God, as the good Father and great Master of the family of the world, allots to every one his proper place and office in it; and it is in this variety of states by which it subsists; and in their mutual dependence upon each other that its good order and beauty consist. It is the most holy and wise appointment of providence and the order of nature, that the different stations in the world be filled. Kings and subjects, rich and poor, reciprocally depend upon each other; and it is the command of God that every one perform well the part which is assigned him. It is then by the constant attendance on all the duties of his state that a person is to be sanctified. By this all his ordinary actions will be agreeable sacrifices to God, and his whole life a continued chain of good works. It is not only in great actions, or by fits and starts, but in all that we do, and in every moment, that we are bound to live to God. The regulation of this point is of essential importance in a virtuous life, that every action may be performed with regularity, exactitude in all its circumstances, and the utmost fervour, and by the most pure motive, referred solely to divine honour, in union with the most holy actions and infinite merits of Christ. Hence St. Hilary says, "When the just man performs all his actions with a pure and simple view to the divine honour and glory, as the apostle admonishes us, his whole life becomes an uninterrupted prayer; and as he passes his days and nights in the accomplishment of the divine will, it is true to say that the whole course of a holy life is a constant meditation on the law of God." Nevertheless this axiom, that the best devotion is the constant practice of a person's ordinary duties, is abused by some, to excuse a life of dissipation. Every one is bound to live to himself in the first place, and to reserve leisure for frequent exercises of devotion; and it is only by a spirit of perfect self-denial, humility, compunction, and prayer, and by an assiduous attention of the soul to God, that our exterior ordinary actions will be animated by the motives of divine faith and charity, and the spirit of true piety nourished in our breasts; in this consists the secret of a Christian life in all states.

ST. ARCADIUS, MARTYR.

The time of this saint's martyrdom is not mentioned in its acts; some place it under Valerian, others under Dioclesian; he seems to have suffered in some city of Mauritania, probably the capital, Cæsárea. The fury of the tyrant raged violently, and the devil had instigated his soldiers to wage, like so many wolves, a bloody war against the servants of Jesus. Upon the least suspicion they broke into houses, made rigorous searches, and if they found a Christian, they treated him upon the spot with the greatest cruelty, their impatience not suffering them to wait the bringing him before a judge. Every day new sacrileges were committed; the faithful were compelled to assist at superstitious sacrifices, to lead victims crowned with flowers through the streets, to burn incense before idols, and to celebrate the enthusiastic feasts of Bacchus. Arcadius, seeing his city in great confusion, left his estate, and withdrew to a solitary place in the neighbouring country, serving Jesus Christ in watching, prayer, and other exercises of a penitential life. His flight could not be long a secret; for his not appearing at the public sacrifices made the governor send soldiers to his house, who surrounded it, forced open the doors, and finding one of his relations in it, who said all he could to justify his kinsman's absence, they seized him, and the governor ordered him to be kept in close custody till Arcadius should be taken. The martyr, informed of his friend's danger, and burning with a desire to suffer for Christ, went into the city, and presenting himself to the judge, said: "If on my account you detain my innocent relation in chains, release him: I, Arcadius, am come in person to give an account of myself, and do declare to you, that he knew not where I was." "I am willing," answered the judge, "to pardon not only him, but you also, on condition that you will sacrifice to the gods." Arcadius replied, "How can you propose to me such a thing? Do you not know the Christians, or do you believe that the fear of death will ever make me swerve from my duty? Jesus Christ is my life, and death is my gain. Invent what torments you please; but know that nothing shall make me a traitor to my God." The governor, in a rage, paused to devise some unheard-of torment for him. Iron hooks seemed too easy; neither plummets of lead nor cudgels could satisfy his fury; the very rack he thought by much too gentle. At last, imagining he had found a manner of death suitable to his purpose, he said to the ministers of his cruelty, "Take him, and let him see and desire death, without being able to obtain it. Cut off his limbs joint by joint, and execute this so slowly, that the wretch may know what it is to abandon the gods of his ancestors for an unknown deity." The executioners dragged Arcadius to the place where many other victims of Christ had already suffered; a place dear and sweet to all who sigh after eternal life. Here the martyr lifts up his eyes to heaven, and implores strength from above: then stretches out his neck, expecting to have his head cut off; but the executioner bid him hold out his hand, and joint after joint chopped off his fingers, arms, and shoulders. Laying the saint afterward on his back, he in the same barbarous manner cut off his toes, feet, legs, and thighs. The holy martyr held out his limbs and joints, one after another, with invincible patience and courage, repeating these words, "Lord, teach me thy wisdom;" for the tyrants had forgot to cut out his tongue. After so many martyrdoms, his body lay a mere trunk weltering in its own blood. The executioners themselves, as well as the multitude, were moved to tears and admiration at this spectacle, and at such an heroic patience. But Arcadius, with a joyful countenance, surveying his scattered limbs all around him, and offering them to God, said, "Happy members, now dear to me, as you at last truly belong to God, being all made a sacrifice to him!" Then turning to the people, he said, "You who have been present at this bloody tragedy, learn that all torments seem as nothing to one who has an everlasting crown before his eyes. Your gods are not gods; renounce their worship. He alone for whom I suffer and die is the true God. He comforts and upholds me in the condition you see me. To die for him is to live; to suffer for him is to enjoy the greatest delights." Discoursing in this manner to those about him, he expired on the 12th of January, the pagans being struck with astonishment at such a miracle of patience. The Christians gathered together his scattered limbs, and laid them in one tomb. The Roman and other Martyrologies make honourable mention of him.

We belong to God by numberless essential titles of interest, gratitude, and justice, and are bound to be altogether his, and every moment to live to him alone, with all our powers and all our strength: whatever it may cost us to make this sacrifice perfect and complete, if we truly love him, we shall embrace it with joy and inexpressible ardour. In these sentiments we ought, by frequent express acts, and by the uninterrupted habitual disposition of our souls, to give all we are and have to God, all the powers of our souls, all the senses and organs of our bodies, all our actions, thoughts, and affections. This oblation we may excellently comprise in any of the first petitions of our Lord's prayer; the following is a form of an oblation to our divine Redeemer, which St. Ignatius of Loyola drew up and used to repeat: "O sovereign King, and absolute Lord of all things, though I am most unworthy to serve you, nevertheless, relying on your grace and boundless mercy, I offer myself up entire to you, and subject whatever belongs to me to your most holy will; and I protest in presence of your infinite goodness, and in presence of the glorious Virgin your mother, and your whole heavenly court, that it is my most earnest desire, and unshaken resolution, to follow and imitate you the nearest I am able, in bearing all injuries and crosses with meekness and patience, and in labouring to die to the world and myself in a perfect spirit of humility and poverty, that I may be wholly yours, and you may reign in me in time and eternity."

ST. LUCIAN,

PRIEST AND MARTYR.

A. D. 312.

St. Lucian, surnamed of Antioch, was born at Samosata, in Syria. He lost his parents while very young; and being come to the possession of his estate, which was very considerable, he distributed all among the poor. He became a great proficient in rhetoric and philosophy, and applied himself to the study of the Holy Scriptures under one Macarius at Edessa. Convinced of the obligation annexed to the character of priesthood, which was that of devoting himself entirely to the service of God and the good of his neighbour, he did not content himself with inculcating the practice of virtue both by word and example; he also undertook to purge the Scriptures, that is, both the Old and New Testament, from the several faults that had crept into them, either by reason of the inaccuracy of transcribers, or the malice of heretics. Some are of opinion, that as to the Old Testament, he only revised it, by comparing different editions of the Septuagint: others contend, that he corrected it upon the Hebrew text, being well versed in that language. Certain, however, it is, that St. Lucian's edition of the Scriptures was much esteemed, and was of great use to St. Jerom.

St. Alexander, bishop of Alexandria, says that Lucian remained some years separated from the catholic communion, at Antioch, under three successive bishops, namely, Domnus, Timæus, and Cyril. If it was for too much favouring Paul of Samosata, condemned at Antioch in the year 269, he must have been deceived, for want of a sufficient penetration into the impiety of that dissembling heretic. It is certain, at least, that he died in the catholic communion; which also appears from a fragment of a letter written by him to the church of Antioch, and still extant in the Alexandrian Chronicle. Though a priest of Antioch, we find him at Nicomedia, in the year 303, when Dioclesian first published his edicts against the Christians. He there suffered a long imprisonment for the faith; for the Paschal Chronicle quotes these words from a letter which he wrote out of his dungeon to Antioch:—" All the martyrs salute you. I inform you that the Pope Anthimus (bishop of Nicomedia) has finished his course by martyrdom." This happened in 303. Yet Eusebius informs us, that St. Lucian did not arrive himself at the crown of martyrdom till after the death of St. Peter of Alexandria, in 311, so that he seems to have continued nine years in prison. At length he was brought before the governor, or, as the acts intimate, the emperor himself, for the word which Eusebius uses may imply either. On his trial he presented to the judge an excellent apology for the Christian faith. Being remanded to prison, an order was given that no food should be allowed him; but, when almost dead with hunger, dainty meats that had been offered to idols, were set before him, which he would not touch. It was not in himself unlawful to eat of such meats, as St. Paul teaches, except where it would give scandal to the weak, or when it was exacted as an action of idolatrous superstition, as was the case here. Being brought a second time before the tribunal, he would give no other answer to all the questions put to him, but this: "I am a Christian." He repeated the same while on the rack, and he finished his glorious course in prison, either by famine, or, according to St. Chrysostom, by the sword. His acts relate many of his miracles, with other particulars; as that when bound and chained down on his back in prison, he consecrated the divine mysteries upon his own breast, and communicated the faithful that were present: this we also read in Philostorgius, the Arian historian. St. Lucian suffered at Nicomedia, where Maximus II. resided.

His body was interred at Drepanum, in Bithnyia, which, in honour of him, Constantine the Great soon after made a large city, which he exempted from all taxes, and honoured with the name of Helenopolis, from his mother. St. Lucian was crowned in 312, on the 7th of January, on which day his festival was kept at Antioch immediately after his death, as appears from St. Chrysostom. It is the tradition of the church of Arles, that the body of St. Lucian was sent out of the East to Charlemagne, who built a church under his invocation at Arles, in which his relics are preserved. See Saussaye, Mart. Gallic. t. 1, p. 17. Chatelain, p. 114.

The first thing that is necessary in the service of God, is earnestly to search his holy will, by devoutly reading, listening to, and meditating on his eternal truths. This will set the divine law in a clear and full light, and conduct us by unerring rules to discover and accomplish every duty. It will awake and continually increase a necessary tenderness of conscience, which will add light and life to its convictions, oblige us to a more careful trial and examination of all our actions, keep us not only from evil, but from every appearance of it, render us steadfast and immovable in every virtuous practice, and always preserve a quick and nice sense of good and evil. For this reason the word of God is called in holy Scripture, *Light*, because it distinguisheth between good and evil, and like a lamp, manifesteth the path which we are to choose, and disperseth that mist with which the subtilty of our enemy and the lusts of our heart have covered it. At the same time, a daily repetition of contrition and compunction washes off the stains which we discover in our souls, and strongly incites us, by the fervour and fruitfulness of our following life, to repair the sloth and barrenness of the past. Prayer must be made our main assistant in every step of this spiritual progress. We must pray that God would enable us to search out and discover our own hearts, and reform whatever is amiss in them. If we do this sincerely, God will undoubtedly grant our requests—will lay open to us all our defects and infirmities, and, showing us how far short we come of the perfection of true holiness of life, will not suffer any latent corruptions in our affections to continue undiscovered, nor permit us to forget the stains and ruins which the sins of our life past have left behind them.

ST. FRANCIS OF ASSISIUM, C.

A. D. 1226.

THE life of the glorious St. Francis, which was a miracle of humility, loudly condemns the wise ones of this world, to whom the sincere practice of this virtue, and the imitation of the cross of Christ appears a scandal and a folly, as the cross itself did to the Jews and Gentiles. For, among Christians, they who walk enemies to the cross are strangers to the spirit of Christ, glory in vain in his name, and falsely call themselves his followers. He communicates himself, and imparts the riches of his graces and holy love to those whose hearts are most perfectly disengaged from all earthly things; and on souls which are grounded in sincere humility and simplicity of heart his divine Spirit rests. The blessed St. Francis was one of these happy little ones, whom God chose to enrich with spiritual knowledge and heavenly gifts of virtue. He was born at Assisium, in Umbria, in the Ecclesiastical State, in 1182. His father, Peter Bernardon, was descended of a gentleman's family originally settled at Florence, but was himself a merchant, and lived at Assisium, a town situated on the brow of a hill called Assi. The saint's mother was called Pica. Both his parents were persons of great probity. They were in good circumstances, but so taken up with their business as to neglect giving their son any tincture of learning. Their trade lying in part with the French, they made him learn that language; and from the readiness with which he acquired and spoke it, he was called Francis, though the name of John had been given him at his baptism. In his youth he was too much led away with vain amusements, and was very intent on temporal gain; but he never let loose the reins of his sensual appetites, nor placed his confidence in worldly riches; and it was his custom never to refuse an alms to any poor man who asked it of him for the love of God. One day being very busy about his affairs, he let a beggar go away without any alms, but, immediately reproaching himself with want of charity, ran after the poor man, gave him an alms, and bound himself by a vow never to refuse it to any poor man that should ask it for the love of God: this vow he kept to his death. Francis, while he yet lived in the world, was meek, patient, very tractable, and liberal to the poor beyond what his circumstances seemed to allow. Whenever he heard the love of God named, he felt in his soul an interior spiritual jubilation. His patience, under two accidents which befell him, contributed greatly to the improvement of his virtue. The one was, that in a war between the cities of Perugia and Assisium, he, with several others, was carried away prisoner by the Perugians. This affliction he suffered a whole year with great alacrity, and comforted his companions. The second was a long and dangerous sickness, which he suffered with so great patience and piety, that by the weakness of his body his spirit gathered greater strength, and improved in the unction of the Holy Ghost and the divine gift of prayer. After his recovery, as he rode out one day in a new suit of clothes, meeting on the road a decayed gentleman then reduced to poverty and very ill clad, he was touched with compassion to the quick, and changed clothes with him. The night following, he seemed to see in his sleep a magnificent palace, filled with rich arms, all marked with the sign of the cross; and he thought he heard one tell him that these arms belonged to him and his soldiers, if they would take up the cross and fight courageously under its banner. After this, he gave himself much to prayer, by which he felt in his soul a great contempt of all transitory things, and an ardent desire of selling his goods, and buying the precious jewel of the gospel. He knew not yet how he should best do this, but he felt certain strong inspirations by which our Lord gave him to understand that the spiritual warfare of Christ is begun by mortification and the victory over one's self. These interior motions awakened him, and inflamed him every day more and more to desire to attain to the perfect mortification of his senses, and contempt of himself. Riding one day in the plains of Assisium, he met a leper whose sores were so loathsome that at the sight of them he was struck with horror, and suddenly recoiled; but overcoming himself, he alighted, and as the leper stretched forth his hand to receive an alms, Francis, while he bestowed it, kissed his sores with great tenderness.

Resolving with fresh ardour to aim at Christian perfection, he had no relish but for solitude and prayer, and besought our Lord with great fervour to reveal to him his will. Being one day wholly absorbed in God, he seemed to behold Christ hanging upon his cross; from which vision he was so tenderly affected, that he was never afterward able to remember the sufferings of Christ without shedding many tears; and, from that time, he was animated with an extraordinary spirit of poverty, charity, and piety. He often visited the hospitals, served the sick, as if in them he had served Christ himself, and kissed the ulcers of the lepers with great affection and humility. He gave to the poor sometimes part of his clothes, and sometimes money. He took a journey to Rome to visit the tombs of the apostles, and finding a multitude of poor before the door of Saint Peter's church, he gave his clothes to one whom he thought to be most in need among them; and clothing himself with the rags of that poor man, he remained all that day in the company of those beggars, feeling an extraordinary comfort and joy in his soul. Having interiorly the cross of Christ imprinted on his heart, he endeavoured earnestly to mortify and crucify his flesh. One day as he was praying in the church of St. Damian, without the walls of Assisium, before a crucifix, he seemed to hear a voice coming from it, which said to him three times: "Francis, go and repair my house, which thou seest falling." The saint seeing that church was old and ready to fall to the ground, thought our Lord commanded him to repair it. He therefore went home, and, by an action which was only justifiable by the simplicity of his heart, and the right of a partnership with his father in trade, (for he was then twenty-five years old,) took a horse-load of cloth out of his father's warehouse, and sold it, with the horse, at Foligni, a town twelve miles from Assisium. The price he brought to the old poor priest of St. Damian's, desiring to stay with him. The priest consented to his staying, but would not take the money, which Francis therefore laid in a window. His father hearing what had been done, came in a rage to St. Damian's, but was somewhat pacified, upon recovering his money, which he found in the window. Francis, to shun his anger, had hid himself; but, after some days spent in prayer and fasting, appeared again in the streets, though so disfigured and ill clad, that the people pelted him, and called him madman; all which he bore with joy.

Bernardon, more incensed than ever, carried him home, beat him unmercifully, put fetters on his feet, and locked him up in a chamber till his mother set him at liberty while his father was gone out. Francis returned to St. Damian's, and his father following him thither, insisted that he should either return home, or renounce before the bishop all his share in his inheritance, and all manner of expectations from his family. The son accepted the latter condition with joy, gave his father whatever he had in his pockets, told him he was ready to undergo more blows and chains for the love of Jesus Christ, whose disciple he desired to be, and cheerfully went with his father before the bishop of Assisium, to make a legal renunciation of his inheritance in form. Being come into his presence, Francis, impatient of delays, while the instrument was drawing up, made the renunciation by the following action, carrying it in his fervour further than was required. He stripped himself of his clothes, and gave them to his father, saying cheerfully and meekly: "Hitherto I have called you father on earth; but now I say with more confidence, Our Father, who art in heaven, in whom I place all my hope and treasure." He renounced the world with greater pleasure than others can receive its favours, hoping now to be freed from all that which is most apt to make a division in our hearts with God, or even to drive him quite out. The bishop admired his fervour, covered him with his cloak, and shedding many tears, ordered some garment or other to be brought in for him. The cloak of a country labourer, a servant of the bishop, was found next at hand. The saint received this first alms with many thanks, made a cross on the garment with chalk or mortar, and put it on. This happened in the twenty-fifth year of his age, in 1206.

Francis went out of the bishop's palace in search of some convenient retirement, singing the divine praises along the highways. He was met by a band of robbers in a wood, who asked him who he was.

He answered with confidence: "I am the herald of the Great King." They beat him, and threw him into a ditch full of snow. He rejoiced to have been so treated, and went on singing the praises of God. He passed by a monastery, and there received an alms as an unknown poor man. In the city of Gubbio, one who knew him, took him into his house, and gave him an entire suit of clothes, which were decent, though poor and mean. These he wore two years with a girdle and shoes, and he walked with a staff in his hand like a hermit. At Gubbio he visited the hospital of lepers, and served them, washing their feet, and wiping and kissing their ulcers. For the repairs of the church of St. Damian, he gathered alms and begged in the city of Assisium, where all had known him rich. He bore with joy the railleries and contempt with which he was treated by his father, brother, and all his acquaintance, and if he found himself to blush upon receiving any confusion, he endeavoured to court and increase his disgrace, in order to humble himself the more, and to overcome all inclinations of pride in his heart. For the building of St. Damian's he himself carried stones, and served the masons, and saw that church put in good repair. Having a singular devotion to St. Peter, he next did the same for an old church which was dedicated in honour of that great apostle. After this, he retired to a little church called Portiuncula, belonging to the abbey of Benedictine monks of Subiaco, who gave it that name because it was built on a small estate or parcel of land which belonged to them. It stands in a spacious open plain, almost a mile from Assisium, and was at that time forsaken and in a very ruinous condition. The retiredness of this place was very agreeable to St. Francis, and he was much delighted with the title which this church bore, it being dedicated in honour of our Lady of Angels; a circumstance very pleasing to him for his singular devotion to the holy angels, and to the queen of angels. Francis repaired this church in 1207, in the same manner he had done the two others; he fixed his abode by it, made it the usual place of his devotions, and received in it many heavenly favours. He had spent here two years in sighs and tears, when hearing one day those words of Christ: *Do not carry gold, or silver, or a scrip for your journey, or two coats, or a staff*, read in the gospel at mass, he desired of the priest, after mass, an exposition of them; and applying them literally to himself, he gave away his money, and leaving off his shoes, staff, and leathern girdle, contented himself with one poor coat, which he girt about him with a cord.

This was the habit which he gave to his friars the year following. It was the dress of the poor shepherds and country peasants in those parts. The saint added a short cloak over the shoulders, and a capouch to cover the head. St. Bonaventure, in 1260, made this capouch or mozetta a little longer to cover the breast and shoulders. Some of the very habits which the saint wore are still shown at Assisium, Florence, and other places. In this attire he exhorted the people to penance with such energy, that his words pierced the hearts of his hearers. Before his discourses he saluted the people with these words: "Our Lord give you peace;" which he sometimes said he had learned by divine revelation. They express the salutation which Christ and St. Paul used. God had already favoured the saint with the gifts of prophecy and miracles. When he was begging alms to repair the church of St. Damian, he used to say: "Assist me to finish this building. Here will one day be a monastery of holy virgins, by whose good fame our Lord will be glorified over the whole church." This was verified in St. Clare five years after, who inserted this prophecy in her last will and testament. Before this, a man in the duchy of Spoletto was afflicted with a horrible running cancer, which had gnawed both his mouth and cheeks in a hideous manner. Having, without receiving any benefit, had recourse to all remedies that could be suggested, and made several pilgrimages to Rome for the recovery of his health, he came to St. Francis, and would have thrown himself at his feet; but the saint prevented him, and kissed his ulcerous sore, which was instantly healed. "I know not," says St. Bonaventure, "which I ought most to admire, such a kiss, or such a cure." The sufferings of our Divine Redeemer were a principal object of our saint's devotions, and, in his assiduous meditation on them, he was not able to contain the torrents of his tears. A stranger passing by the Portiuncula, heard his sighs, and stepping in, was astonished to see the abundance of tears in which he found him bathed; for which he reproached him as for a silly weakness. The saint answered: "I weep for the sufferings of my Lord Jesus Christ. I ought not to blush to weep publicly over the whole earth at the remembrance of this wonderful mystery." Does not a Christian die of grief and shame who feels not these sentiments of love, gratitude, and compunction in this contemplation? Only the impious can be insensible of this great spectacle. "For my part," says St. Austin to his flock, "I desire to mourn with you over it. The passion of our Lord calls for our sighs, our tears, our supplications. Who is able to shed such abundance of tears as so great a subject deserves? Certainly no one, though a fountain was placed in his eyes. Let us consider what Christ suffered; that we may accompany him with more vehement sighs and abundant tears." It was from the passion of Christ that St. Francis learned his perfect sentiments of Christian humility and piety.

Many began to admire the heroic and uniform virtue of this great servant of God, and some desired to be his companions and disciples. The first of these was Bernard of Quintaval, a rich tradesman of Assisium, a person of singular prudence, and of great authority in that city, which had been long directed by his counsels. Seeing the extraordinary conduct of St. Francis, he invited him to sup at his house, and had a good bed made ready for him near his own. When Bernard seemed to be fallen asleep, the servant of God arose, and falling on his knees, with his eyes lifted up, and his arms across, repeated very slow, with abundance of tears, the whole night: *Deus meus et Omnia*—"My God and my All." The ardour with which he poured forth his soul in these words, by most fervent acts of adoration, love, praise, thanksgiving, and compunction, was admirable; and the tender and vehement manner of his prayer expressed strongly how much the divine love filled the whole capacity of his heart. Bernard secretly watched the saint all night, by the light of a lamp, saying to himself, "This man is truly a servant of God," and admiring the happiness of such a one, whose heart is entirely filled with God, and to whom the whole world is nothing. After many other proofs of the sincere and admirable sanctity of Francis, being charmed and vanquished by his example, he begged the saint to make him his companion. Francis recommended the matter to God for some time; they both heard mass together, and took advice, that they might learn the will of God. The design being approved, Bernard sold all his effects, and divided the sum among the poor in one day. Peter of Catana, a canon of the cathedral of Assisium, desired to be admitted with him. The saint gave his habit to them both together on the 16th of August, 1209, which is called the foundation of this order, though some date it a year sooner, when the saint himself, upon hearing the gospel read, embraced this manner of life. The third person who joined them was Giles, a person of great simplicity and virtue. The first joined St. Francis in his cell at the Portiuncula; the two first soon after he had changed his habit; upon which he went to Rome and obtained a verbal approbation of his order from Innocent IV., in the same year 1209, a little before Otho IV. was crowned emperor at Rome about the close of September. The saint at his return settled at Rivo-Torto, near Assisium, where he inhabited with his disciples an abandoned cottage. After an excursion into the marquisate of Ancona to preach penance, he brought back his disciples to the Portiuncula. When their number was augmented to one hundred and twenty-seven, St. Francis, assembling them together, spoke to them in a most pathetic manner of the kingdom of God, the contempt of the world, the renouncing their own will, and the mortification of their senses; adding, in the end of his discourse: "Fear not to appear little and contemptible, or to be called by men fools and madmen; but announce penance in simplicity, trusting in Him who overcame the world by humility; it is He that will speak in you by his spirit. Let us take care that we do not lose the kingdom of heaven for any temporal interest, and that we never despise those who live otherwise than we do. God is their master, as he is ours, and he can call them to himself by other ways."

The saint composed a rule for his order, consisting of the gospel counsels of perfection, to which he added some things necessary for uniformity in their manner of life. He exhorts his brethren to manual labour, but will have them content to receive for it things necessary for life, not money. He bids them not be ashamed to beg alms, remembering the poverty of Christ; and he forbids them to preach in any place without the bishop's license. He carried his rule to Rome, to obtain the pope's approbation. Innocent III., who then sat in St. Peter's chair, appeared at first averse, and many of the cardinals alleged that the orders already established ought to be reformed, but their number not multiplied; and that the intended poverty of this new institute was impracticable. Cardinal Colonna, bishop of Salina, pleaded in its favour, that it was no more than the evangelical counsels of perfection. The pope consulted for some time, and had the affair recommended to God. He afterward told his nephew, from whom St. Bonaventure heard it, that in a dream he saw a palm-tree growing up at his feet; in another vision, some time after, he saw St. Francis propping up the Lateran church, which seemed ready to fall; as he saw St. Dominic, in another vision, five years after. He therefore sent again for St. Francis, and approved his rule, but only by word of mouth, in 1210, and he ordained him deacon. The first design of St. Francis and his companions was to form a holy society with no other view than that of studying most perfectly to die to themselves, that they might live only by the life of Jesus Christ, in holy solitude, having no commerce but with God; but it pleased God afterward to inspire the zealous founder with an earnest desire of labouring to bring sinners to repentance. He deliberated with his brethren upon this subject, and they consulted God by devout prayer. The result was that St. Francis was persuaded that God had manifested his will to him by his holy inspiration during his fervent prayers, that he had called him and his brethren to preach penance to the world by word and example.

St. Francis, having obtained of his Holiness an oral approbation of his institute, left Rome with his twelve disciples, and returned with them, first to the valley of Spoletto, and thence to Assisium, where they lived together in a little cottage at Rivo-Torto, without the gates of the town; and they sometimes went into the country to preach. Soon after, the Benedictines of Monte Soubazo bestowed on the founder the church of the Portiuncula, upon condition that it should always continue the head church of his order. The saint refused to accept the property or dominion, but would only have the use of the place; and, in token that he held it of the monks, he sent them every year, as an acknowledgment, a basket of little fish, called laschi, of which there is great plenty in a neighbouring river. The monks always sent the friars, in return, a barrel of oil. St. Francis would not suffer any dominion or property of temporal goods to be vested even in his order, or in any community or convent in it, (as in other religious orders,) that he might more perfectly and more affectionately say in his heart, that the house in which he lived, the bread which he ate, and the poor clothes which he wore, were none of his; and that he possessed nothing of any earthly goods, being a disciple of Him who, for our sakes, was born a stranger in an open stable, lived without a place of his own wherein to lay his head, subsisting by the charity of good people, and died naked on a cross in the close embraces of holy poverty, in order to expiate our sins, and to cure our passions of covetousness, sensuality, pride, and ambition. The motives which recommended to St. Francis so high an esteem of holy poverty, and made him so great a lover of that virtue, were, first, the resemblance which we bear by this state to the life of our Divine Redeemer, who was pleased to become voluntarily poor for us, and lived in extreme poverty from his first to his last breath in his mortal life—secondly, the spiritual advantage which this state affords for the perfecting in our souls the habits of humility, patience, meekness, and other heroic virtues, by their repeated acts, which are exercised under the inconveniences, privations, sufferings, and humiliations which attend that condition—thirdly, the powerful remedies which holy poverty offers for the cure of our irregular desires, especially of all inordinate love of the world; but this virtue consists not in an exterior poverty, which may be very vicious, and full of irregular desires, but in that poverty which is called holy, that is, in the spirit and love of poverty, and of its privations and humiliations, resulting from perfect motives of virtue. It is this alone which deserves the recompense promised by Christ, extirpates the passions, and is the mistress of many other virtues.

This spirit and love of holy poverty our saint learned by assiduous humble meditation on the life and passion of Christ, the great book of a spiritual life; and this is the poverty which he assiduously and most earnestly recommended to his followers. When they one day asked him which of all virtues is the most agreeable to God, he answered: "Poverty is the way to salvation, the nurse of humility, and the root of perfection. Its fruits are hidden, but they multiply themselves infinite ways." He speaks of the spirit of poverty as the root of humility and divine charity, in the same sense that some others speak of humble obedience, inasmuch as both spring from and reciprocally entertain a sincere and cordial affection of humility. St. Francis called the spirit of holy poverty the foundation of his order; and, in his habit, in every thing that he used, and in all his actions, he carried his affection for it to the greatest nicety. He sometimes ordered houses already built for his religious to be pulled down, because he thought them too large and sumptuous for their state of the most severe evangelical poverty. Returning once from a journey to the Portiuncula, he found a new building made there, which he judged to be too neat and commodious. He therefore insisted that it should be demolished, till the citizens of Assisium declared that they had built it for the lodgings of strangers, who must otherwise lie in the fields, and that it was in no way intended for his Order. In his rule he prescribed that the churches of his religious should be low and small, and all their other buildings of wood; but some person representing to him that in certain countries wood is dearer than stone, he struck out this last condition, requiring only that all their buildings should be suitable to that strict poverty which they professed. God is glorified by every spirit that is founded upon sincere motives of humility, penance, and charity; and this saint's admirable love of holy poverty, which confounds the sensuality, pride and avarice which reign so much among men, derogates not from the merit of their virtue who make a just and holy use of the things of this world to the glory of God, so as still to maintain a disengagement of heart, and a true spirit of poverty, compunction, penance, humility, and all other virtues, which are never perfect, if any one in the whole train be wanting or imperfect.

Holy poverty was dearer to St. Francis through his extraordinary love of penance. He scarce allowed his body what was necessary to sustain life, and found out every day new ways of afflicting and mortifying it. If any part of his rough habit seemed too soft, he sewed it with packthread, and was wont to say to his brethren that the devils easily tempted those that wore soft garments. His bed was ordinarily the ground, or he slept sitting, and used for his bolster a piece of wood or a stone. Unless he was sick, he very rarely ate any thing that was dressed with fire, and, when he did, he usually put ashes or water upon it; often his nourishment was only a little coarse bread, on which he sometimes strewed ashes. He drank clear water, and that very moderately, how great thirst or heat soever he suffered. He fasted rigorously eight lents in the year. Seculars were much edified that, to conform himself to them, he allowed his religious to eat flesh meat, which the end of his institute made necessary. He called his body brother Ass, because it was to carry burdens, to be beaten, and to eat little and coarsely. When he saw any one idle, eating of other men's labours, he called him brother Fly, because he did no good, but spoiled the good which others did, and was troublesome to them. As a man owes a discreet charity to his own body, the saint, a few days before he died, asked pardon of his for having treated it perhaps with too great rigour, excusing himself that he had done it the better to secure and guard the purity of his soul, and for the greater service of God. Indiscreet or excessive austerities always displeased him. When a brother, by immoderate abstinence, was not able to sleep, the saint brought him some bread, and, that he might eat it with less confusion, began himself to eat with him.

The care with which he watched over himself to preserve the virtue of purity, ought not to be passed over. In the beginning of his conversion, finding himself assailed with violent temptations of concupiscence, he often cast himself into ditches full of snow. Once, under a more grievous assault than ordinary, he presently began to discipline himself sharply; then with great fervour of spirit he went out of his cell, and rolled himself in the snow; after this, having made seven great heaps of snow, he said to himself: "Imagine these were thy wife and children ready to die of cold; thou must then take great pains to maintain them." Whereupon he set himself again to labour in the cold. By the vigour and fervour with which he on that occasion subdued his domestic enemy, he obtained so complete a victory, that he never felt any more assaults. Yet he continued always most wary in shunning every occasion of danger; and, in treating with women, kept so strict a watch over his eyes, that he scarce knew any woman by sight. It was a usual saying with him, that "by occasions the strong became weak. To converse too frequently with women, and not suffer by it, is as hard as to take fire into one's bosom and not to be burnt. What has a religious man to do," says he, "to treat with women, unless it be when he hears their confessions, or gives them necessary spiritual instructions? He that thinks himself secure is undone; the devil finding somewhat to take hold on, though it be but a hair, raises a dreadful war."

With extreme austerity, St. Francis joined the most profound humility of heart. He was, in his own eyes, the basest and most despicable of all men, and desired to be reputed such by all; he loved contempt, and sincerely shunned honour and praise. If others commended him, and showed any esteem of his virtue, he often said to himself: "What every one is in the eyes of God, that he is, and no more." He frequently commanded some friar to revile him with reproachful language. Thus he once repeated: "O brother Francis, for thy sins thou hast deserved to be plunged into hell;" and ordered brother Leo as often to reply: "It is true, you have deserved to be buried in the very bottom of hell." When he was not able to avoid the esteem of others, he was overwhelmed with secret confusion. "I refer honours and praises," said he once to another, "entirely to God, to whom they are due. I take no share in them, but behold myself in the filth of my own baseness and nothingness, and sink lower and lower in it. Statues of wood or stone take nothing to themselves, and are insensible to the respect and honour which is given them, not at all on their own account, but for the sake of those whom they represent. And if men honour God in his creatures, even in me, the last and vilest among them, I consider him alone." When he preached, he often published his own faults, that he might be despised. He was very careful to conceal the gifts of God; and to those who seemed to express an esteem for his person, he would sometimes say: "No one can justly be praised who is not yet secure of himself, and while we know not what he will be." At other times he said: "No one can boast, because he does those things which a sinner can do, as fasting, weeping, and chastising his flesh. There is one thing which no sinner does; which is, if we faithfully serve the Lord, and ascribe purely to him, whatever he gives us." A certain holy friar, and companion of Saint Francis, was favoured with a vision at prayer, in which he saw a bright throne prepared in heaven, and heard a voice telling him, that it was for the humble Francis. After having received this vision, he asked the saint how he could with truth think and call himself the greatest sinner in the world? To which the saint answered: "If God had bestowed on the greatest sinner the favours he has done me, he would have been more grateful than I am; and if he had left me to myself, I should have committed greater wickedness than all other sinners." From this humility it was that he would not be ordained priest, but always remained in the degree of deacon; he bore the greatest reverence to all priests. An effect of the same humility was his extreme love of obedience, and his often asking counsel of his lowest subjects, though he had the gift of prophecy, and was endued with an extraordinary heavenly discretion and light. In his journeys from place to place he used to promise obedience to the brother whom he took with him for his companion. He said once, that among the many favours God had done him, one was, that he would as willingly and as diligently obey a novice who had lived but one hour in a religious state, (if he was set over him by his warden or guardian,) as he would the most ancient and discreet among the fathers, because a subject is not to regard the person whom he obeys, but God, whose place every superior holds with regard to us. Being asked how one that is truly obedient ought to behave, he said, he ought to be like a dead body. He was a great enemy to all singularity. In a certain convent of his order he was told, that one of the friars was a man of admirable virtue, and so great a lover of silence, that he would only confess his faults by signs. The saint did not like it, and said: "This is not the spirit of God, but of the devil; a foul temptation, not a divine virtue." It afterward appeared, by the misconduct of this poor religious man, by how deceitful a singularity he separated himself from the conversation of his brethren. Like instances happened on other occasions. The saint's extreme aversion to the least shadow of dissimulation or hypocrisy appeared in his whole conduct. In the greatest sicknesses he would not allow himself the least indulgence which was not made public; and refused to wear any clothing to cover his breast in a dangerous cold, unless it was visible to others.

This saint, who by humility and self-denial, was perfectly crucified and dead to himself, seemed by the ardour of his charity to be rather a seraph incarnate than a frail man in a mortal state. Hence he seemed to live by prayer, and was assiduously employed in holy contemplation; for he that loves much, desires to converse with the person whom he loves; in this he places his treasure and his happiness, and finds no entertainment or delight like that of dwelling upon his excellences and greatness.

St. Francis retired every year, after the feast of the Epiphany, in honour of the forty days which Christ spent in the desert, and shutting himself up in his cell, he spent all that time in rigorous fasting and devout prayer. He communicated very often, and ordinarily with ecstasies, in which his soul was rapt and suspended in God. He recited the canonical hours with great devotion and reverence, always standing with his head bare, and usually with his eyes bathed in tears, never leaning upon any thing, even when he was very weak and sick. When he travelled, he always stopped at the canonical hours of prayer, for the sake of greater recollection and attention; and he used to say, that if the body, when it eats corruptible food, desires to be at rest, why should not this be granted the soul when it takes heavenly sustenance. Out of tender devotion and reverence to the names of God and of Jesus Christ, if he found them written in any paper thrown on the ground, he took it up, and put it in some decent place. For his trial, God once abandoned him to a violent desolation of soul and spiritual dryness during two months, till, by assiduous prayer, he suddenly found himself again replenished with the delights of the Holy Ghost, and his sensible presence. Though he felt a wonderful tenderness of devotion to all the mysteries of the life of our Saviour, yet he was most affected, next to those of his sacred passion, with that of his holy nativity, by reason of the poverty, cold, and nakedness in which the divine infant made his appearance in the stable and crib at Bethlehem. One Christmas-night the saint having sung the gospel at mass, preaching to the people on the nativity of the poor King, he was not able to satiate the tender affection of his heart by repeating often with incredible sweetness his holy name under the appellation of the Little Babe of Bethlehem. He never spoke or heard mention made of the holy mystery of the Incarnation without feeling the most tender affection of devotion. He was particularly affected with those words: *The Word was made flesh.* He had a singular devotion to the Mother of God, (whom he chose for the special patroness of his order,) and in her honour he fasted from the feast of SS. Peter and Paul to that of her Assumption. After this festival he fasted forty days, and prayed much out of devotion to the angels, especially the Archangel Michael; and at All Saints he fasted other forty days. Under the name of these lents, he spent almost the whole year in fasting and prayer, though he at no time interrupted his penitential austerities and devout recollection. Notwithstanding many great troubles which the devils, both interiorly, and sometimes visibly, raised to disturb him, and withdraw him from prayer, he always persevered constant in that heavenly exercise; nor were they ever able to make him interrupt his devotion. According to the measure of his great affection and tenderness for God, he was favoured by him with the abundance of his spiritual comforts and graces. Many times, being in prayer, he fell into raptures; often on the road as he travelled, he was visited by our Lord with a ravishing inexpressible sweetness, with which his soul was quite overwhelmed; and he usually made those that went with him go before, both for the sake of closer recollection, and to conceal the visits and favours of the Lord. Because he humbled himself, and his heart was disengaged from the love of all creatures, God exalted him above others. He illuminated the understanding of his servant with a light and wisdom that is not taught in books, but comes down from heaven, and he infused into him an uncommon knowledge of the Holy Scriptures, and of the ineffable mysteries of our divine religion. He moreover gave him the spirit of prophecy; for Saint Francis foretold many things which happened a long time after. He was endowed with an extraordinary gift of tears. His eyes seemed two fountains of tears, which were almost continually falling from them, insomuch that at length he almost lost his sight. When physicians advised him to repress his tears, for otherwise he would be quite blind, the saint answered: "Brother physician, the spirit has not received the benefit of light for the flesh, but the flesh for the spirit; we ought not, for the love of that sight which is common to us and flies, to put an impediment to spiritual sight and celestial comfort." When the physician prescribed that, in order to drain off the humours by an issue, he should be burnt with a hot iron,* the saint was very well pleased, because it was a painful operation and a wholesome remedy. When the surgeon was about to apply the searing-iron, the saint spoke to the fire, saying: "Brother fire, I beseech thee to burn me gently, that I may be able to endure thee." He was seared very deep, from the ear to the eyebrow, but seemed to feel no pain at all.

Whatever he did, or wherever he was, his soul was always raised to heaven, and he seemed continually to dwell with the angels. He consulted God before every thing he did, and he taught his brethren to set a high value upon, and by humility, self-denial, and assiduous recollection, to endeavour to obtain the most perfect spirit of prayer, which is the source of all spiritual blessings, and without which a soul can do very little good. The practice of mental prayer was the favourite exercise which he strongly recommended. Persons who laboured under any interior weight of sadness, or spiritual dryness, he vehemently exhorted to have recourse to fervent prayer, and to keep themselves as much as possible in the presence of their heavenly Father, till he should restore to them the joy of salvation. Otherwise, said he, a disposition of sadness, which comes from Babylon, that is, from the world, will gain ground, and produce a

---

* This method was used before the invention of blistering plasters, or even that more ancient of cupping-glasses.

great rust in the affections of the soul, while she neglects to cleanse them by tears, or a spiritual desire of them. After extraordinary visits of the Holy Ghost, the saint taught men to say: "It is thou, O Lord, who by thy gracious goodness, hast vouchsafed to give this consolation to me a sinner, most unworthy of thy mercy. To thee I commend this favour, that thou preserve its fruit in my heart; for I tremble lest, by my wretchedness, I should rob thee of thy own gift and treasure." He was accustomed to recite our Lord's prayer very slowly, with singular gust in each petition, and in every word. The doxology, *Glory be to the Father*, &c., was a beloved aspiration of this saint, who would repeat it often together at work, and at other times, with extraordinary devotion, and he advised others to use the same. A certain lay-brother once asking him leave to study, the saint said to him: "Repeat assiduously the doxology, *Glory be to the Father*, &c., and you will become very learned in the eyes of God." The brother readily obeyed, and became a very spiritual man. St. Francis sometimes cried out in the fervour of his love: "Grant, O Lord, that the sweet violence of thy most ardent love may disengage and separate me from every thing that is under heaven, and entirely consume me, that I may die for the love of thy infinite love. This I beg by thyself, O Son of God, who diedst for love of me. My God, and my All! who art thou, O sweetest Lord? and who am I, thy servant, and a base worm? I desire to love thee, most holy Lord. I have consecrated to thee my soul and my body with all that I am. Did I know what to do, more perfectly to glorify thee, this I would most ardently do. Yes; this I most ardently desire to accomplish, O my God." St. Francis sometimes expressed his pious breathings in Canticles. St. Teresa writes: "I know a person who, without being a poet, has sometimes composed, upon the spot, stanzas of very exact metre, on spiritual subjects, expressing the pain which her soul felt in certain transports of divine love, and the joy with which she was overwhelmed in this sweet pain." Several among the sacred writers, under the influence of the divine inspiration, delivered the heavenly oracles in verse. St. Francis, in raptures of love, poured forth the affections of his soul, and of the divine praises, sometimes in animated verse. Two such canticles composed by him are still extant, and express, with wonderful strength and sublimity of thought, the vehemence and tenderness of divine love in his breast, in which he found no other comfort than, could it be gratified, to die of love, that he might be for ever united to the great object of his love. His thirst for the conversion of souls was most ardent. He used to say, that for this, example has much greater force than words, and that those preachers are truly to be deplored, who, in their sermons, preach themselves rather than Christ, seeking their own reputation more than the salvation of souls; and much more those who pull down, by their wicked and slothful lives, what they build by their good doctrine. He prayed and wept continually for the conversion of sinners with extraordinary fervour, and recommended to his religious to do the same, saying that many sinners are converted and saved by the prayers and tears of others; and that even simple laymen, who do not preach, ought not to neglect employing this means of obtaining the divine mercy in favour of infidels and sinners. So great was the compassion and charity of this holy man for all such, that, not contenting himself with all that he did and suffered for that end in Italy, he resolved to go to preach to the Mohammedans and other infidels, with an extreme desire of laying down his life for our Lord. With this view he embarked, in the sixth year after his conversion, for Syria, but straight there arose a tempest, which drove him upon the coast of Dalmatia; and finding no convenience to pass on farther, he was forced to return back again to Ancona. Afterward, in 1214, he set out for Morocco, to preach to the famous Mohammedan king Miramolin, and went on his way with so great fervour and desire of martyrdom, that though he was very weak and much spent, his companion was not able to hold pace with him. But it pleased God that in Spain he was detained by a grievous fit of sickness, and afterward by important business of his order, and various accidents, so that he could not possibly go into Mauritania. But he wrought several miracles in Spain, and founded there some convents; after which he returned through Languedoc into Italy.

It will be related below how, in the thirteenth year after his conversion, he passed into Syria and Egypt. In the mean time, upon motives of the same zeal, he laboured strenuously to advance the glory of God among Christians, especially in his own order. With incredible pains he ran over many towns and villages, instructing and exhorting all persons to the divine love. He often said to his brethren, especially in his last sickness: "Let us begin to serve the Lord our God; for hitherto we have made very little progress." No man in this life ever arrived at perfection; and that Christian has climbed the highest toward it who labours the most strenuously and with the most sincere humility to advance higher. St. Francis, preaching penance to all the world, used often to repeat the following words, with inimitable fervour and energy: "My love is crucified," meaning that Christ is crucified, and we ought to crucify our flesh. The holy founder out of humility gave to his order the name of Friars Minors, desiring that his brethren should be disposed, in the affection of sincere humility, to strive, not for the first, but for the last and lowest places. Many cities became suitors that they might be so happy as to possess some of his disciples animated with his spirit, and St. Francis founded convents at Cortona, Arezzo, Vergoreta, Pisa, Bologna, Florence, and other places; and in less than three years his order was multiplied to sixty monasteries. In 1212 he gave his habit to St. Clare, who, under his direction, founded the institute of holy virgins, which was called the second order of St. Francis. He took upon himself the care of her monastery as St. Damian's in Assisium, but would never consent that his friars should serve any other nunnery of this or any other order, in which resolution he persisted to his death; though Cardinal Hugolin, the protector of his order, was not so scrupulous in that particular. The founder carried his precaution and severity so far, in imitation of many ancient saints, the better to secure in his religious a perfect purity of heart, which a defect in many small circumstances may sometimes tarnish. All familiar or unnecessary conversation is certainly to be cut off in such stations, and by the strictest watchfulness all dangerous sparks are to be prevented. To give his brethren to understand this, when, by the authority of the protector, one of them had visited a nunnery, St. Francis ordered him to plunge into the river, and afterward to walk two miles in his wet clothes. This spirit was inherited by that holy disciple and priest whom the founder had sent with some others into Spain, and in whose favour the Princess Sancia, sister to Alfonsus II., then king of Portugal, had given her own house at Alenquer for a convent. A lady of honour, belonging to the court of that princess, desired to speak to the holy man in the church about the affairs of her conscience, and when he refused to come, burst into tears and cries almost of despair. The holy priest therefore went to her, but carried in one hand a wisp of straw, and in the other a burning torch, with which he set the straw on fire as soon as he came into her presence, saying: "Though your conversation be on piety and devotion, if it be frequent, a religious man ought to dread lest it should have on his heart the same effect this fire produced in the straw. At least he will lose by it the fruit of conversing with God in prayer." Notwithstanding the reluctancy of the holy founder, several houses of the Poor Clares found means to procure, through powerful mediations, directors out of this order to be allowed them, especially after the death of St. Francis. St. Dominic being at Rome in 1215, met there St. Francis, and these two eminent servants of God honoured each other, had frequent spiritual conferences together, and cemented a close friendship between their orders, which they desired to render perpetual, as we are informed by contemporary writers of the life of St. Dominic; some say that St. Dominic assisted at St. Francis's chapter of Matts and some others; but this is not supported by ancient vouchers, and is denied by the most judicious Dominican historians.

Ten years after the first institution of his order, in 1219, St. Francis held near the Portiuncula the famous general chapter called of Matts, because it was assembled in booths in the fields, being too numerous to be received in any building of the country. We are assured by four companions of St. Francis, and by St. Bonaventure, that five thousand friars met there, though some remained at home who could not leave their convents. In this chapter several of the brethren prayed St. Francis to obtain for them of the pope a license to preach everywhere without the leave of the bishops of each diocess. The saint, shocked at the proposal, answered: "What, my brethren! do not you know the will of God? It is that by our humility and respect we gain the superiors, that we may by words and example draw the people to God. When the bishops see that you live holily, and attempt nothing against their authority, they will themselves entreat you to labour for the salvation of the souls committed to their charge. Let it be your singular privilege to have no privilege which may puff up the hearts of any with pride, or raise contests and quarrels." St. Francis had sent some of his friars into Germany in 1216, where they met with small success. Afterward from this chapter he commissioned some to go into Greece, others into Africa, others into France, Spain, and England, to all whom he gave zealous instructions. He reserved for himself the mission of Syria and Egypt, in hopes of receiving there the crown of martyrdom; but the affairs of his order obliged him to defer his departure some time.

The orders of St. Francis and St. Dominic had been approved by word of mouth, by Innocent III., who died in 1209, having sat eighteen years. Honorius III., who succeeded him, confirmed that of St. Dominic by two bulls dated the 22d of December, 1216. St. Francis obtained of this pope an approbation of his missions; and in 1219 set sail with B. Illuminatus of Reate and other companions from Ancona, and having touched at Cyprus, landed at Acon or Ptolemais in Palestine. The Christian army in the sixth crusade lay at that time before Damiata in Egypt, and the soldan of Damascus or Syria led a numerous army to the assistance of Meledin, soldan of Egypt or Babylon; for so he was more commonly called, because he resided at Babylon in Egypt, a city on the Nile, opposite to the ruins of Memphis: Grand Cairo rose out of the ashes of this Babylon. St. Francis, with brother Illuminatus, hastened to the Christian army, and upon his arrival endeavoured to dissuade them from giving the enemy battle, foretelling their defeat, as we are assured by three of his companions; also by St. Bonaventure, Cardinal James of Vitri, who was then present in the army, and Marin Sanut. He was not heard, and the Christians were drove back into their trenches with the loss of six thousand men. However, they continued the siege, and took the city on the 5th of November the same year. In the mean time St. Francis, burning with zeal for the conversion of the Saracens, desired to pass to their camp, fearing no dangers for Christ. He was seized by the scouts of the infidels, to whom he cried out: "I am a Christian, conduct me to your master." Being brought before the soldan, and asked by him his errand, he said with wonderful intrepidity and fervour: "I am sent, not by men, but by the most high God, to show you and your people the way of salvation, by announcing to you the truth of the gospel." The soldan appeared to be moved, and invited him to stay with him. The man of God replied: "If you and your people will listen to the word of God, I will with joy stay with you. If yet you waver between Christ and Mohammed, cause a great fire to be kindled, and I will go into it with your Imans, (or priests,) that you may see which is the true faith." The soldan answered that he did not believe any of their priests would be willing to go into the fire, or to suffer torments for their religion, and that he could not accept his condition for fear of a sedition. He offered him many presents, which the saint refused. After some days, the soldan apprehending lest some should be converted by his discourse, and desert to the Christians, sent him, escorted by a strong guard, to their camp before Damiata, saying to him privately: "Pray for me, that God may make known to me the true religion, and conduct me to it." The soldan became from that time very favourable to the Christians, and, according to some authors, was baptized a little before his death.

St. Francis returned by Palestine into Italy, where he heard with joy that the five missionaries, whom he had sent to preach to the Moors, had been crowned with martyrdom in Morocco. But he had the affliction to find that Elias, whom he had left vicar-general of his order, had introduced several novelties and mitigations, and wore himself a habit of finer stuff than the rest, with a longer capouch or hood, and longer sleeves. St. Francis called such innovators bastard children of his order, and deposed Elias from his office. Resigning the generalship that year, 1220, he caused the virtuous Peter of Cortona to be chosen minister-general, and after his death, in 1221, Elias to be restored. But Peter, and after him Elias, out of respect for the saint, were only styled vicars-general till his death, who, by the sole weight of his authority, continued always to direct the government of his order, as long as he lived. In 1223 he obtained of Pope Honorius III. the confirmation of the famous indulgence granted a little time before to the church Portiuncula. His order, as has been mentioned, was verbally approved by Innocent III., in 1210; a like approbation was given it in 1215, by the fourth Lateran council, to which St. Francis repaired for that purpose, as F. Helyot mentions, though this does not appear in the acts of that council, because it was no more than a verbal declaration. The founder, therefore, revised his rule, which breathed throughout the most profound humility and an entire renunciation of the world, and presented it to Pope Honorius III., who confirmed it by a bull dated the 29th of November, 1223. On which occasion the saint preached extempore, at the suggestion of the dean of the cardinals, before the pope and the consistory of cardinals, with great dignity and energy, so as to move the whole audience to compunction.

When St. Francis returned from Spain, and laid aside the thoughts of his intended mission to Morocco in 1215, Count Orlando of Catona bestowed on him a close agreeable solitude on Mount Alverno, a part of the Apennines, not very far from Camaldoli and Vale Umbrosa. This virtuous count built there a convent and a church for the Friar Minors, and St. Francis was much delighted with the retirement of that high mountain. The solitude of the valley of Fabriano also pleased him much, and he frequently hid himself there. The raptures and other extraordinary favours which he received from God in contemplation, he was careful to conceal from men. St. Bonaventure and other writers of his life assure us that he was frequently raised from the ground at prayer. F. Leo, his secretary and confessor, testified that he had seen him in prayer sometimes raised above the ground so high, that this disciple could only touch his feet, which he held and watered with his tears; and that sometimes he saw him raised much higher. Toward the festival of the Assumption of the Blessed Virgin, in 1224, St. Francis retired into a most secret place in Mount Alverno, where his companions made him a little cell. He kept Leo with him, but forbade any other person to come to him before the feast of St. Michael; it was then the lent which he kept before the feast of that archangel, and he desired to devote himself in it entirely to the delights of heavenly contemplation. He ordered Leo to bring him a little bread and water every evening, and lay it at the entry of his cell: "And when you shall come to matins," said he, "do not come in, only say, *Domine, labia mea aperies.* If I answer, *Et os meum annuntiabit laudem tuam,* you shall come in; otherwise you will go away again." The pious disciple was very punctual in obeying; but was often obliged to go back again, the saint being in raptures, as he did not doubt; and once, when he did not answer, he saw him lying prostrate on the ground, encompassed with a bright light, and heard him often repeat these words: "Who art thou, O my God, and my most sweet Lord? And who am I, a base worm, and thy most unworthy servant?" The saint afterward told Leo that nothing gave him so perfect a knowledge and sense of his own nothingness as the contemplation of the abyss of the divine perfections; for nothing so much improves the knowledge of ourselves as the clear knowledge of God's infinite greatness and goodness, and his spotless purity and sanctity. Heavenly visions and communications of the Holy Ghost were familiar to our saint; but in this retreat on Mount Alverno, in 1224, he was favoured with extraordinary raptures, and inflamed with burning desires of heaven in a new and unusual manner. Then it was that this saint deserved, by his humility, and his ardent love of his crucified Saviour, to be honoured with the extraordinary favour of the marks of his five wounds imprinted on his body by the vision of a seraph.

About the feast of the Exaltation of the Cross, on the 15th day of September, Francis being in prayer on the side of the mountain, raised himself toward

God with the seraphic ardour of his desires, and was transported by a tender and affective compassion of charity into Him, who, out of love, was crucified for us. In this state he saw, as it were, a seraph, with six shining wings blazing with fire, bearing down from the highest part of the heavens toward him, with a most rapid flight; and placing himself in the air near the saint. There appeared between his wings the figure of a man crucified, with his hands and feet stretched out, and fastened to the cross. The wings of the seraph were so placed, that two he stretched above his head, two others he extended to fly, and with the other two he covered his whole body. At this sight, Francis was extremely surprised; a sudden joy, mingled with sorrow, filled his heart. The familiar presence of his Lord under the figure of a seraph, who fixed on him his eyes in the most gracious and tender manner, gave him an excessive joy; but the sorrowful sight of his crucifixion pierced his soul with a sword of compassion. At the same time he understood by an interior light, that though the state of crucifixion noway agreed with that of the immortality of the seraph, this wonderful vision was manifested to him, that he might understand he was not to be transformed into a resemblance with Jesus Christ crucified by the martyrdom of the flesh, but in his heart, and by the fire of his love. After a secret and intimate conversation, the vision disappearing, his soul remained interiorly inflamed with a seraphic ardour, and his body appeared exteriorly to have received the image of the crucifix, as if his flesh, like soft wax, had received the mark of a seal impressed upon it. For the marks of nails began to appear in his hands and feet, resembling those he had seen in the vision of the man crucified. His hands and feet seemed bored through in the middle with four wounds, and these holes appeared to be pierced with nails of hard flesh; the heads were round and black, and were seen in the palms of his hands, and in his feet in the upper part of the instep. The points were long, and appeared beyond the skin on the other side, and were turned back as if they had been clenched with a hammer. There was also in his right side a red wound, as if made by the piercing of a lance; and this often threw out blood, which stained the tunic and drawers of the saint. This relation is taken from St. Bonaventure, who (chap. 13) calls the wound of the side a scar; but means not a scar covered, but a wound left visible and open; for he calls it (chap. 14) a wound, and a hole in his side; and such he again describes it as seen after the saint's death. (Chap. 15.) The circumstance of its often bleeding confirms the same; which does not agree to a wound that is healed and covered, or to a callous scar raised after the healing of a wound, as Baillet, with many other mistakes, pretends this to have been. This wonderful miracle was performed while the saint's understanding was filled with the strongest ideas of Christ crucified, and his love employed in the utmost strength of his will in entertaining its affections on that great object, and assimilating them to his beloved in that suffering state; so that in the imaginative faculty of his soul he seemed to form a second crucifix, with which impression it acted upon, and strongly affected the body. To produce the exterior marks of the wounds in the flesh, which the interior love of his burning heart was not able to do, the fiery seraph, or rather Christ himself, in that vision (by darting bright piercing rays from his wounds represented in the vision) really formed them exteriorly in him, which love had interiorly imprinted in his soul, as St. Francis of Sales explains it.

St. Francis endeavoured nothing more than to conceal this singular favour of heaven from the eyes of men; and for this purpose he ever after covered his hands with his habit, and wore shoes and the feet of stockings on his feet. Yet having first asked the advice of brother Illuminatus and others, by their counsel, he, with fear, disclosed to them this wonderful vision, but added, that several things had been manifested to him in it, which he never would discover to any one; secrets, says St. Bonaventure, which perhaps could not be expressed by words, or which men, who are not supernaturally enlightened, are not capable of understanding. Notwithstanding the precautions of the saint, these miraculous wounds were seen be several during the two years which he survived, from 1224 to 1226, and by great multitudes after his death. The account of them the vicar-general of his order published in a circular letter addressed to all his brethren, immediately after St. Francis's death; the original copy of which was seen by Wadding. Luke of Tuy, bishop of that city in Spain, published his work against the Albigenses in 1231, in which he tells us that he went to Assisium the year after the saint's death, and that this vision was attested to him by many religious men and seculars, clergymen and laymen, who had seen these nails of flesh in the saint's hands and feet, and the wound in his side, and with their hands had felt them; he infers from them that Christ was fastened on the cross with four nails, and that it was his right side which was opened with the lance. He confirms this wonderful miracle from the life of the saint, written by F. Thomas de Celano, a disciple and companion of the saint, by the order of Pope Gregory IX., from which work St. Bonaventure took his relation. When some in Bohemia called it in question, Pope Gregory IX. rebuked them by a bull in 1237, attesting the truth of those miraculous wounds upon his own certain knowledge, and that of his cardinals. The same he affirms in two letters recited by Wadding and Chalippe; and says, these wounds, after his death, were publicly shown to every one. Pope Alexander IV., in a sermon to the people in 1254, declared that he had been himself an eye-witness of those wounds in the body of the saint while he was yet living. St. Bonaventure, who with other friars was present at this discourse, heard this authentic declaration made by his

Holiness. That pope assures the same in a bull in 1255, addressed to the whole church. St. Bonaventure, who wrote his life in 1261, and who had lived long with the most familiar disciples of the servant of God, says, that while the saint was alive, many of his brethren and several cardinals saw the marks of the nails in his hands and feet; some also, by secret artifices, found the means to see and feel the wound in his side. After his death, every one openly saw it and the other four wounds. Fifty friars, St. Clare and all her sisters, and an innumerable multitude of seculars, saw and kissed them; and some, for greater certainty, touched them with their hands. St. Bonaventure relates many miracles, and a vision of St. Francis to Pope Gregory IX., by which the truth of these miraculous wounds was confirmed. In honour of this miracle, and to excite in the hearts of the faithful a more ardent love of our crucified Saviour, and devotion to his sacred passion, Pope Benedict IX., in 1304, instituted a festival and office in memory of them; which were extended to the whole church by Sixtus IV., in 1475, Sixtus V. and Paul V., in 1615, the 17th of September being the day chosen for this annual commemoration. The ancient church of St. Francis on Mount Alverno, with another new one more spacious, and a large convent, are places of great devotion on account of this miracle, and enjoy great privileges by the grants of several popes and emperors.

It appears manifest that this wonderful favour was in part a recompense of the great love which St. Francis bore to the cross of Christ. From the beginning of his conversion his heart was so inflamed with divine love, that the sufferings of his Saviour almost continually filled his thoughts, in which meditation, sighs and tears frequently expressed the sentiments of his soul. It was to render himself more perfectly conformed to his crucified Jesus, that he with great fervour stripped himself of every thing, made of his body a victim of penance, and thrice sought an opportunity of giving his life for Christ by martyrdom. This adorable object was all his science, all his glory, all his joy, all his comfort in this world. To soothe the sharp pains of a violent distemper, he was one day desired to let some one read a book to him; but he answered: "Nothing gives me so much delight as to think on the life and passion of our Lord; I continually employ my mind on this object, and were I to live to the end of the world, I should stand in need of no other books." In the school of his crucified Lord he learned so vehement a love of holy poverty, that meeting one day a beggar almost naked, he with sighs said to his companion: "Here is a poor man, whose condition is a reproach to us. We have chosen poverty to be our riches; yet in it he outdoes us." He called poverty his lady, his queen, his mother, and his spouse, and earnestly begged it of God as his portion and privilege. "O Jesus," said he, "who wast pleased to embrace extreme poverty, the grace I beg of thee is, that thou bestow on me the privilege of poverty. It is my most ardent desire to be enriched with this treasure. This I ask for me and mine, that for the glory of thy holy name we never possess any thing under heaven, and receive our subsistence itself from the charity of others, and be in this also very sparing and moderate." He extended his rule of poverty to what is interior and spiritual, fearing lest any one among his friars should regard his science as his own property and fund, for so it feeds self-love, and produces inordinate complacency in itself, and secret attachments, very contrary to that entire disengagement of the heart which opens it to the divine grace. The saint indeed exhorted those that were best qualified to apply themselves to sacred studies; but always with this caution, that they still spent more time in prayer, and studied not so much how to speak to others, as how to preach to themselves, and how to practise virtue. Studies which feed vanity rather than piety he abhorred, because they utterly extinguish charity and devotion, and drain and puff up the heart. Humiliations, reproaches, and sufferings he called the true gain and the most perfect joy of a religious man, especially a friar minor, who, according to this saint, ought to be not so much in name, as in spirit, the lowest among men.

St. Francis came down from Mount Alverno, bearing in his flesh the marks of the sacred wounds, and more inflamed than ever with the seraphic ardours of divine charity. The two years that he survived his heavenly vision, seemed a martyrdom of love. He was moreover much afflicted in them with sickness, weakness, and pains in his eyes. In this suffering state he used often to repeat that the most rigorous appointments of Providence are often the most tender effects of the divine mercy in our favour. In 1225, his distemper growing dangerous, Cardinal Hugolin and the Vicar-general Elias obliged him to put himself in the hands of the most able surgeons and physicians of Rieti, wherein he complied with great simplicity. In his sickness he scarce allowed himself any intermission from prayer, and would not check his tears, though the physician thought it necessary for the preservation of his sight; which he entirely lost upon his death-bed. Under violent pains, when another exhorted him to beg of God to mitigate them, notwithstanding his extreme weakness, he arose, and falling on the ground, and kissing it, prayed as follows: "O Lord, I return thee thanks for the pains which I suffer; I pray that thou add to them a hundred times more, if such be thy holy will. I shall rejoice that thou art pleased to afflict me without sparing my carcass here; for what sweeter comfort can I have, than that thy holy will be done!" He foretold his death long before it happened, both to several of his brethren, and in a letter which he dictated on Sunday the 28th of September, to a pious lady of Rome, his great friend. The saint earnestly requested that he might be buried at the common place of execution, among the bodies of the malefactors, on a hill then without the walls of the town of Assisium, called Colle d'Inferno. St. Francis, a little before his death, dictated his testament to his religious brethren, in which he recommends to them, that they always honour the priests and pastors of the church as their masters, that they faithfully observe their rule, and that they work with their hands, not out of a desire of gain, but for the sake of good example, and to avoid idleness. "If we receive nothing for our work," says he, "let us have recourse to the table of the Lord, the begging alms from door to door." He orders that they who do not know how to work, learn some trade. Pope Nicholas III. declared that this precept of manual labour does not regard those who are in holy orders, and are employed in preaching, and in other spiritual functions, which is clear from the rule itself, the example of St. Francis, and the apology wrote by St. Bonaventure. Having finished his testament, the saint desired a spiritual song of thanksgiving to God for all his creatures, which he had composed, to be sung. Then he insisted upon being laid on the ground, and covered with an old habit, which the guardian gave him. In this posture he exhorted his brethren to the love of God, holy poverty, and patience, and gave his last blessing to all his disciples, the absent as well as those that were present, in the following words: "Farewell, my children; remain always in the fear of the Lord. That temptation and tribulation which is to come, is now at hand; and happy shall they be who shall persevere in the good they have begun. I hasten to go to our Lord, to whose grace I recommend you." He then caused the history of the passion of our Lord in the Gospel of St. John to be read; after which he began to recite the hundred forty-first psalm, *I have cried with my voice to the Lord*, &c. Having repeated the last verse: *Bring my soul out of prison, that I may praise thy name: the just shall wait for me till thou reward me*, he yielded up his soul on the 4th of October, in the year 1226, the twentieth after his conversion, and the forty-fifth of his age, as De Calano assures us. Great multitudes flocked to see and kiss the prints of the sacred wounds in his flesh, which were openly shown to all persons. A certain learned man of rank, named Jerom, doubted of the reality of these miraculous wounds till he had touched and examined them with his hands, and moved the nails of flesh backward and forward; by which he was so evidently convinced, that he confirmed by a solemn oath his attestation of them, as St. Bonaventure mentions. The next morning, which was Sunday, the saint's body was carried with a numerous and pompous procession from the convent of the Portiuncula to Assisium. The procession stopped at St. Damian's, where St. Clare and her nuns had the comfort of kissing the marks of the wounds in his flesh. St. Clare attempted to take out one of the nails of flesh, but could not, though the black head was protuberant above the palm of the hand, and she easily thrust it up and down, and dipped a linen cloth in the blood which issued out. The body was carried thence, and buried at St. George's. Pope Honorius III. dying in 1227, Cardinal Hugolin was chosen pope the same year, and took the name of Gregory IX. Two years after the saint's death, this pope went to Assisium, and after a rigorous examination and solemn approbation of several miraculous cures wrought through the merits of St. Francis, he performed the ceremony of his canonization in the church of St. George, on the 16th of July, 1228, and commanded his office to be kept in 1229. His Holiness gave a sum of money for building a new church on the place which he would have called from that time Colle del Paradiso. Elias the general, by contributions and exactions, much increased the sum, and raised a most magnificent pile, which was finished in 1230, and that year the body of the saint was translated thither on the 25th of May. Pope Gregory IX. came again to Assisium in 1235. But the ceremony of the dedication of this church was not performed by him, as some mistake, but by Pope Innocent IV., in 1253, when he passed the summer in this convent, as is related at length by Nicolas de Curbio, a Franciscan, that pope's confessarius and sacristan, in his life. Pope Benedict XIV., in 1754, by a prolix most honourable bull confirms the most ample privileges granted to this church by former popes, and declares it a patriarchal church and a papal chapel with apostolic penitentiaries. The body of the saint still lies in this church, and it is said under a sumptuous chapel of marble, curiously wrought, standing in the middle of this spacious church, which is dedicated in honour of St. Francis. In the sacristy, among many other relics, was shown, in 1745, some of the writings of St. Francis, and also of St. Bonaventure. Over this church is a second, adorned with rich paintings, dedicated in honour of the twelve apostles. We are told there is a third subterraneous church under it, like that under St. Peter's on the Vatican hill, made in vaults; but that of St. Francis is not open. The body of St. Francis has never been discovered or visited since the time of Gregory IX., and was concealed in some secret vault, for the better securing so precious a treasure. In this patriarchal convent the general of the Conventual Franciscans resides.

ST. ELIZABETH,

OF HUNGARY, WIDOW.

A. D. 1231.

ELIZABETH, daughter to Alexander II., the valiant and religious king of Hungary, and his queen, Gertrude, daughter to the duke of Carinthia, was born in Hungary in 1207. Herman, landgrave of Thuringia and Hesse, had a son born about the same time, and named Lewis. This prince obtained, by ambassadors, a promise from the king of Hungary that his daughter should be given in marriage to this newborn son; and, to secure the effect of this engagement, at the landgrave's request, the princess, at four years of age, was sent to his court, and there brought up under the care of a virtuous lady. Five years after, Herman died, and Lewis became landgrave. Elizabeth, from her cradle, was so happily prevented with the love of God, that no room for creatures could be found in her heart; and, though surrounded, and, as it were, besieged by worldly pleasures in their most engaging shapes, she had no relish for them, prayed with an astonishing recollection, and seemed scarce to know any other use of money than to give it to the poor; for her father allowed her, till her marriage was solemnized, a competent yearly revenue for maintaining a court suitable to her rank. This child of heaven, in her very recreations, studied to practise frequent humiliations and self-denials; and stole often to the chapel, and there knelt down and said a short prayer before every altar, bowing her body reverently, or, if nobody was there, prostrating herself upon the ground. If she found the doors of the chapel in the palace shut, not to lose her labour, she knelt down at the threshold, and always put up her petition to the throne of God. Her devotion she indulged with more liberty in her private closet. She was very devout to her angel guardian and the saints, particularly St. John the Evangelist. . She was educated with Agnes, sister to the young landgrave, and upon their first appearing together at church, they were dressed alike, and wore coronets set with jewels. At their entering the house of God, Sophia, the landgrave's mother, observing our saint take off her coronet, asked why she did so; to which the princess replied. that she could not bear to appear with jewels on her head, where she saw that of Jesus Christ crowned with thorns. Agnes and her mother, who were strangers to such kind of sentiments, and fond of what Elizabeth trampled upon, conceived an aversion for the young princess, and said that since she seemed to have so little relish for a court, a convent would be the properest place for her. The courtiers carried their reflections much further, and did all in their power to bring the saint into contempt, saying that neither her fortune nor her person were such as the landgrave had a right to expect, that he had no inclination for her, and that she would either be sent back to Hungary, or married to some nobleman in the country. These taunts and trials were more severe and continual, as the landgrave, Herman, dying when Elizabeth was only nine years old, the government fell into the hands of his widow in the name of her son till he should be of age. These persecutions and injuries were, to the saint, occasions of the greatest spiritual advantages; for by them she daily learned a more perfect contempt of all earthly things, to which the heavenly lover exhorts his spouse, saying: "Hearken, daughter, forget thy people." She learned also the evangelical hatred of herself, and crucifixion of self-love; by which she was enabled to say with the apostles: *Behold, we have left all things.* In this entire disengagement of her heart, she learned to take up her cross and follow Christ by the exercise of meekness, humility, patience, and charity toward unjust persecutors; and to cleave to God by the closest union of her soul to him, by resignation, love, and prayer, contemning herself, and esteeming the vanity of the world as filth and dung. She desired to please God only, and in this spirit she was wont to pray: "O sovereign Spouse of my soul, never suffer me to love any thing but in thee, or for thee. May every thing which tends not to thee, be bitter and painful, and thy will alone sweet. May thy will be always mine; as in heaven thy will is punctually performed, so may it be done on earth by all creatures, particularly in me and by me. And as love requires a union, and entire resignation of all things into the hands of the beloved, I give up my whole self to thee without reserve. In my heart I renounce all riches and pomp; if I had many worlds,

I would leave them all, to adhere to thee alone in poverty and nakedness of spirit, as thou madest thyself poor for me. O Spouse of my heart, so great is the love I bear thee, and holy poverty for thy sake, that with joy I leave all that I am, that I may be transformed into thee, and enter that abandoned state so amiable to thee."

The saint was in her fourteenth year when Lewis, the young landgrave, returned home, after a long absence on account of his education. Address in martial exercises and other great accomplishments introduced the young prince into the world with a mighty reputation; but nothing was so remarkable in him as a sincere love of piety. The eminent virtue of Elizabeth gave him the highest esteem for her person. However, he seldom saw or spoke to her, even in public, and never in private, till the question was one day put to him, what his thoughts were with regard to marrying her, and he was told what rumours were spread in the court to her disadvantage. Hereat he expressed much displeasure, and said that he prized her virtue above all the mountains of gold and rubies that the world could afford. Forthwith he sent her by a nobleman a glass garnished with precious stones of inestimable value, with two crystals opening on each side, in the one of which was a looking-glass; on the other a figure of Christ crucified was most curiously wrought. And not long after, he solemnized his marriage with her, and the ceremony was performed with the utmost pomp, and with extraordinary public rejoicings. The stream of public applause followed the favour of the prince; the whole court expressed the most profound veneration for the saint, and all the clouds which had so long hung over her head were at once dispersed. Conrad of Marpurg, a most holy and learned priest, and an eloquent pathetic preacher, whose disinterestedness and love of holy poverty, mortified life, and extraordinary devotion and spirit of prayer, rendered him a model to the clergy of that age, was the person whom she chose for her spiritual director, and to his advice she submitted herself in all things relating to her spiritual concerns. This holy and experienced guide, observing how deep root the seeds of virtue had taken in her soul, applied himself by cultivating them to conduct her to the summit of Christian perfection, and encouraged her in the path of mortification and penance, but was obliged often to moderate her corporal austerities by the precept of obedience. The landgrave also reposed an entire confidence in Conrad, and gave this holy man the privilege of disposing of all ecclesiastical benefices in the prince's gift. Elizabeth, with her pious husband's consent, often rose in the night to pray, and consecrated great part of her time to her devotions, insomuch that on Sundays and holydays she never allowed herself much leisure to dress herself. The rest of her time which was not spent in prayer or reading, she devoted to works of charity, and to spinning or carding wool, in which she would only work very coarse wool for the use of the poor, or of the Franciscan friars. The mysteries of the life and sufferings of our Saviour were the subject of her most tender and daily meditation. Weighing of what importance prayer and mortification, or penance are in a spiritual life, she studied to make her prayer virtually continual, by breaking forth into fervent acts of compunction and divine love amid all her employments. The austerity of her life surpassed that of recluses. When she sat at table, next to the landgrave, to dissemble her abstinence from flesh and savoury dishes, she used to deceive the attention of others by discoursing with the guests, or with the prince, carving for others, sending her maids upon errands, often changing her plates, and a thousand other artifices. Her meal frequently consisted only of bread and honey, or a dry crust, with a cup of the smallest wine, or the like; especially when she dined privately in her chamber, with two maids, who voluntarily followed her rules as to diet. She never ate but what came out of her own kitchen, that she might be sure nothing was mixed contrary to the severe rules she had laid down; and this kitchen she kept out of her own private purse, not to be the least charge to her husband. She was a great enemy to rich apparel, though, in compliance to the landgrave, she on certain public occasions conformed in some degree to the fashions of the court. When ambassadors came from her father, the king of Hungary, her husband desired her not to appear in that homely apparel which she usually wore; but she prevailed upon him to suffer it; and God was pleased to give so extraordinary a gracefulness to her person, that the ambassadors were exceedingly struck at the comeliness and majesty of the appearance she made. In the absence of her husband, she commonly wore only coarse cloth, not dyed, but in the natural colour of the wool, such as the poor people used. She so strongly recommended to her maids of honour simplicity of dress, penance, and assiduous prayer, that several of them were warmed into an imitation of her virtues; but they could only follow her at a distance, for she seemed inimitable in her heroic practices, especially in her profound humility, with which she courted the most mortifying humiliations. In attending the poor and the sick, she cheerfully washed and cleansed the most filthy sores, and waited on those that were infected with the most loathsome diseases.

Her alms seemed at all times to have no bounds; in which the good landgrave rejoiced exceedingly, and gave her full liberty. In 1225, Germany being severely visited by a famine, she exhausted the treasury and distributed her whole crop of corn among those who felt the weight of that calamity heaviest. The landgrave was then in Apulia with the emperor; and at his return the officers of his household complained loudly to him of her profusion in favour of the poor. But the prince was so well assured of her piety and prudence, that, without examining into the matter, he asked if she had alienated his dominions. They answered: "No."

"As for her charities," said he, "they will entail upon us the divine blessings; and we shall not want, so long as we suffer her to relieve the poor as she does." The castle of Marpurg, the residence of the landgrave, was built on a steep rock, which the infirm and weak were not able to climb. The holy margravine therefore built a hospital at the foot of the rock for their reception and entertainment, where she often fed them with her own hands, made their beds, and attended them even in the heat of summer, when that place seemed insupportable to all those who were strangers to the sentiments of her generous and indefatigable charity. The helpless children, especially all orphans, were provided for at her expense. Elizabeth was the foundress of another hospital, in which twenty-eight persons were constantly relieved; she fed nine hundred daily at her own gate, besides an incredible number in the different parts of the dominions, so that the revenue in her hands was truly the patrimony of the distressed. But the saint's charity was tempered with discretion; and instead of encouraging in idleness such as were able to work, she employed them in a way suitable to their strength and capacity. Her husband, edified and charmed with her extraordinary piety, not only approved of all she did, but was himself an imitator of her charity, devotion, and other virtues; insomuch that he is deservedly styled by historians the pious Landgrave. He had by her three children, Herman, Sophia, who was afterward married to the duke of Brabant, and Gertrude, who became a nun, and died abbess of Aldemburg. Purely upon motives of religion the landgrave took the cross to accompany the Emperor Frederic Barbarossa, in the holy war, to Palestine. The separation of this pious and loving couple was a great trial, though moderated by the heroic spirit of religion with which both were animated. The landgrave joined the emperor in the kingdom of Naples; but, as he was going to embark, fell ill of a malignant fever at Otranto, and, having received the last sacraments at the hands of the patriarch of Jerusalem, expired in great sentiments of piety, on the 11th of September, 1227. Many miracles are related to have been wrought by him, in the history of Thuringia, and in that of the Crusades. Elizabeth, who at his departure had put on the dress of a widow, upon hearing this melancholy news, wept bitterly, and said: "If my husband be dead, I promise to die henceforth to myself, and to the world with all its vanities." God himself was pleased to complete this her sacrifice by a train of other afflictions into which she fell, being a sensible instance of the instability of human things, in which nothing is more constant than an unsteadiness of fortune, the life of man being a perpetual scene of interludes, and virtue being his only support, a check to pride in prosperity, and a solid comfort in adversity.

Envy, jealousy, and rancour, all broke loose at once against the virtuous landgravine, which, during her husband's life, for the great love and respect which he bore her, had been raked up and covered over as fire under the ashes. As pretences are never wanting to cloak ambition, envy, and other passions, which never dare show themselves barefaced, it was alleged that the saint had squandered away the public revenue upon the poor; that the infant Herman, being unfit for the government of the state, it ought to be given to one who was able to defend and even extend the dominions of the landgraviate; and that therefore Henry, younger brother to the late landgrave, ought to be advanced to the principality. The mob being soothed by the fine speeches of certain powerful factious men, Henry got possession, and turned Elizabeth out of the castle, without furniture, provision, or necessaries for the support of nature, and all persons in the town were forbid to let her any lodgings. The princess bore this unjust treatment with a patience far transcending the power of nature, showing nothing in her gestures which was not as composed as if she had been in the greatest tranquillity possible. And rejoicing in her heart to see herself so ill treated, she went down the castle-hill to the town, placing her whole confidence in God, and with her damsels and maids went into a common inn, or, as others say, a poor woman's cottage, where she remained till midnight, when the bell ringing to matins at the church of the Franciscan friars, she went thither, and desired the good fathers to sing a *Te Deum* with solemnity, to give God thanks for his mercies to her in visiting her with afflictions. Though she sent about the next day, and used all her endeavours to procure some kind of lodging in the town, no one durst afford her any, for fear of the usurper and his associates. She stayed the whole day in the church of the friars, and at evening had the additional affliction to see her three children, whom their barbarous uncle had sent out of the castle, coming down the hill. She received them in the church porch, with undaunted fortitude, but could not refrain from tenderly weeping to see the innocent babes so insensible of their condition as to smile upon her, rejoicing that they had recovered their mother. Reduced to the lowest ebb, she applied to a priest for relief, who received her into his humble dwelling, where she had but one strait poor chamber for herself, her maids, and children. Her enemies soon forced her from thence, so that, with thanks to those who had given her and hers some kind of shelter from the severities of a very sharp winter season, she returned to the inn or cottage. Thus she, who had entertained thousands of poor, could find no entertainment or harbour; and she, who had been a mother to so many infants and orphans of others, was glad to beg an alms for her own, and to receive it from her enemies. God failed not to comfort her in her distress, and she addressed herself to him in raptures of love, praying that she might be wholly converted into his love, and that his pure love might reign in her. Melting in the sweetness of divine love, she poured forth her soul in inflamed ejaculations, saying, for example: "Ah, my Lord and my God, may thou be all mine, and I all thine. What is this, my God and my love? Thou all mine, and I all thine. Let me love thee, my God, above all things, and let me not love myself but for thee, and all other things in thee. Let me love thee, with all my soul, with all my memory," &c. In these fervent aspirations, overflowing with interior joy, she sometimes fell into wonderful raptures, which astonished Hentrude, a lady of honour, particularly beloved by her, and her companion in her devotions and mortifications.

The abbess of Kitzingen, in the diocess of Wurtzburg, our saint's aunt, sister to her mother, hearing of her misfortunes, invited her to her monastery, and, being extremely moved at the sight of her desolate condition and poverty, advised her to repair to her uncle, the bishop of Bamberg, a man of great power, charity, and prudence. The bishop received her with many tears, which compassion drew from his eyes, and from those of all the clergy that were with him; and provided for her a commodious house near his palace. His first views were, as she was young and beautiful, to endeavour to look out for a suitable party, that marrying some powerful prince, she might strengthen her interest, and that of her family, by a new alliance, which might enable her to recover her right; but such projects she entirely put a stop to, declaring it was her fixed resolution to devote herself to the divine service in a state of perpetual chastity. In the mean time the body of her late husband, which had been buried at Otranto, was taken up, and, the flesh being entirely consumed, the bones were put into a rich chest, and carried into Germany. The hearse was attended by a great many princes and dukes, and by counts, barons, and knights without number, marching in martial order, with ensigns folded up, the mournful sound of drums, all covered with black, and other warlike instruments in like manner. Where some of these princes left the corpse, to return home, the nobility of each country through which it passed took their place; and every night it was lodged in some church or monastery, where masses and dirges were said and gifts offered. When the funeral pomp approached Bamberg, the bishop went out with the clergy and monks in procession to meet it, having left the nobility and knights with the disconsolate pious margravine. At the sight of the hearse, her grief was inexpressible; yet, while there was not a dry eye in the church, she showed, by restraining her sorrow, how great command she had of her passions. Yet, when the chest was opened, her tears burst forth against her will. But, recollecting herself in God, she gave thanks to his Divine Majesty for having so disposed of her honoured husband, as to take him into his eternal tabernacles, so seasonably for himself, though to her severe trial. The corpse remained several days at Bamberg, during which the funeral rites were continued with the utmost solemnity, and it was then conducted with great state into Thuringia. The princess entreated the barons and knights that attended it to use their interest with her brother-in-law to do her justice, not blaming him for the treatment she had received, but imputing it to evil counsellors. Fired with indignation at the indignities she had received, they engaged to neglect no means of restoring her to her right; so that it was necessary for her to moderate their resentment, and to beg they would only use humble remonstrances. This they did, reproaching Henry for having brought so foul a blot and dishonour upon his house, and having violated all laws, divine, civil, and natural, and broke the strongest ties of humanity. They conjured him by God, who beholds all things, and asked him in what point a weak woman, full of peace and piety, could offend him; and what innocent princely babes, who were his own blood, could have done, the tenderness of whose years made them very unfit to suffer such injuries. Ambition strangely steels a heart to all sentiments of justice, charity, or humanity. Yet these remonstrances, made by the chief barons of the principality, softened the heart of Henry, and he promised them to restore to Elizabeth her dower and all the rights of her widowhood, and even to put the government of the dominions into her hands. This last she voluntarily chose to renounce, provided it was reserved for her son. Hereupon, she was conducted back to the castle out of which she had been expelled, and from that time Henry began to treat her as princess, and obsequiously executed whatever she intimated to be her pleasure. Yet her persecutions were often renewed till her death.

The devout priest Conrad had attended her in great part of her travels, and returned to Marpurg, which was his usual residence. Elizabeth, loathing the grandeur and dreading the distractions of the world, with his advice, bound herself by a vow, which she made in his presence, in the church of the Franciscans, to observe the third rule of St. Francis, and secretly put on a little habit under her clothes. Her confessor relates that, laying her hands on the altar in the church of the friars minors, she by vow renounced the pomps of the world; she was going to add the vow of poverty, but he stopped her, saying she was obliged, in order to discharge many obligations of her late husband, and what she owed to the poor, to keep in her own hands the disposal of her revenues. Her dower she converted to the use of the poor; and, as her director Conrad, in whom she reposed an entire confidence, was obliged to live in the town of Marpurg, when she quitted her palace, she made that which was on the boundary of her husband's dominions her place of residence, living first in a little cottage near the town, while a house was building for her, in which she spent the last three years of her life in the most fervent practices of devotion, charity, and penance. In her speech she was so reserved and modest that if she affirmed or denied any thing, her words seemed to imply a fear of some mistake. She spoke little, always with gravity, and most commonly of God; and never let drop any thing that tended to her own praise. Out of a love of religious silence, she shunned tattlers; in all things she praised God, and being intent on spiritual things, was never puffed up with prosperity, or troubled at adversity. She tied herself by vow to obey her confessor Conrad, and received at his hands a habit made of coarse cloth, of the natural colour of the wool without being dyed. Whence, Pope Gregory IX., who had corresponded with her, says she took the religious habit, and subjected herself to the yoke of obedience. Thus she imitated the state of nuns, though, by the advice of her confessor, she remained a secular, that she might better dispose of her alms for the relief of the poor. Conrad, having observed that her attachment to her two principal maids, Isentrude and Guta, seemed too strong, and an impediment to her spiritual progress, proposed to her to dismiss them; and, without making any reply, she instantly obeyed him, though the sacrifice cost mutual tears. The saint, by spinning coarse wool, earned her own maintenance, and, with her maids, dressed her own victuals, which were chiefly herbs, bread, and water. While her hands were busy, in her heart she conversed with God. The king of Hungary, her father, earnestly invited her to his court; but she preferred a state of humiliation and suffering. She chose by preference to do every kind of service in attending the most loathsome lepers among the poor. Spiritual and corporal works of mercy occupied her even to her last moments, and by her moving exhortations many obstinate sinners were converted to God. It seemed, indeed, impossible for any thing to resist the eminent spirit of prayer with which she was endowed. In prayer she found her comfort and her strength in her mortal pilgrimage, and was favoured in it with frequent raptures and heavenly communications. Her confessor, Conrad, assures us that, when she returned from secret prayer, her countenance often seemed to dart forth rays of light from the divine conversation. Being forewarned by God of her approaching passage to eternity, which she mentioned to her confessor four days before she fell ill, as he assures us, she redoubled her fervour, by her last will made Christ her heir in his poor, made a general confession of her whole life on the twelfth day, survived yet four days, received the last sacraments, and, to her last breath, ceased not to pray, or to discourse in the most pathetic manner on the mysteries of the sacred life and sufferings of our Redeemer, and on his coming to judge us. The day of her happy death was the 19th of November, in 1231, in the twenty-fourth year of her age. Her venerable body was deposited in a chapel near the hospital which she had founded. Many sick persons were restored to health at her tomb; an account of which miracles Siffrid, archbishop of Mentz, sent to Rome, having first caused them to be authenticated by a juridical examination before himself and others. Pope Gregory IX., after a long and mature discussion, performed the ceremony of her canonization on Whit Sunday, in 1235, four years after her death. Siffrid, upon news hereof, appointed a day for the translation of her relics, which he performed at Marpurg in 1236. The Emperor Frederic II. would be present, took up the first stone of the saint's grave, and gave and placed on the shrine with his own hands a rich crown of gold. St. Elizabeth's son, Herman, then landgrave, and his two sisters, Sophia and Gertrude, assisted at this august ceremony; also the archbishops of Cologne and Bremen, and an incredible number of other princes, prelates, and people, so that the number is said to have amounted to above two hundred thousand persons. The relics were enshrined in a rich vermilion case, and placed upon the altar in the church of the hospital. A Cistercian monk affirmed upon oath that, a little before this translation, praying at the tomb of the saint, he was cured of a palpitation of the heart and grievous melancholy, with which he had been grievously troubled for forty years, and had in vain sought remedies from physicians and every other means. Many instances are mentioned by Montanus, and by the archbishop of Mentz, and the confessor Conrad, of persons afflicted with palsies, and other inveterate diseases, who recovered their health at her tomb, or by invoking her intercession; as, of a boy blind from his birth, by the mother's invocation of St. Elizabeth at her sepulchre, applying some of the dust to his eyes, upon which a skin which covered his eye burst, and he saw, as several witnesses declared upon oath, and Master Conrad saw the eyes thus healed; of a boy three years old, dead, cold and stiff a whole night, raised to life the next morning by a pious grandmother praying to God through the intercession of St. Elizabeth, with a vow of an alms to her hospital, and of dedicating the child to the divine service, attested in every circumstance by the depositions of the mother, father, grandmother, uncle, and others, recorded by Conrad; of a boy, dead and stiff for many hours, just going to be carried to burial, raised by the invocation of St. Elizabeth; of a youth drowned, restored to life by the like prayer; of a boy drawn out of a well, dead, black, &c.; and a child still-born, brought to life; others cured of palsies, falling-sickness, fevers, madness, lameness, blindness, the bloody flux, &c., in the authentic relation. A portion of her relics is kept in the church of the Carmelites at Brussels; another in the magnificent chapel of La Roche-Guyon, upon the Seine, and a considerable part in a precious shrine is in the electoral treasury of Hanover. Some persons of the third order of St. Francis having raised that institute into a religious order long after the death of our saint, (without prejudice to the secular state of this order, which is still embraced by many who live in the world,) the religious women of this order chose her for their patroness, and are sometimes called the nuns of St. Elizabeth.

Perfection consists not essentially in mortification, but in charity; and he is most perfect who is most united to God by love. But humility and self-denial remove the impediments to this love, by retrenching the inordinate appetites and evil inclinations which wed the heart to creatures. The affections must be untied by mortification, and the heart set at liberty by an entire disengagement from the slavery of the senses, and all irregular affections. Then will a soul, by the assistance of grace, easily raise her affections to God, and adhere purely to him; and his holy love will take possession of them. A stone cannot fall down to its centre so long as the lets which hold it up are not taken away. So neither can a soul attain to the pure love of God, while the strings of earthly attachments hold her down. Hence, the maxims of the gospel, and the example of the saints, strongly inculcate the necessity of dying to ourselves, by humility, meekness, patience, self-denial, and obedience. Nor does any thing so much advance this inteior crucifixion of the old man as the patient suffering of afflictions.

ST. IGNATIUS OF LOYCLA, C.

FOUNDER OF THE SOCIETY OF JESUS.

A. D. 1556.

THE conversion of many barbarous nations, several heretofore unknown to us, both in the most remote eastern and western hemisphere, the education of youth in learning and piety, the instruction of the ignorant, the improvement of all the sciences, and the reformation of the manners of a great part of Christendom, is the wonderful fruit of the zeal with which this glorious saint devoted himself to labour in exalting the glory of God, and in spreading over the whole world that fire which Christ himself came to kindle on earth. St. Ignatius was born in 1491, in the castle of Loyola, in Guipuscoa, a part of Biscay that reaches to the Pyrenean mountains. His father, Don Bertram, was lord of Ognez and Loyola, head of one of the most ancient and noble families of that country. His mother, Mary Saez de Balde, was not less illustrious by her extraction. They had three daughters and eight sons. The youngest of all these was Inigo or Ignatius; he was well shaped, and in his childhood gave proofs of a pregnant wit, and discretion above his years; was affable and obliging, but of a warm or choleric disposition, and had an ardent passion for glory. He was bred in the court of Ferdinand V., in quality of page to the king, under the care and protection of Antony Manriquez, duke of Najara, grandee of Spain, who was his kinsman and patron; and who, perceiving his inclinations, led him to the army, and took care to have him taught all the exercises proper to make him an accomplished officer. The love of glory, and the example of his elder brothers, who had signalized themselves in the wars of Naples, made him impatient till he entered the service. He behaved with great valour and conduct in the army, especially at the taking of Najara, a small town on the frontiers of Biscay; yet he generously declined taking any part of the booty, in which he might have challenged the greatest share. He hated gaming as an offspring of avarice, and a source of quarrels and other evils; was dexterous in the management of affairs, and had an excellent talent in making up differences among the soldiers. He was generous, even toward enemies, but addicted to gallantry, and full of the maxims of worldly honour, vanity, and pleasures. Though he had no tincture of learning, he made tolerably good verses in Spanish, having a natural genius for poetry. A poem which he composed in praise of St. Peter was much commended.

Charles V., who had succeeded King Ferdinand, was chosen emperor, and obliged to go into Germany. Francis I., king of France, a martial prince, having been his competitor for the empire, resented his disappointment, and became an implacable enemy to the emperor and the house of Austria. He declared war against Charles, with a view to recover Navarre, of which Ferdinand had lately dispossessed John of Albert, and which Charles still held, contrary to the treaty of Noyon, by which he was obliged to restore it in six months. Francis, therefore, in 1521, sent a great army into Spain, under the command of Andrew de Foix, younger brother of the famous Lautrec, who, passing the Pyrenees, laid siege to Pampeluna, the capital of Navarre. Ignatius had been left there by the viceroy, not to command, but to encourage the garrison. He did all that lay in his power to persuade them to defend the city, but in vain. However, when he saw them open the gates to the enemy, to save his own honour, he retired into the citadel with one only soldier who had the heart to follow him. The garrison of this fortress deliberated likewise whether they should surrender, but Ignatius encouraged them to stand their ground. The French attacked the place with great fury, and with their artillery made a wide breach in the wall, and attempted to take it by assault. Ignatius appeared upon the breach, at the head of the bravest part of the garrison, and, with his sword in his hand, endeavoured to drive back the enemy; but, in the heat of the combat, a shot from a cannon broke from the wall a bit of stone, which struck and bruised his left leg; and the ball itself, in the redound, broke and shivered his right leg. The garrison, seeing him fall, surrendered at discretion.

The French used their victory with moderation, and treated the prisoners well, especially Ignatius, in consideration of his quality and valour. They carried him to the general's quarters, and soon after sent him, in a litter carried by two men, to the castle of Loyola, which was not far from Pampeluna. Being arrived there, he felt great pain; for the bones had been ill set, as is often the case in the hurry after a battle. The surgeons therefore judged it necessary to break his leg again, which he suffered without any concern. But a violent fever followed the second setting, which was attended with dangerous symptoms, and reduced him to an extreme degree of weakness, so that the physicians declared that he could not live many days. He received the sacraments on the eve of the feast of SS. Peter and Paul, and it was believed he could not hold out till the next morning. Nevertheless, God, who had great designs of mercy upon him, was pleased to restore him to his health in the following manner. Ignatius always had a singular devotion to St. Peter, and implored his intercession in his present distress with great confidence. In the night he thought he saw, in a dream, that apostle touch him and cure him. When he awaked he found himself out of danger; his pains left him, and his strength began to return, so that he ever after looked upon this recovery as miraculous; yet he still retained the spirit of the world. After the second setting of his leg, the end of a bone stuck out under his knee, which was a visible deformity. Though the surgeons told him the operation would be very painful, this protuberance he caused to be cut off, merely that his boot and stockings might sit handsomely; and he would neither be bound nor held, and scarce ever changed countenance whilst the bone was partly sawed and partly cut off, though the pain must have been excessive. Because his right leg remained shorter than the left, he would be, for many days together, put upon a kind of rack, and with an iron engine he violently stretched and drew out that leg; but all to little purpose, for he remained lame his whole life after.

During the cure of his knee, he was confined to his bed, though otherwise in perfect health, and, finding the time tedious, he called for some book of romances, for he had been always much delighted with fabulous histories of knight-errantry. None such being then found in the castle of Loyola, a book of the lives of our Saviour and of the saints was brought him. He read them first only to pass away the time, but afterward began to relish them, and to spend whole days in reading them. He chiefly admired, in the saints, their love of solitude and of the cross. He considered among the anchorets many persons of quality, who buried themselves alive in caves and dens, pale with fasting, and covered with haircloth; and he said to himself: "These men were of the same frame I am of; why then should not I do what they have done?" In the fervour of his good resolutions, he thought of visiting the Holy Land, and becoming a hermit. But these pious motions soon vanished; and his passion for glory, and a secret inclination for a rich lady in Castile, with a view to marriage, again filled his mind with thoughts of the world, till, returning to the lives of the saints, he perceived in his own heart the emptiness of all worldly glory, and that only God could content the soul. This vicissitude and fluctuation of mind continued some time; but he observed this difference, that the thoughts which were from God filled his soul with consolation, peace, and tranquillity; whereas the others brought indeed some sensible delight, but left a certain bitterness and heaviness in the heart. This mark he lays down in his book of Spiritual Exercises, as the ground of the rules for the discernment of the Spirit of God, and the world, in all the motions of the soul; as does Cardinal Bona, and all other writers who treat of the discernment of spirits in the interior life. Taking at last a firm resolution to imitate the saints in their heroic practice of virtue, he began to treat his body with all the rigour it was able to bear; he rose at midnight, and spent his retired hours in weeping for his sins.

One night, being prostrate before an image of the Blessed Virgin, in extraordinary sentiments of fervour, he consecrated himself to the service of his Redeemer under her patronage, and vowed an inviolable fidelity. When he had ended his prayer he heard a great noise; the house shook, the windows of his chamber were broken, and a rent was made in the wall which remains to this day, says the latest writer of his life. God might by this sign testify his acceptance of his sacrifice; as a like sign happened in the place where the faithful were assembled after Christ's ascension, and in the prison of Paul and Silas; or this might be an effect of the rage of the devil. Another night, Ignatius saw the mother of God environed with light, holding the infant Jesus in her arms; this vision replenished his soul with spiritual delight, and made all sensual pleasure and worldly objects insipid to him ever after. The saint's eldest brother, who was then, by the death of their father, lord of Loyola, endeavoured to detain him in the world, and to persuade him not to throw away the great advantages of the honour and reputation which his valour had gained him. But Ignatius, being cured of his wounds, under pretence of paying a visit to the duke of Najara, who had often come to see him during his illness, and who lived at Navarret, turned another way, and sending his two servants back from Navarret to Loyola, went to Montserrat. This was a great abbey of near three hundred Benedictine monks, of a reformed austere institute, situate on a mountain of difficult access, about four leagues in circumference and two leagues high, in the diocess of Barcelona. The monastery was first founded for nuns by the sovereign counts of Barcelona about the year 880, but was given to monks in 990. It has been much augmented by several kings of Spain, and is very famous for a miraculous image of the Blessed Virgin, and a great resort of pilgrims.

There lived at that time in this monastery a monk of great sanctity, named John Chanones, a Frenchman, who, being formerly vicar-general to the bishop of Mirepoix, in the thirty-first year of his age, resigned his ecclesiastical preferments, and took the monastic habit in this place. He lived to the age of eighty-eight years, never eating any flesh, watching great part of the night in prayer, dividing his whole time between heavenly contemplation and the service of his neighbour; and giving to all Spain an example of the most perfect obedience, humility, charity, devotion, and all other virtues. To this experienced director Ignatius addressed himself, and after his preparation, was three days in making to him a general confession, which he often interrupted by the abundance of his tears. He made a vow of perpetual chastity, and dedicated himself with great fervour to the divine service. At his first coming to this place, he had bought, at the village of Montserrat, a long coat of coarse cloth, a girdle, a pair of sandals, a wallet, and a pilgrim's staff, intending, after he had finished his devotions there, to make a pilgrimage to Jerusalem. Disguised in this habit, he remained at the abbey. He communicated to his director a plan of the austerities he proposed to practise, and was confirmed by him in his good resolutions. He received the blessed eucharist early in the morning on the feast of the Annunciation of our Lady in 1522; and, on the same day, left Montserrat, for fear of being discovered, having given his horse to the monastery, and hung up his sword on a pillar near the altar in testimony of his renouncing the secular warfare and entering himself in that of Christ. He travelled with his staff in his hand, a scrip by his side, bareheaded, and with one foot bare, the other being covered because it was yet tender and swelled. He went away infinitely pleased that he had cast off the livery of the world and put on that of Jesus Christ. He had bestowed his rich clothes on a beggar at his coming out of Montserrat; but the poor man was thrown into prison on suspicion of theft. Ignatius, being sent after by the magistrates, and brought back, told the truth to release him, but would not discover his own name.

Three leagues from Montserrat is a large village called Manresa, with a convent of Dominicans, and a hospital without the walls for pilgrims and sick persons. Ignatius went to this hospital, and rejoicing to see himself received in it unknown and among the poor, began to fast on water and bread (which he begged) the whole week, except Sundays, when he ate a few boiled herbs, but sprinkled over with ashes. He wore an iron girdle and a hair shirt; disciplined himself thrice a day, slept little, and lay on the ground. He was every day present at the whole divine office, spent seven hours on his knees at prayer, and received the sacraments every Sunday. To add humiliation to his bodily austerities, he affected a clownishness in his behaviour, and went begging about the streets with his face covered with dirt, his hair rough, and his beard and nails grown out to a frightful length. The children threw stones at him, and followed him with scornful shouts in the streets. Ignatius suffered these insults without saying one word, rejoicing secretly in his heart to share in the reproaches of the cross. The more mortifying the noisomeness of the hospital and the company of beggars were, the more violence he offered to himself that he might bear them cheerfully. The story of the fine suit of clothes given to the beggar at Montserrat, and the patience and devotion of the holy man, made him soon be reverenced as some fervent penitent in disguise. To shun this danger he privately hid himself in a dark, deep cave, in a solitary valley, called The Vale of Paradise, covered with briers, half a mile from the town. Here he much increased his mortifications till he was accidentally found half dead, and carried back to Manresa and lodged in the hospital.

After enjoying peace of mind and heavenly consolations from the time of his conversion, he was here visited with the most terrible trial of fears and scruples. He found no comfort in prayer, no relief in fasting, no remedy in disciplines, no consolation from the sacraments, and his soul was overwhelmed with bitter sadness. The Dominicans, out of compassion, took him out of the hospital into their convent; but his melancholy only increased upon him. He apprehended some sin in every step he took, and seemed often on the very brink of despair; but he was in the hands of Him whose trials are favours. He most earnestly implored the divine assistance, and took no sustenance for seven days, till his confessor obliged him to eat. Soon after this his tranquillity of mind was perfectly restored, and his soul overflowed with spiritual joy. From this experience he acquired a particular talent for curing scrupulous consciences, and a singular light to discern them. His prayer was accompanied with many heavenly raptures, and he received from God a supernatural knowledge and sense of sublime divine mysteries; yet he concealed all from the eyes of men, only disclosing himself to his two confessors, the pious monk of Montserrat, and the Dominican of Manresa; however, the people began to reverence him as a living saint, which they particularly testified during a violent fever into which his austerities cast him three times.

Too nice a worldly prudence may condemn the voluntary humiliations which this saint sometimes made choice of; but the wisdom of God is above that of the world, and the Holy Ghost sometimes inspires certain heroic souls to seek perfectly to die to themselves by certain practices which are extraordinary, and which would not be advisable to others; and if effected or undertaken with obstinacy and against advice, would be pernicious and criminal. Ignatius, by perfect compunction, humility, self-denial, contempt of the world, severe interior trials, and assiduous meditation, was prepared, by the divine grace, to be raised to an extraordinary gift of supernatural prayer. He afterward assured F. Lainez, that he had learned more of divine mysteries by prayer in one hour at Manresa, than all the doctors of the schools could ever have taught him. He was there favoured with many raptures, and divine illustrations concerning the Trinity, of which he afterward spoke with so much light and unction, that the most learned admired him, and the ignorant were instructed. In like manner, in various wonderful ecstasies, he was enlightened concerning the beauty and order of the creation, the excess of divine love which shines forth to man in the sacrament of the altar, and many other mysteries. So imperfect was his knowledge of his duties when he first renounced the world, that hearing a certain Moresco or Mohammedan speak injuriously of the holy Mother of God, when he set out from Loyola for Montserrat, he deliberated whether, being an officer, he ought not to kill him, though the divine protection preserved him from so criminal an action. But at Manresa he made so good a progress in the school of virtue, as to become qualified already to be a guide to others. He stayed there almost a year, during which time he governed himself by the advice of the holy monk of Montserrat, whom he visited every week, and that of his Dominican director.

Spain, in that and the foregoing age, abounded with many learned and experienced persons in that way, endowed with an eminent spirit, and a perfect experimental knowledge of Christian piety; witness the works of St. Peter of Alcantara, John of Avila, St. Teresa, Bartholomew de Martyribus, Lewis of Granada, and others. Our saint had the happiness to fall into the hands of prudent and able guides, and giving his heart to God without reserve, became himself in a short time an accomplished master; and whereas he at first openly proposed to himself his own perfection, he afterward burned with an ardent desire of contributing to the salvation of others; and commiserating the blindness of sinners, and considering how much the glory of God shines in the sanctification of souls purchased with the blood of his Son, he said to himself: "It is not enough that I serve the Lord; all hearts ought to love him, and all tongues ought to praise him." With this view, in order to be admitted more freely to converse with persons in the world, he chose a dress which, being more decent than the penitential garments which he at first wore, might not be disagreeable to others; and he moderated his excessive austerities.

He began then to exhort many to the love of virtue, and he there wrote his Spiritual Exercises, which he afterward revised, and published at Rome in 1548. Though the saint was at that time unacquainted with learning any further than barely to read and write, yet this book is so full of excellent maxims and instructions in the highest points of a spiritual life, that it is most clear that the Holy Ghost supplied abundantly what was yet wanting in him of human learning and study. The spirit which reigns in this book was that of all the saints. Frequent religious retirement had been practised by pious persons, in imitation of Christ and all the saints from the beginning; likewise the use and method of holy meditation were always known, but the excellent order of these meditations, prescribed by Ignatius, was new; and, though the principal rules and maxims are found in the lessons and lives of the ancient fathers of the desert, they are here judiciously chosen, methodically digested, and clearly explained. One of these is, that a person must not abridge the time, or desist from meditating, on account of spiritual dryness; another, that no one make any vow in sudden sentiments of fervour, but wait some time, and first ask advice. St. Ignatius establishes in this book the practices of a daily particular examination against a person's predominant passion, or on the best means and endeavours to acquire some particular virtue, besides the daily general examination of conscience. He lays down this excellent maxim: "When God hath appointed out a way, we must faithfully follow it, and never think of another, under pretence that it is more easy and safe. It is one of the devil's artifices to set before a soul some state, holy indeed, but impossible to her, or at least different from hers; that, by this love of novelty, she may dislike or be slack in her present state, in which God hath placed her, and which is best for her. In like manner he represents to her other actions as more holy and profitable, to make her conceive a disgust of her present employment." When some pretended to find fault with this book of St. Ignatius's Spiritual Exercises, Pope Paul III., at the request of St. Francis Borgia, by a brief in 1548, approved it, as full of the Spirit of God, and very useful for the edification and spiritual profit of the faithful.

The pestilence which raged in Italy having ceased, Ignatius, after a stay of ten months at Manresa, left that place for Barcelona, neither regarding the tears of those who sought to detain him, nor admitting any to bear him company, nor consenting to accept any money for the expenses of his journey. He took shipping at Barcelona, and in five days landed at Gaeta, whence he travelled on foot to Rome, Padua, and Venice, through villages, the towns being shut for fear of the plague. He spent the Easter at Rome, and sailed from Venice on board the admiral's vessel, which was carrying the governor to Cyprus. The sailors were a profligate crew, and seemed entirely to neglect prayer and all duties of religion, and their discourse was often lewd and profane. Ignatius having reproved them for their licentiousness, his zeal made them conspire to leave him ashore in a desert island; but a gust of wind from the land hindered the ship from touching upon it. He arrived at Cyprus, and found in the port a vessel full of pilgrims, just ready to hoist sail. Going immediately on board, he made a good voyage, and landed at Jaffa, the ancient Joppe, on the last day of August, 1523, forty days after he had left Venice. He went on foot from thence to Jerusalem in four days. The sight of the holy places filled his soul with joy and the most ardent sentiments of devotion and compunction, and he desired to stay there to labour in the conversion of the Mohammedans. The provincial of the Franciscans, by virtue of his authority from the holy see over the pilgrims, commanded him to leave Palestine. Ignatius obeyed, but slipped privately back to satisfy his devotion again in visiting twice more the print of our Saviour's feet on Mount Olivet.

He returned to Europe in winter, in extreme cold weather, poorly clad, and came to Venice at the end of January in 1524; from whence he continued his journey by Genoa to Barcelona. Desiring to qualify himself for the functions of the altar, and for assisting spiritually his neighbour, he began at Barcelona to study grammar, and addressed himself to a famous master named Jerom Ardebal, being assisted in the mean time in his maintenance by the charities of a pious lady of that city, called Isabel Rosella. He was then thirty-three years old; and it is not hard to conceive what difficulties he must go through in learning the rudiments of grammar at that age. Moreover, he seemed, by his military employments, and after his retreat by his contemplative life, very unfit for such an undertaking. At first, his mind was so fixed only on God, that he forgot every thing he read, and conjugating *amo*, for example, could only repeat to himself, "I love God; I am loved by God," and the like: but resisting this as a temptation, he began to make some progress, still joining contemplation and extraordinary austerities with his studies. He bore the jeers and taunts of the little boys, his schoolfellows, with joy. Hearing that a poor man called Lasano had hanged himself on a beam in his chamber, he ran to him, cut the rope, and prayed by him till the man returned to himself, though he had before seemed perfectly dead to all the bystanders. Lasano made his confession, received the sacraments, and soon after expired. This fact was regarded in the city as miraculous.

Some persons persuaded Ignatius to read Erasmus's Christian Soldier, an elegant book, wrote by that master of style at the request of an officer's pious lady, for the use of her husband, a man of loose morals. The saint always found his heart dry after reading this or any other of that author's works; which made him afterward caution those of his society against reading them, at least very much. Though in that writer's paraphrase on the Lord's prayer and other such treatises of piety, we find very pious sentiments collected from great authors, and elegantly and concisely expressed, yet a devout reader finds the language of the heart wanting. On the other side, it is well known how much St. Ignatius read daily, and recommended to all others the incomparable book, of the Imitation of Christ, which he made frequent use of to nourish and increase the fervour of his soul. He lodged at the house of one Agnes Pascal, a devout woman. Her son, John Pascal, a pious youth, would sometimes rise in the night to observe what Ignatius did in his chamber, and saw him sometimes on his knees, sometimes prostrate on the ground, his countenance on fire, and often in tears, repeating such words as these: "O God, my love, and the delight of my soul, if men knew thee, they could never offend thee! My God, how good art thou to bear with such a sinner as I am!"

The saint, after studying two years at Barcelona, went to the university of Alcala, which had been lately founded by Cardinal Ximenes, where he attended at the same time to lectures in logic, physics, and divinity; by which multiplicity he only confounded his ideas, and learned nothing at all, though he studied night and day. He lodged in a chamber of an hospital, lived by begging a small subsistence, and wore a coarse gray habit, in which he was imitated by four companions. He catechised children, held assemblies of devotion in the hospital, and by his mild reprehensions converted many loose livers, and among others one of the richest prelates in Spain. Some accused him of sorcery, and of the heresy of certain visionaries lately condemned in Spain under the name of the Illuminati, or Men of New Light; but, upon examination, he was justified by the inquisitors. After this, for teaching the catechism, being a man without learning or authority, he was accused to the bishop's grand vicar, who confined him to close prison two-and-forty days, but declared him innocent of any fault by a public sentence on the 1st day of June, 1527, yet forbidding him and his companions to wear any singular habit, or to give any instructions in religious matters, being illiterate persons. Ignatius rejoiced in his jail that he suffered though innocent, but spoke with such piety that many called him another St. Paul in prison. Being enlarged, he went about the streets with a public officer to beg money to buy a scholar's dress, in which action he rejoiced at the insults and affronts which he met with. However, he went himself to the archbishop of Toledo, Alphonsus de Fonseca, who was much pleased with him, but advised him to leave Alcala, and go to Salamanca, promising him his protection. Ignatius, in this latter place, began to draw many to virtue, and was followed by great numbers, which exposed him again to suspicions of introducing dangerous practices, and the grand-vicar of Salamanca imprisoned him; but, after two-and-twenty days, declared him innocent, and a person of sincere virtue. Ignatius looked upon prisons, sufferings, and ignominy as the height of his ambition; and God was pleased to purge and sanctify his soul by these trials. Recovering his liberty again, he resolved to leave Spain.

He from that time began to wear shoes, and received money sent him by his friends, but in the middle of winter travelled on foot to Paris, where he arrived in the beginning of February, 1528. He spent two years in perfecting himself in the Latin tongue; then went through a course of philosophy. He lived first in Montaigue college; but being robbed of his money, was oblige to lodge in the hospital of St. James, to beg his bread from day to day, and in the vacation time to go into Flanders, and once into England, to procure charities from the Spanish merchants settled there, from whom and from some friends at Barcelona he received abundant supplies. He studied his philosophy three years and a half in the college of St. Barbara. He had induced many of his schoolfellows to spend the Sundays and holy-days in prayer, and to apply themselves more fervently to the practice of good works. Pegna his master thought he hindered their studies, and finding him not corrected by his admonitions, prepossessed Govea, principal of the college of St. Barbara, against him, so that he was ordered by him to undergo the greatest punishment then in use in that university, called *The Hall*, which was a public whipping; that this infamy might deter others from following him. The regents came all into the hall with rods in their hands, ready to lash this seditious student. Ignatius offered himself joyfully to suffer all things; yet, apprehending lest the scandal of this disgrace should make those whom he had reclaimed fall back, when they saw him condemned as a corrupter of youth, went to the principal in his chamber, and modestly laid open to him the sentiments of his soul, and the reasons of his conduct; and offered himself, as much as concerned his own person, that any sacrifice should be made of his body and fame, but begged of him to consider the scandal some might receive, who were yet young and tender in virtue. Govea made him no answer, but taking him by the hand led him into the hall, where, at the ringing of the bell, the whole college stood ready assembled. When all saw the principal enter, and expected the sign for the punishment, he threw himself at the feet of Ignatius, begging his pardon for having too lightly believed such false reports; then rising, he publicly declared that Ignatius was a living saint, and had no other aim or desire than the salvation of souls, and was ready to suffer joyfully any infamous punishment. Such a reparation of honour gave the saint the highest reputation, and even the ancient and experienced doctors asked his advice in spiritual matters. Pegna himself was ever after his great admirer and friend, and appointed another scholar, who was more advanced in his studies, and a young man of great virtue and quick parts, to assist him in his exercises. This was Peter Faber, a Savoyard, a native of the diocess of Geneva, by whose help he finished his philosophy, and took the degree of master of arts with great applause, after a course of three years and a half, according to the custom of the times. After this, Ignatius began his divinity at the Dominicans.

Peter Faber had from his childhood made a vow of chastity, which he had always most faithfully kept, yet was troubled with violent temptations, from which the most rigorous fasts did not deliver him. He was also tempted to vainglory, and laboured under great anxiety and scruples about these temptations, which he at length disclosed to Ignatius his holy pupil, whose skilful and heavenly advice was a healing balsam to his soul. The saint at last prescribed him a course of his spiritual exercises, and taught him the practices of meditation, of the particular examination, and other means of perfection, conducting him through all the paths of an interior life. St. Francis Xavier, a young master of philosophy, full of the vanity of the schools, was his next conquest. St. Ignatius made him sensible that all mortal glory is emptiness, only that which is eternal deserving our regard. He converted many abandoned sinners. When a young man, engaged in a criminal commerce with a woman of the city, was proof against his exhortations, Ignatius stood in a frozen pond by the wayside up to the neck, and as he passed by in the night, cried out to him: "Whither are you going? Do not you hear the thunder of divine justice over your head, ready to break upon you? Go then; satisfy your brutish passion; here I will suffer for you, to appease heaven." The lewd young man, at first affrighted, then confounded, returned back, and changed his life. By the like pious stratagems the saint recovered many other souls from the abysses into which they were fallen. He often served the sick in the hospitals; and one day finding a repugnance to touch the ulcers of one sick of a contagious distemper, to overcome himself, he not only dressed his sores, but put his hand from them to his mouth, saying: "Since thou art afraid for one part, thy whole body shall take its share." From that time he felt no natural repugnance in such actions.

James Laynez, of Almazan, twenty-one years of age, Alphonsus Salmeron, only eighteen, and Nicholas Alphonso, surnamed Bobadilla, from the place of his birth, near Valencia, all Spaniards of great parts, at that time students in divinity at Paris, associated themselves to the saint in his pious exercises. Simon Rodriguez, a Portuguese, joined them. These fervent students, moved by the pressing instances and exhortations of Ignatius, made all together a vow to renounce the world, to go to preach the gospel in Palestine, or if they could not go thither within a year after they had finished their studies, to offer themselves to his holiness to be employed in the service of God in what manner he should judge best. They fixed for the end of all their studies the 25th day of January in 1537, and pronounced this vow aloud, in the holy subterraneous chapel at Montmartre, after they had all received the holy communion from Peter Faber, who had been lately ordained priest. This was done on the feast of the Assumption of our Lady, in 1534. Ignatius continued frequent conferences, and joint exercises, to animate his companions in their good purposes; but soon after was ordered by the physicians to try his native air, for the cure of a lingering indisposition. He left Paris in the beginning of the year 1535, and was most honourably and joyfully received in Guipuscoa by his eldest brother Garcias, and his nephews, and by all the clergy in processions. He refused to go to the castle of Loyola, taking up his quarters in the hospital of Azpetia. The sight of the places where he had led a worldly life excited in him the deepest sentiments of compunction, and he chastised his body with a rough hair shirt, iron chains, disciplines, watching, and prayer. He recovered his health in a short time, and catechised and instructed the poor with incredible fruit. Ignatius, in his childhood, had with some companions robbed an orchard, for which another man had been condemned to pay the damages. In the first discourse he made he accused himself publicly of this fact, and calling the poor man, who was present, declared that he had been falsely accused, and for reparation gave him two farms which belonged to him, begging his pardon before all the people, adding that this was one of the reasons of his journeying thither.

In the mean time, three others, all doctors in divinity, by the exhortations of Faber, joined the saint's companions in Paris: Claudius le Jay, a Savoyard, John Codure, a native of Dauphiné, and Pasquier Brouet, of Picardy; so that with Ignatius they were now ten in number. The holy founder, after a tedious and dangerous journey both by sea and land, arrived at Venice about the end of the year 1536, and his nine companions from Paris met him there on the 8th of January, 1537. They employed themselves in the hospitals; but all except Ignatius went to Rome, where Pope Paul III. received them graciously, and granted them an indult, that those who were not priests might receive holy orders from what bishop they pleased. They were accordingly ordained at Venice by the bishop of Arbe. Ignatius was one of this number. After their ordination, they retired into a cottage near Vicenza, to prepare themselves in solitude by fasting and prayer for the holy ministry of the altar. The rest said their first masses in September and October, but Ignatius deferred his from month to month till Christmas-day, overflowing in his retirement with heavenly consolations, and in danger of losing his sight through the abundance of his tears. Thus he employed a whole year in preparing himself to offer that adorable sacrifice. After this they dispersed themselves into several places about Verona and Vicenza, preaching penance to the people, and living on a little bread which they begged. The emperor and the Venitians having declared war against the Turks, their pilgrimage into Palestine was rendered impracticable. The year therefore being elapsed, Ignatius, Faber, and Laynez went to Rome, threw themselves at his holiness's feet, and offered themselves to whatever work he should judge best to employ them in. St. Ignatius told his companions at Vicenza, that if any one asked what their institute was, they might answer, "the Society of Jesus;" because they were united to fight against heresies and vice under the standard of Christ. In his road from Vicenza to Rome, praying in a little chapel between Sienna and Rome, he, in an ecstasy, seemed to see the eternal Father, who affectionately recommended him to his Son. Jesus Christ appeared at the same time also shining with an unspeakable light, but loaded with a heavy cross, and sweetly said to Ignatius: "I will be favourable to you at Rome." This St. Ignatius disclosed to F. Lainez, in a transport, when he came out of the chapel; and F. Lainez, when he was general, related it to all the fathers in Rome in a domestic conference, at which F. Ribadeneira, who records it, was present. The same was attested by others to whom the saint had discovered this signal favour. Pope Paul III. accordingly received them graciously, and appointed Faber, called in French Le Fevre, to teach in the Sapienza at Rome scholastic divinity, and Lainez to explain the Holy Scripture; while Ignatius laboured, by means of his spiritual exercises and instructions, to reform the manners of the people.

The holy founder, with a view to perpetuate the work of God, called to Rome all his companions, and proposed to them his design and motives of forming themselves into a religious order. After recommending the matter to God by fasting and prayer, all agreed in the proposal, and resolved, first, besides the vows of poverty and chastity already made by them, to add a third of perpetual obedience, the more perfectly to conform themselves to the Son of God, who was obedient even to death; and to establish a general whom all, by their vow, should be bound to obey, who should be perpetual, and his authority absolute, subject entirely to the pope, but not liable to be restrained by chapters. He likewise determined to prescribe a fourth vow of going wherever the pope should send them for the salvation of souls, and even without money if it should so please him; also, that the professed Jesuits should possess no real estates or revenues, either in particular or in common; but that colleges might enjoy revenues and rents for the maintenance of students of the order. In the mean while Govea, principal of the college of St. Barbara, at Paris, had recommended the Jesuits to the king of Portugal as proper missionaries for the conversion of the Indies, and that prince asked of Ignatius six labourers for that purpose. The founder having only ten, could send him no more than two, Simon Rodriguez, who remained in Portugal, and Xavier, afterward the apostle of the Indies. The three cardinals appointed by the pope to examine the affair of this new order, at first opposed it, thinking religious orders already too much multiplied, but changed their opinion on a sudden, and Pope Paul III. approved it, under the title of "The Society of Jesus," by a bull, dated the 27th of September, 1540. Ignatius was chosen the first general, but only acquiesced in obedience to his confessor. He entered upon his office on Easter-day, 1541, and the members all made their religious vows, according to the bull of the institution.

Ignatius then set himself to write constitutions or rules for his society, in which he lays down its end to be, in the first place, the sanctification of their own souls by joining together the active and the contemplative life; for nothing so much qualifies a minister of God to save others, as the sanctification of his own soul in the first place: Secondly, to labour for the salvation and perfection of their neighbour, and this first, by catechising the ignorant, (which work is the basis and ground of religion and virtue, and though mean and humble, is the most necessary and indispensable duty of every pastor;) secondly, by the instruction of youth in piety and learning, (upon which the reformation of the world principally depends;) and, thirdly, by the direction of consciences, missions, and the like.

St. Ignatius would have the office of general to be

perpetual, or for life, being persuaded this would better command the respect of inferiors, and more easily enable him to undertake and carry on great enterprises for the glory of God, which require a considerable time to have them well executed. Nevertheless, he often strenuously endeavoured to resign that dignity, but was never able to compass it; and at length the pope forbade him any more to attempt it. He had no sooner taken that charge upon him than he went into the kitchen, and served as scullion under the cook, and he continued for forty-six days to catechise poor children in the church of the society. By preaching he gained such an ascendant over the hearts of the people as produced many wonderful conversions. Among the pious establishments which he made at Rome, he founded a house for the reception of Jews, who should be converted, during the time of their instruction, and another for the reception and maintenance of lewd women who should be desirous to enter upon virtuous courses, yet were not called to a religious state among the Magdalens or penitents. When one told him that the conversion of such sinners is seldom sincere, he answered: "To prevent only one sin would be a great happiness, though it cost me ever so great pains." He procured two houses to be erected at Rome for the relief of poor orphans of both sexes, and another for the maintenance of young women whose poverty might expose their virtue to danger. The heart of this blessed man so burned with charity, that he was continually thinking and speaking of what might most contribute to promote the divine honour and the sanctification of souls; and he did wonders by the zealous fathers of his society in all parts of the globe. He was entreated by many princes and cities of Italy, Spain, Germany, and the Low Countries, to afford them some of his labourers. Under the auspicious protection of John III., king of Portugal, he sent St. Francis Xavier into the East Indies, where he gained a new world to the faith of Christ. He sent John Nugnez and Lewis

Gonzales into the kingdoms of Fez and Morocco, to instruct and assist the Christian slaves; in 1547, four others to Congo in Africa; in 1555, thirteen into Abyssinia, among whom John Nugnez was nominated, by Pope Julius III., patriarch of Ethiopia, and two others bishops; lastly, others into the Portuguese settlements in South America.

Pope Paul III. commissioned the fathers James Lainez and Alphonsus Salmeron to assist, in quality of his theologians, at the Council of Trent. Before their departure, St. Ignatius, among other instructions, gave them a charge in all disputations to be careful above all things to preserve modesty and humility, and to shun all confidence, contentiousness, or empty display of learning. F. Claudius Le Jay appeared in the same council as theologian of Cardinal Otho, bishop of Ausberg. Many of the first disciples of St. Ignatius distinguished themselves in divers kingdoms of Europe, but none with greater reputation, both for learning and piety, than Peter Canisius, who was a native of Nimeguen, in the Low Countries, and having with wonderful success employed his zealous labours at Ingolstadt, and in several other parts of Germany, and in Bohemia, died in the odour of sanctity, at Fribourg, in 1597, seventy-seven years old. While F. Claudius Le Jay was at Trent, Ferdinand, king of the Romans, nominated him bishop of Trieste. The good father seemed ready to die of grief at this news, and wrote to St. Ignatius, humbly requesting him to put some bar to this promotion. The holy founder was himself alarmed, and by a pressing letter to the king, prevailed upon him not to do what would be an irreparable prejudice to his young society. He urged to the pope and sacred college many reasons why he desired that all the fathers of his society should be excluded from all ecclesiastical dignities, alleging that this would be a means more easily to preserve among them a spirit of humility and poverty, which is the very soul and perfection of their state; and that, being missionaries, it was more advantageous to the church that they should remain such, always ready to fly from pole to pole, as the public necessities should require. The pope being satisfied with his reasons, the saint obliged all professed Jesuits to bind themselves by a simple vow never to seek prelatures, and to refuse them when offered, unless compelled by a precept of the pope to accept them.

In 1546 the Jesuits first opened their schools in Europe, in the college which St. Francis Borgia had erected for them at Gandia, with the privileges of an university. The seminary of Goa in Asia, which had been erected some years before for the Indian missions, was committed to the Jesuits, under the direction of St. Francis Xavier, the preceding year. King John also founded for them, in 1546, a noble college at Coïmbra, the second which they had in Europe. F. Simon Rodriguez directed this establishment, and many others in Portugal, Spain, and Brazil, and died at Lisbon in the highest reputation for sanctity and learning in 1579. Among the rules which St. Ignatius gave to the masters, he principally inculcated the lessons of humility, modesty, and devotion; he prescribed that all their scholars should hear mass every day, go to confession every month, and always begin their studies by prayer; that their masters should take every fit occasion to inspire them with the love of heavenly things; and that, by daily meditation, self-examinations, pious reading, retreat, and the constant exercise of the divine presence, they should nourish in their own souls a fervent spirit of prayer, which, without the utmost care, is extinguished by a dry course of studies and school disputations; and with it is destroyed the very soul of a religious or spiritual life. He recommended nothing more earnestly, both to professors and scholars, than that they should dedicate all their labours, with the greatest fervour, to the greater glory of God, which intention will make studies equal to prayer. He treated very harshly all those whom learning rendered self-conceited, or less devout; and removed all those masters who discovered any fondness for singular opinions. It is incredible with what attention and industry he prompted emulation and every means that could be a spur to scholars. He required that copies of some of the principal literary performances should be sent from all the colleges to Rome, where he had them examined before him, that he might better judge of the progress both of masters and scholars.

He encouraged every branch of the sciences, and would have the fathers in his society applied to those functions, whether in teaching, preaching, or the missions, for which God seemed chiefly to qualify and destine them by their genius, talents, and particular graces; yet so that no one should neglect the duties either of assiduous prayer and an interior life, or of instructing and catechising others. He recommended to them all, especially to the masters of novices, &c., to read diligently the conferences, lives, and writings of the fathers of the desert, and other pious ascetics, in order to learn their spirit. With what success many among them did this, appears from the Practice of Christian Perfection, compiled by F. Alphonsus Rodriguez, one of the most eminent persons whom our saint had admitted into his society. In this excellent work he gathered and digested, in a clear and easy method, the most admirable maxims and lessons of the ancient monks; and having many years trained up, according to them, the novices of his order in Spain, died holily in the year 1616, the ninetieth of his age. We have other eminent instances of this holy spirit and science among the primitive disciples of St. Ignatius, in the works of F. Lewis de Ponte or Puente, who died in 1624, and whose canonization has been often desired by the kings of Spain; in those of F. Alvarez de Paz, who died in Peru in 1620; and in the writings and life of F. Baltassar Alvarez, who died in Spain in 1580, in the odour of sanctity.

St. Francis Borgia, in 1551, gave a considerable sum toward building the Roman college for the Jesuits. Pope Julius III. contributed largely to it;

Paul IV., in 1555, founded it for perpetuity with great munificence; afterward Gregory XIII. much augmented its buildings and revenues. St. Ignatius, intending to make this the model of all his other colleges, neglected nothing to render it complete, and took care that it should be supplied with the ablest masters in all the sciences, and with all possible helps for the advancement of literature. He made it a strict rule in the society, that every one should study to speak correctly the language of the country where he lives; for, without being perfect in the vulgar tongue, no one can be qualified to preach or perform many other functions with profit. On this account he established in the Roman college daily lessons in the Italian tongue, and he carefully studied that language, and appointed others to put him in mind of all the faults which he should commit in speaking. St. Ignatius also directed the foundation of the German college in Rome made by Julius III., but afterward finished by Gregory XIII. He often met with violent persecutions, but overcame them by meekness and patience. When the French king Henry II. gave the society letters-patent to settle in France, the parliament of Paris made the most outrageous remonstrances, and the faculty of Sorbon, though not without opposition, passed a virulent decree against it. The other fathers at Rome thought it necessary to answer these censures; but St. Ignatius would have nothing printed or written in their defence, saying, that it was better to commit their cause to God, and that the slanders raised against them would fall of themselves; and so it happened. Indeed the storm was too violent to last. Upon other occasions the saint modestly defended his institute against slanderers.

The prudence and charity of the saint in his conduct toward his religious, won him all their hearts. His commands seemed rather entreaties. The address with which he accommodated himself to every one's particular genius, and the mildness with which he tempered his reproofs, gave to his reprehensions a sweetness which gained the affections while it corrected a fault. Thus, chiding one for too little guard over his eyes, he said to him with tenderness: "I have often admired the modesty of your deportment, yet observe that unguarded glances often escape you." When another had fixed his eye steadfastly upon him a long time, the saint enjoined him to make the government of his eye the subject of his particular examination, and to say every day a short prayer for fifteen months. He extremely recommended a strict modesty in the whole exterior as the index of the interior, and a means absolutely necessary for the regulating of it, and the government of the senses and passions. He always showed the affection of the most tender parent toward all his brethren, especially toward the sick, for whom he was solicitous to procure every spiritual and even temporal succour and comfort, which it was his great delight to give them himself. The most perfect obedience and self-denial were the two first lessons which he inculcated to his novices, whom he told at the door as they entered, that they must leave behind them all self-will and private judgment. In his famous letter to the Portuguese Jesuits, on the Virtue of Obedience, he says, this alone bringeth forth and nourisheth all other virtues; and calls it the peculiar virtue and distinguishing mark and characteristic of his society, in which, if any member suffer himself to be outdone by those of other orders in fasting or watching, he must yield to none in obedience. He adds, true obedience must reach the understanding as well as the will, and never suffer a person even secretly to complain of, or censure the precept of a superior, whom he must always consider as vested with the authority of Jesus Christ over him. He says, it is not a less fault to break the laws of obedience in watching than in sleeping, in labouring than in doing nothing.

When F. Araos, whose spiritual labours were very successful in the court of Spain, seemed to seek the conversation of the great ones of the world, upon pretence of conciliating their favour to his ministry, St. Ignatius sent him a sharp reprimand, telling him, that the necessary authority for the ministers of the word of God, is to be gained only by a spirit of recollection and the exercises of Christian humility; for the loss of every thing is to be feared in an intercourse with the great ones of the world. He used to say that prosperity caused in him more fear than joy; that when persecution ceased, he should be in apprehension lest the society should somewhat relax in the observance of its regular discipline; that good fortune is never to be trusted; and that we have most to fear when things go according to our own desires. He made a most severe regulation, that in the society no one should even visit women, even of the highest quality, alone; and that when they discoursed with them, or heard their confessions, this should be so ordered, that the companion might see all that passed, without hearing what ought to be secret, this being a means to prevent the possibility of evil suspicions or slanders. In assigning the employments of those under his charge, he had usually a regard to their inclinations, though he always required that, on their parts, they should be wholly indifferent, and disposed cheerfully to accept and discharge any.

Notwithstanding the fatigue and constant application which the establishment of his order in all parts of the world, and so many other great enterprises undertaken to promote the glory of God required, he was all on fire with an excess of charity and a restless desire of gaining souls to God, and wearied himself out in the service of his neighbour, always labouring to extirpate vice, and to promote virtue in all, and set on foot several practices which might conduce to the divine service and salvation of men. It is not to be believed how many and how great affairs this blessed man was able to go through, and with what courage and spirit he bore so continual a burden, and this with so weak health and infirm body. But he was assisted by the powerful hand of our Lord, that furnished him with strength for all his labours; so that he then appeared strongest and most courageous, when he was weary, sickly, and unprovided of human and natural helps; for, in his infirmity, the power of God manifested itself, and the saint seemed to support the weakness of his body with the vigour of his soul. This interior strength he chiefly maintained by an eminent spirit of prayer, and the constant and closest union of his soul with God. For he was favoured with an extraordinary grace of devotion, which he, out of humility, thought God had given him out of compassion for his weakness and misery, which he said was greater than that of any other. In saying the holy mass, and reciting the divine office, the abundance of heavenly delights which God poured into his soul, was often so great, and made such showers of tears stream from his eyes, that he was obliged to stop in a manner at every word, sometimes to make a considerable interruption while he gave vent to his tears. It was once feared lest his continual effusion of tears should hurt his eyesight. At other times, though his eyes were dry at his devotion, and the sluices of his tears were shut up, yet their influence and effect were not wanting; for his spirit was still watered with heavenly dew, and the divine illustrations ceased not to flow copiously into his soul.

In matters of concern, though reasons were ever so convincing and evident, he never took any resolution before he had consulted God by prayer. He let not an hour pass in the day without recollecting himself interiorly, and examining his conscience, for this purpose banishing for a while all other thoughts. He never applied his mind so much to exterior affairs as to lose the sweet relish of interior devotion. He had God always and in all things present to his mind. Every object served him for a book, wherein he read the divine perfections, and by that means raised his heart to his Creator. He recommended this manner of prayer to every one, especially to those who are employed in spiritual functions for the help of their neighbour. Before he betook himself to public or private prayer, he prepared his soul with great fervour, and entering into the oratory of his heart, enkindled his affections, so that this appeared in his countenance, and he seemed to be all on fire, as we ourselves frequently observed, says Ribadeneira. The saint being once asked by F. Lainez what manner of prayer he used, gave this answer, that in matters concerning Almighty God he behaved himself rather passively than actively. He prayed sometimes standing, and profoundly adored the majesty of God present to his soul; he often bowed his body low, and most frequently prayed on his knees. No sooner had he recollected his mind in God, but his countenance put on an air which appeared altogether heavenly, and often streams of tears fell sweetly from his eyes.

He prescribed to the priests of his order to be about half an hour at the altar in saying mass, to avoid on one side the least appearance of indecent hurry and precipitation in that tremendous sacrifice, and on the other, not to be tedious to the people, by unseasonably indulging their private devotion. Nevertheless, he was himself about an hour in saying mass, to excuse which he alleged the plea of necessity, being often obliged to make pauses through an irresistible tenderness of devotion. After mass he spent two hours in private prayer, during which time no one was admitted to speak to him, except on some pressing necessity. F. Lewis Gonzales, who for some time governed the college under him, says: "As often as I went to him at that time, which necessity frequently obliged me to do, I always saw his face shining with an air so bright and heavenly, that, quite forgetting myself, I stood astonished in contemplating him. Nor was his countenance like that of many devout men in whom I have admired a wonderful serenity at their prayers, but it breathed something quite unusual, and, as it were, divine." On other occasions the like was remarked in him; on which account F. Lainez compared him to Moses when he came from conversing with God. Nicholas Lanoy testified that he one day saw a fire flame on his head while he was saying mass. Saint Philip Neri, who often visited St. Ignatius, used to assure his friends that he had seen his face shining with bright rays of light, as F. Antony Galloni, his disciple and confidant in all his concerns, and Marcellus Vitelleschi declared they had often heard from his own mouth; of which Cardinal Taurusius, archbishop of Sienna, published an authentic certificate. John Petronius, a famous physician in Rome, declared publicly that, when sick, he once saw his own chamber, which was then very dark by reason of the windows being shut, filled with a dazzling light from such rays, upon the blessed man's coming into it. Isabel Rosella, John Pascal, and several other persons testified that they had sometimes beheld his countenance, at prayer, sparkling with radiant beams of light, the abundant consolations which replenished his soul redounding on his body. John Pascal added that he had seen him in prayer raised more than a foot above the ground, and heard him say at the same time, "O my God! O my Lord! O that men knew thee!" The saint was often favoured, amid the tears and fervour of his devotion, with wonderful raptures, visions, and revelations; and some of these visions and other supernatural favours St. Ignatius mentioned himself in short notes which he wrote, and which were found, in his own hand, after his death, some of which notes are published by F. Bartoli. Others are mentioned by Ribadeneira, who inserted in the saint's life, as he declares, only what himself had seen, or had heard from his mouth, or from persons of unquestionable authority, and whose life of his holy founder, by the order of Saint Francis Borgia, was carefully examined and approved by the principal persons then living, who had frequently conversed with the saint, as Salmeron, Bobadilla, Polancus, who had been the saint's secretary, Natalis, &c.

If the spirit of prayer was that virtue by which our saint was admitted to the familiar intercourse with

God, was the key which unlocked to him the treasure of all other virtues and graces, and was the continual comfort and light of his soul, and the constant advancement of its supernatural life in his mortal pilgrimage, this spirit was itself founded in the most perfect self-denial. The Holy Ghost never communicates himself, by the infusion of this grace, but to a heart that is entirely dead to itself and its passions, and crucified to the world. This St. Ignatius understood so well, that, hearing another once say that a certain person was endowed with a great gift of contemplation, and was eminently a man of prayer, he corrected the expression, saying, "call him rather a man of the most perfect self-denial;" because the spirit of grace and prayer requires a perfect purity and disengagement from all inordinate affections, and a heart empty of itself. This victory over himself the saint obtained by an habitual practice of the exterior mortification of his senses, and by that perfect patience, resignation, and confidence in God, and constancy with which he bore the most severe interior and exterior trials. To complete the most essential interior mortification of his will and passions, he added the practice of an unlimited obedience to his directors and superiors, and of the most profound and sincere humility. Even when broken with age and infirmities, he said, that should his holiness command it, he would with joy go on board the first ship he could find; and, if he were so ordered, though it had neither sails nor rudder, and without any warning, would immediately set out for any part of the globe. It was his perpetual lesson to his novices—"Sacrifice your will and judgment by obedience. Whatever you do without the consent of your spiritual guide, will be imputed to wilfulness, not to virtue, though you were to exhaust your bodies by labours or austerities."

Humility is the sister virtue of obedience, the foundation of a spiritual life, and the distinguishing mark or characteristic of all the saints. This virtue St. Ignatius embraced with the utmost ardour, from his first entering upon a spiritual course of life. He went a long time in old tattered rags, and lived in hospitals, despised, affronted, and persecuted; this he desired, and in it he found his great joy and satisfaction. He ever retained this affection for humiliations, out of a sincere contempt for himself; for, acknowledging himself a sinner, he was thoroughly persuaded that contempt and injuries from all creatures, as instruments of the divine justice, were his due, and that he was most unworthy of all comforts, favour, or regard. Nothing but charity and zeal to procure his neighbour's good, restrained him from doing ridiculous things on purpose to be laughed at by all; and he practised such humiliations as were consistent with prudence and his other duties. All his actions, and whatever belonged to him, breathed an air of sincere humility. His apparel was poor, though clean; his bed was very mean, and his diet coarse, and so temperate, that it was a perpetual abstinence. He employed himself often, most cheerfully, in the meanest offices about the house, as in making beds, and in cleansing the chambers of the sick. It was his great study to conceal his virtues, and nothing was more admirable in his life than the address with which he covered his most heroic actions under the vail of humility. Though he was superior, he frequently submitted to inferiors with wonderful meekness and humility, when he could do it without prejudice to his authority. In things of which he was not certain, he readily acquiesced in the judgment of others; and was a great enemy to all positiveness, and to the use of superlatives in discourse. He received rebukes from any one with cheerfulness and thanks. If in his presence any thing was said that redounded to his praise, he showed an extreme confusion, which was usually accompanied with many tears. He was seldom heard to speak of himself, and never but on very pressing occasions. Though visions, revelations, and the like favours were frequently vouchsafed him, he scarce ever mentioned such things;

but all his discourse was of humility, charity, patience, divine zeal, prayer, mortification, and other such virtues, of which we are to make the greatest account, and by which alone men become saints and friends of God. Ribadeneira heard him say that every one in the house was to him an example of virtue, and that he was not scandalized at any one besides himself. It was his usual saying, that he did not think there was a man in the world, that on one side received from God so great and continued favours, and yet, on the other side, was so ungrateful and so slothful in his service as himself. It was his desire that, after his death, his body might be thrown upon some dunghill, in punishment of the sins he had committed by pampering it. The chief reasons why he would have his order called The Society of Jesus, were lest his name should be given it, and that his followers might be known by their love and zeal for the Redeemer. As often as he spoke of his order, he called it This least Society; for he would have his children to look upon themselves as the last and least of all persons in the church.

From the perfect mortification of all his passions and inordinate affections, resulted an admirable peace and evenness of mind, which nothing seemed able ever to disturb or ruffle. His contempt of the world appeared by the disinterestedness with which he rejected legacies and presents whenever they might give occasion to complaints. When he looked up toward the heavens, he used feelingly to repeat: "How contemptible doth earth appear when I behold the heavens!" Charity, or the most ardent and pure love of God, was the most conspicuous, and the crown of all his other virtues. He had often in his mouth those words which he took for his motto or device, "To the greater glory of God," referring to this end, with all his strength, himself, his society, and all his actions, in which he always chose that which appeared to him the most perfect. He often said to God:

"Lord, what do I desire, or what can I desire besides thee!" True love is never idle; and always to labour to promote God's honour, or to suffer for his sake, was this saint's greatest pleasure. He said that no created thing can bring to a soul such solid joy and comfort as to suffer for Christ. Being asked what was the most certain and the shortest way to perfection, he answered: "To endure for the love of Christ many and grievous afflictions. Ask this grace of our Lord; on whomsoever he bestoweth it, he does him many other signal favours, that always attend this grace." Out of this burning love of God, he most ardently desired the separation of his soul from his mortal body, when it should be God's will; and, when he thought of death, he could not refrain from tears of joy, because he should then see his loving Redeemer, and, beholding God face to face, should love and praise him eternally, without let, abatement, or intermission.

From this same love of God sprang his ardent thirst for the salvation of men, for which he undertook so many and so great things, and to which he devoted his watchings, prayers, tears, and labours. When he dismissed any missionaries to preach the word of God, he usually said to them: "Go, brethren, inflame the world, spread about that fire which Jesus Christ came to kindle on earth." To gain others to Christ, he, with admirable address, made himself all to all, going in at *their* door, and coming out at *his own*. He received sincere penitents with the greatest sweetness and condescension, so as often to take upon himself part of their penance. When a brother, growing weary of the yoke of Christ, had determined to leave the society, St. Ignatius, by his remonstrances, made such an impression upon his heart, that, falling at the feet of the general, he offered to undergo whatever punishment he would impose upon him. To which the saint replied: "One part of your penance shall be, that you never repent more of having served God. For the other part, I take it upon myself, and will discharge it for you." He endeavoured to bring all his penitents to make, without reserve, the perfect sacrifice of themselves to God, telling them that it is not to be expressed what precious treasures God reserves for, and with what effusion he communicates himself to, those who give themselves to him with their whole heart. He proposed to them for their model this prayer, which he used often to recite: "Receive, O Lord, all my liberty, my memory, my understanding, and my whole will. Thou hast given me all that I have, all that I possess, and I surrender all to thy divine will, that thou dispose of me. Give me only thy love, and thy grace. With this I am rich enough, and I have no more to ask."

St. Ignatius was general of the society fifteen years, three months, and nine days; but was in the end so worn out with infirmities that he procured that the society should choose him an assistant in that office. This was F. Jerom Nadal. After which, the saint reserved to himself only the care of the sick, and spent his time in continual prayer, and in preparing himself for death. By way of his last will and testament, he dictated certain holy maxims concerning the obligation and conditions of religious obedience, which he bequeathed to his brethren of the society. The saint, on the day before he died, charged F. Polancus to beg his Holiness's blessing for him at the article of death, though others at that time did not think it so near. The next morning, having lifted up his eyes and hands to heaven, and pronouncing, both with his tongue and heart, the sweet name of Jesus, with a serene countenance, he calmly gave up his happy soul into the hands of his Creator on the last day of July, in the year 1556, the sixty-fifth of his age, the thirty-fifth after his conversion, and the sixteenth after the confirmation of the society. The people esteemed him a saint both living and after his death; and the opinion of his sanctity was confirmed by many miracles. He saw his society in very few years divided into twelve provinces, with above one hundred colleges, and spread over almost the whole world. In 1626, it contained thirty-six provinces, and in them eight hundred houses, and fifteen thousand Jesuits, since which time it is much increased. St. Ignatius's body was buried first in the little church of the Jesuits, dedicated in honour of the blessed Virgin in Rome. When Cardinal Alexander Farnesius had built the stately church of the professed house called Il Giesu, it was translated thither in 1587; and, in 1637, was laid under the altar of the chapel, which bears his name. This church is one of the most magnificent piles of building in the world next to the Vatican, and is not less admired for the elegance of the architecture than for its riches, consisting in costly beautiful ornaments of gold, silver, jewels, exquisite paintings, statues, and carving, and a great profusion of fine marble. Among the many chapels which it contains, those of the blessed Virgin, of the Angels, of SS. Abundius and Abundantius, martyrs, of St. Francis Borgia, and of St. Ignatius, are the admiration of travellers, especially the last; in which the remains of the holy founder lie, in a rich silver shrine under the altar, exposed to view. The other glittering rich ornaments of this place seem almost to lose their lustre when the statue of the saint is uncovered. It is somewhat bigger than the life, because raised high. Its bright shining gold, silver, and sparkling diamonds, especially in the crown of glory over the head, dazzle the eye. In the professed house are shown the pictures of St. Ignatius and St. Philip Neri, taken from the life. St. Ignatius's chamber is now a chapel, his study is another, in which prelates, and sometimes popes, come to say mass on the saint's festival. He was beatified by Paul V., in 1609, and canonized by Gregory XV., in 1622, though the bull was only published the year following by Urban VIII.

The example of the saints evinces that to disengage our affections from earthly things, and to converse much in heaven by the constant union of our hearts to God, is the short road to Christian perfection. Those who are employed in the active life, ought to learn the art of accompanying all their actions with a lively attention to the divine presence, as our guardian angels are faithful in discharging every duty of that external ministry which God hath committed to them, yet so as never to intermit their contemplation of the Godhead, and their incessant homages of praise and love, which are the uninterrupted employment of their happy state. Without this precaution, by the hurry of dry studies, and even the discharge of the sacred ministry itself, the spirit of piety and devotion is extinguished in the heart, and the more sacred functions are easily profaned.

ST. ARSENIUS.

ANCHORET.

HE was a Roman by birth, and was related to senators. He had been trained up in learning and piety, was sincerely virtuous, and well skilled, not only in the Holy Scriptures, but also in the profane sciences, and in the Latin and Greek languages and literature. He was in deacon's orders, and led a retired life at home with his sister, in Rome, when the emperor, Theodosius the Great, wanted a person to whom he might intrust the care of his children, and desired the Emperor Gratian to apply for that purpose to the bishop of Rome, who recommended Arsenius. Gratian sent him to Constantinople, where he was kindly received by Theodosius, who advanced him to the rank of a senator, with orders that he should be respected as the father of his children, whose tutor and preceptor he appointed him. No one in the court at that time wore richer apparel, had more sumptuous furniture, or was attended by a more numerous train of servants than Arsenius; he was attended by no fewer than a thousand, all richly clad. Theodosius coming one day to see his children at their studies, found them sitting, while Arsenius talked to them standing. Being displeased thereat, he took from them for some time the marks of their dignity, and caused Arsenius to sit, and them to listen to him standing.

Arsenius had always a great inclination to a retired life, which the care of his employment and the encumbrances of a great fortune made him desire the more ardently; for titles and honours were burdensome to him. At length, about the year 390, an opportunity offered itself. Arcadius having committed a considerable fault, Arsenius whipped him for it. The young prince, resenting the chastisement, grew the more obstinate. Arsenius laid hold of this occasion to execute the project he had before formed of forsaking the world. The Lives of the Fathers, both in Rosweide and Cotelier, make no mention of this resentment of Arcadius, which circumstance is only related by Metaphrastes; on which account it is omitted by Tillemont and others. It is most certain that retirement had long been the object of the saint's most earnest wishes and desires; but before he left the court, he for a long time begged by earnest prayer to know the will of God; and one day making this request with great fervour, he heard a voice, saying: "Arsenius, flee the company of men, and thou shalt be saved." He obeyed the call of heaven without delay, and going on board a vessel, sailed to Alexandria, and thence proceeded to the desert of Sceté, where he embraced an anchoretical life. This happened about the year 394, he being in the fortieth year of his age, and having lived eleven years at the court. There he renewed his prayers to God, begging to be instructed in the way of salvation, having no other desire than to make it his only study to please God in all things. While he prayed thus, he again heard a voice, which said: "Arsenius, flee, hold thy peace, and be quiet; these are the principles of salvation," that is, the main things to be observed in order to be saved. Pursuant to the repeated advice or injunction of fleeing and avoiding human conversation, he made choice of a very remote cell, and admitted very few visits, even from his own brethren. When he went to the church, upward of thirty miles distant from his habitation, he would place himself behind one of the pillars, the better to prevent his seeing or being seen by any one. Theodosius, in great affliction for the loss of him, caused search to be made for him both by sea and land; but being soon after called into the West to revenge the death of Valentinian II., and to extinguish the rebellion of Arbogastus, his murderer, and Eugenius, died of a dropsy, at Milan, in 395. Arcadius being left emperor of the East, advanced Rufin, who was the prefectus-prætorio, and had been his flattering governor, to the rank of prime minister, committing to him the direction not only of his armies, but also of the whole empire. He at the same time earnestly desired to call back to court his holy master Arsenius, that he might be assisted by his wise and faithful counsels. Being informed that he was in the desert of Sceté, he wrote to him, recommending himself to his prayers, begging his forgiveness, and offering him the disposal of all the tribute of Egypt, that he might make a provision for the monasteries and the poor at his discretion; but the saint had no other ambition on earth than to be allowed the liberty of enjoying his solitude, that he might employ his time in bewailing his sins, and in preparing his soul for eternity. He therefore answered the emperor's message only by word of mouth, saying: "God grant us all the pardon of our sins; as to the distribution of the money, I am not capable of such a charge, being already dead to the world." When he first presented himself to the ancients or superiors of the monks of Sceté, and begged to be allowed to serve God under their direction, they recommended him to the care of St. John the dwarf who, when the rest in the evening sat down to take their repast, took his place among them, and left Arsenius standing in the middle without taking notice of him. Such a reception was a severe trial to a courtier; but was followed by another much rougher; for, in the middle of the repast, St. John took a loaf or portion of bread, and threw it on the ground before him, bidding him, with an air of indifference, eat if he would. Arsenius cheerfully fell on the ground, and in that posture took his meal. St. John was so satisfied with his behaviour in this single instance, that he required no further trial for his admission, and said to his brethren: "Return to your cells with the blessing of the Lord. Pray for us. This person is fit for a religious life."

Arsenius after his retreat only distinguished himself among the anchorets by his greater humility and fervour. At first he used, without perceiving it, to do certain things which he had practised in the world, which seemed to savour of levity or immortification, as, for instance, to sit cross-legged, or laying one knee over another. The seniors were unwilling, through the great respect they bore him, to tell him of this in a public assembly, in which they were met to hold a spiritual conference together; but Abbot Pemen or Pastor made use of this stratagem: He agreed with another that he should put himself in that posture; and then he rebuked him for his immodesty; nor did the other offer any excuse. Arsenius perceived that the reproof was meant for him, and corrected himself of that custom. In other respects he appeared from the beginning an accomplished master in every exercise of virtue in that venerable company of saints. To punish himself for his seeming vanity at court, because he had there gone more richly habited than others, his garments were always the meanest of all the monks in Sceté. He employed himself on working-days till noon in making mats of palm-tree leaves; and he always worked with a handkerchief in his bosom, to wipe off the tears which continually fell from his eyes. He never changed the water in which he moistened his palm-tree leaves, but only poured in fresh water upon it as it wasted. When some asked him one day why he did not cast away the corrupted water, he answered: "I ought to be punished by this ill smell for the sensuality with which I formerly used perfumes when I lived in the world." To satisfy for former superfluities, he lived in the most universal poverty, so that in a violent fit of illness having occasion for a small sum to procure him some little necessaries, he was obliged to receive it in alms, whereupon he gave God thanks for being made worthy to be thus reduced to the necessity of asking alms in his name. The distemper continued so long upon him that the priest of this desert of Sceté caused him to be carried to his apartment contiguous to the church, and laid him on a little bed made of the skins of beasts, with a pillow under his head. One of the monks coming to see him, was much scandalized at his lying so easy, and said: "Is this the Abbot Arsenius?" The priest took him aside, and asked him what his employment had been in the village before he was a monk? The old man answered: "I was a shepherd, and lived with much pains and difficulty." Then the priest said: "Do you see this Abbot Arsenius? when he was in the world he was the father of the emperors; he had a thousand slaves clothed in silk, with bracelets and girdles of gold, and he slept on the softest and richest beds. You who were a shepherd, did not find in the world the ease which you now enjoy." The old man, moved by these words, fell down, and said: "Pardon me, father, I have sinned; he is in the true way of humiliation;" and he went away exceedingly edified. Arsenius in his sickness wanting a linen garment, accepted something given him in charity to buy one, saying: "I return thanks to thee, O Lord, for thy grace and mercy, in permitting me to receive alms in thy name." One of the emperor's officers, at another time, brought him the will of a senator, his relation, who was lately dead, and had left him his heir. The saint took the will, and would have torn it to pieces, but the officer threw himself at his feet, and begged him not to tear it, saying, such an accident would expose him to be tried for his life. St. Arsenius, however, refused the estate, saying: "I died before him, and cannot be made his heir."

Though no one knew the saint's fasts, they must have been excessive, as the measure of corn, called thallin, sent him for the year, was exceeding small; this, however, he managed so well as not only to make it suffice for himself, but also to impart some of it to his disciples when they came to visit him. When new fruit was brought him, he just tasted it, and gave thanks to God; but he took so little as to show he did it only to avoid the vanity of singularity. Great abstinence makes little sleep to suffice nature. Accordingly St. Arsenius often passed the whole night in watching and prayer, as we learn from his disciple Daniel. At other times, having watched a considerable part of the night, when nature could hold out no longer, he would allow himself a short repose, which he took sitting, after which he resumed his wonted exercises. On Saturday evenings, as the same disciple relates, it was his custom to go to prayers at sunset, and continue in that exercise with his hands lifted up to heaven till the sun beat on his face the next morning. His affection for the holy exercise of prayer, and his dread of the danger of vainglory gave him the strongest love of retirement. He had two disciples who lived near him, and did all his necessary business abroad. Their names were Alexander and Zoilus; he afterward admitted a third, called Daniel. All three were famous for their sanctity and discretion, and frequent mention is made of them in the histories of the fathers of the deserts of Egypt. St. Arsenius would seldom see strangers who came to visit him, saying, he would only use his eyes to behold the heavens.

Theophilus, the patriarch of Alexandria, came one day in company with a certain great officer and others to visit him, and begged he would entertain them on some spiritual subject for the good of their souls. The saint asked them whether they were disposed to comply with his directions; and being answered in the affirmative, he replied: "I entreat you, then, that wherever you are informed of Arsenius's abode, you would leave him to himself, and spare yourselves the trouble of coming after him." On another occasion, when the same patriarch sent to know if he would open his door to him if he came, St. Arsenius returned for answer, that if he came alone he would; but that if he brought others with him, he would seek out some other place, and would stay there no longer. Melania, a noble Roman lady, travelled as far as Egypt, only to see Arsenius, and by means of Theophilus contrived to meet him as he was coming out of his cell. She threw herself at his feet. The saint said to her: "A woman ought not to leave her house. You have crossed these great seas that you may be able to say at Rome that you have seen Arsenius, and raise in others a curiosity to come and see me." Not daring to lift up her eyes, as she lay on the ground, she begged he would always remember her and pray for her. He answered: "I pray that the remembrance of you be blotted out of my mind." Melania returned to Alexandria in great grief at this answer; but Theophilus comforted her, saying: "He only prayed that he might forget your person on account of your sex; but as for your soul, doubt not but he will pray for you."

The saint never visited his brethren, contenting himself with meeting them at spiritual conferences. The Abbot Mark asked him one day, in the name of the hermits, why he so much shunned their conversation? The saint answered: "God knoweth how dearly I love you all; but I find I cannot be both with God and with men at the same time; nor can I think of leaving God to converse with men." This disposition however did not hinder him from giving short lessons of virtue to his brethren, and several of his apothegms are recorded among those of the ancient fathers. He said often: "I have always something to repent of after having conversed with men; but have never been sorry for having been silent." He had frequently in his mouth those words which St. Euthymius and St. Bernard used also to repeat to themselves, to renew their fervour in the discharge of the obligations of their profession: "Arsenius, why hast thou forsaken the world, and wherefore art thou come hither?" Being asked one day why he, being so well versed in the sciences, sought the instruction and advice of a certain monk who was an utter stranger to all human literature, he replied: "I am not unacquainted with the learning of the Greeks and Romans; but I have not yet learned the alphabet of the science of the saints, whereof this seemingly ignorant person is master."

Though the saint was excellently versed in sacred learning, and in the maxims and practice of perfect Christian virtue, he never would discourse on any point of Scripture, and chose rather to hear than to instruct or speak, making it the first part of his study to divest his mind of all secret opinion of himself, or confidence in his own abilities or learning; and this he justly called the foundation of humility and all Christian virtue. Evagrius of Pontus, who had distinguished himself at Constantinople by his learning, and had retired to Jerusalem, and thence into the deserts of Nitria in 385, expressed his surprise to our saint that many very learned men made no progress in virtue, while many Egyptians, who knew not the very letters of the alphabet, arrived at a high degree of sublime contemplation. To whom Arsenius made this answer: "We make no progress in virtue, because we dwell in that exterior learning which puffs up the mind; but these illiterate Egyptians have a true sense of their own weakness, blindness, and insufficiency; by which they are qualified to labour successfully in the pursuit of virtue." This saint used often to cry out to God with tears, in the most profound sentiment of humility: "O Lord, forsake me not; I have done nothing that can be acceptable in thy sight; but for the sake of thy infinite mercy, enable and assist me that I may now begin to serve thee faithfully."

Nothing is so remarkable or so much spoken of by the ancients concerning our saint, as the perpetual tears which flowed from his eyes almost without intermission. The source from which they sprang was the ardour with which he sighed after the glorious light of eternity, and the spirit of compunction with which he never ceased to bewail the sins of his life past, and the daily imperfections into which he fell. But nothing was more amiable or sweet than these tears of devotion, as appeared in the venerable and majestic serenity of his countenance. His example was a proof of what the saints assure us concerning the sweetness of the tears of divine love. "When you hear tears named," says St. Chrysostom, "do not represent to yourselves any thing grievous or terrible. They are sweeter than any carnal delights which the world can enjoy." St. Austin says to the same purpose: "The tears of devotion are sweeter than the joys of theatres." St. John Climacus unfolds to us at large the incomparable advantages and holy pleasure of pious tears, and among other things writes thus: "I am astonished when I consider the happiness of holy compunction; and I wonder how carnal men can think it affliction. It contains in it a pleasure and spiritual joy as wax does honey. God in an invisible manner visits and comforts the heart that is broken with this holy sorrow." St. Arsenius being asked by a certain person what he must do to deliver himself from a troublesome temptation of impure thoughts, the saint gave him this answer: "What did the Midianites do? They decked and adorned their daughters, and led them to the Israelites, though they used no violence upon them. Those among the servants of God that treated them with severity, and revenged their treachery and criminal designs with their blood, put a stop to their lewdness. Behave in the same manner with regard to your evil thoughts. Repulse them vigorously, and punish yourself for this attempt made in yourself toward a revolt."

This great saint lived in a continual remembrance and apprehension of death and the divine judgment. This made Theophilus, the busy patriarch of Alexandria, cry out when he lay on his death-bed in 312: "Happy Arsenius! who has had this moment always before his eyes." His tears did not disfigure his countenance, which from the inward peace and joy of his soul, mixed with sweet compunction, and from his assiduous conversation with God, appeared to have something angelical or heavenly, being equally venerable for a certain shining beauty and an inexpressible air of majesty and meekness, in a fair and vigorous old age. The great and experienced master in a contemplative life, St. John Climacus, proposes St. Arsenius as an accomplished model, and calls him a man equal to the angels, saying that he shunned so rigorously the conversation of men, only that he might not lose something more precious, which was God, who always filled his soul. Our saint called it a capital and indispensable duty of a monk never to intermeddle in any temporal concerns, and never to listen to any news of the world. He was tall and comely, but stooped a little in his old age; had a graceful mien, his hair was all white, and his beard reached down to his girdle; but the tears which he shed continually had worn away his eyelashes. He was forty years old when he quitted the court, and he lived in the same austere manner from that time to the age of ninety-five; he spent forty years in the desert of Sceté, except that, about the year 395, he was obliged to leave it for a short time, on account of an irruption of the Mazici, a barbarous people of Lybia; but the plunderers were no sooner returned home but he returned back to his former solitude, where he remained till a second inroad of the same barbarians, in which they massacred several hermits, compelled him entirely to forsake this abode about the year 434. He retired weeping to the rock of Troë, called also Petra, over against Memphis, and, ten years after, to Canopus near Alexandria; but not being able to bear the neighbourhood of that great city, he stayed here only three years; then returned to Troë, where he died two years after.

Knowing that his end was drawing near, he said to his disciples: "One only thing I beg of your charity, that when I am dead I may be remembered in the holy sacrifice. If in my life I have done any thing that is accepted by God, through his mercy, that I shall now find again." They were much grieved to hear him speak as if they were going soon to lose him. Upon which he said: "My hour is not yet come. I will acquaint you of it; but you shall answer it at the tribunal of Christ, if you suffer any thing belonging to me to be kept as a relic." They said with tears, (being solicitous for a funeral procession:) "What shall we do alone, father? for we know not how to bury the dead." The saint answered: "Tie a cord to my feet, and drag my carcass to the top of the mountain, and there leave it." His brethren seeing him weep in his agony, said to him: "Father, why do you weep? are you, like others, afraid to die?" The saint answered: "I am seized with great fear; nor has this dread ever forsaken me from the time I first came into these deserts." The saints all serve God in fear and trembling, in the constant remembrance of his judgment; but this is always accompanied with a sweet confidence in his infinite love and mercies. The Holy Ghost indeed so diversifies his gifts and graces as to make these dispositions more sensible in some than in others. Notwithstanding this fear, St. Arsenius expired in great peace, full of faith and of that humble confidence which perfect charity inspires, about the year 449. He was ninety-five years old, of which he had spent fifty-five in the desert. Abbot Pemen having seen him expire, said, with tears: "Happy Arsenius! who have wept for yourself so much here on earth! Those who weep not here shall weep eternally hereafter." This saint was looked upon by the most eminent monks of succeeding ages as a most illustrious pattern of their state. The great St. Euthymius endeavoured in all his exercises to form himself upon the model of his life, and to copy in himself his humility, his meekness and constant evenness of mind, his abstinences and watching, his compunction and tears, his love of retirement, his charity, discretion, fervour, assiduous application to prayer, and that greatness of soul which appeared with so much lustre in all his actions. The name of St. Arsenius occurs in the Roman Martyrology on the 19th of July.

ST. PAMBO OF NITRIA, ABBOT.

A. D. 385.

St. Pambo betook himself in his youth to the great St. Antony in the desert, and desiring to be admitted among his disciples, begged he would give him some lessons for his conduct. The great patriarch of the ancient monks told him he must take care always to live in a state of penance and compunction for his sins, must perfectly divest himself of all self-conceit, and never place the least confidence in himself, or in his own righteousness, must watch continually over himself, and study to act in every thing in such a manner as to have no occasion afterward to repent of what he had done, and that he must labour to put a restraint upon his tongue and his appetite. The disciple set himself earnestly to learn the practice of all these lessons. The mortification of gluttony was usually laid down by the fathers as one of the first steps toward bringing the senses and the passions into subjection; this consisting in something that is exterior and sensible, its practice is more obvious, yet of great importance toward the reduction of all the sensual appetites of the mind, whose revolt was begun by the intemperance and disobedience of our first parents. Fasting is also, by the divine appointment, a duty of the exterior part of our penance. What a reproach are the austere lives which so many saints have led to those slothful and sensual Christians whose God is their belly, and who walk enemies to the cross of Christ, or who have not courage at least by frequent self-denials to curb this appetite? No man can govern himself who is a slave to this base gratification of sense. St. Pambo excelled most other ancient monks in the austerity of his continual fasts. The government of his tongue was no less an object of his watchfulness than that of his appetite. A certain religious brother, to whom he had applied for advice, began to recite to him the thirty-eighth psalm: *I said I will take heed to my ways, that I sin not with my tongue.* Which words Pambo had no sooner heard, but without waiting for the second verse, he returned to his cell, saying, that was enough for one lesson, and that he would go and study to put it into practice. This he did by keeping almost perpetual silence, and by weighing well, when it was necessary to speak, every word before he gave any answer. He often took several days to recommend consultations to God, and to consider what answer he should give to those who addressed themselves to him.

By his perpetual attention not to offend in his words, he arrived at so great a perfection in this particular, that he was thought to have equalled, if not to have excelled, St. Antony himself; and his answers were seasoned with so much wisdom and spiritual prudence, that they were received by all as if they had been oracles dictated by heaven. Abbot Pœman said of our saint: "Three exterior practices are remarkable in Abbot Pambo; his fasting every day till evening, his silence, and his great diligence in manual labour." St. Antony inculcated to all his disciples the obligation of assiduity in constant manual labour in a solitary life, both as a part of penance, and a necessary means to expel sloth, and entertain the vigour of the mind in spiritual exercises. This lesson was confirmed to him by his own experience, and by a heavenly vision related in the lives of the fathers, as follows: "Abbot Antony, as he was sitting in the wilderness, fell into a grievous temptation of spiritual sadness, importunate thoughts, and interior darkness; and he said to God: Lord, I desire to be saved; but my thoughts are a hinderance to me. What shall I do in my present affliction? How shall I be saved? Soon after, he rose up, and going out of his cell, saw a man sitting and working; then rising from his work to pray; afterward sitting down again, and twisting his cord: after this, rising to prayer. He understood this to be an angel sent by God to teach him what he was to do, and he heard the angel say to him: Do so, and thou shalt be saved." Hereat the abbot was filled with joy and confidence, and by this means he cheerfully persevered to the end. St. Pambo most rigorously observed this rule, and feared to lose one moment of his precious time. Out of love of humiliations, and a fear of the danger of vainglory and pride, he made it his earnest prayer for three years that God would not give him glory before men, but rather contempt. Nevertheless God glorified him in this life, but made him by his grace to learn more perfectly to humble himself amid applause. The eminent grace which replenished his soul showed itself in his exterior, by a certain air of majesty, and a kind of light which shone on his countenance, like what we read of Moses, so that a person could not look steadfastly on his face. St. Antony, who admired the purity of his soul, and his mastery over his passions, used to say, that his fear of God had moved the divine Spirit to take up his resting-place in him.

St. Pambo, after he left St. Antony, settled in the desert of Nitria on a mountain, where he had a monastery. But he lived some time in the wilderness of the Cells, where Rufinus says he went to receive his blessing in the year 374. St. Melania the elder, in the visit she made to the holy solitaries who inhabited the deserts of Egypt, coming to St. Pambo's monastery on Mount Nitria, found the holy abbot sitting at his work, making mats. She gave him three hundred pounds weight of silver, desiring him to accept that part of her store for the necessities of the poor among the brethren. St. Pambo, without interrupting his work, or looking at her or her present, said to her that God would reward her charity. Then turning to his disciple, he bade him take the silver, and distribute it among all the brethren in Lybia and the isles who were most needy, but charged him to give nothing to those of Egypt, that country being rich and plentiful. Melania continued some time standing, and at length said: "Father, do you know that here is three hundred pounds weight of silver?" The abbot, without casting his eye upon the chest of silver, replied: "Daughter, he to whom you made this offering, very well knows how much it weighs, without being told. If you give it to God, who did not despise the widow's two mites, and even preferred them to the great presents of the rich, say no more about it." This Melania herself related to Palladius. St. Athanasius once desired St. Pambo to come out of the desert to Alexandria to confound the Arians by giving testimony to the divinity of Jesus Christ. Our saint seeing in that city an actress dressed up for the stage, wept bitterly; and being asked the reason of his tears, said he wept for the sinful condition of that unhappy woman, and also for his own sloth in the divine service; because he did not take so much pains to please God as she did to ensnare men. When Abbot Theodore begged of St. Pambo some words of instruction: "Go," said he, "and exercise mercy and charity toward all men. Mercy finds confidence before God." To the priest of Nitria who asked him how the brethren ought to live, he said: "They must live in constant labour and the exercise of all virtues, watching to preserve their conscience free from stain, especially from giving scandal or offence to any neighbour." St. Pambo said a little before his death: "From the time that I came into this desert, and built myself a cell in it, I do not remember that I have ever eaten any bread but what I had earned by my own labour, nor that I ever spoke any word of which I afterward repented. Nevertheless, I go to God as one who has not yet begun to serve him." He died seventy years old, without any sickness, pain or agony, as he was making a basket, which he bequeathed to Palladius, who was at that time his disciple, the holy man having nothing else to give him. Melania took care of his burial, and having obtained this basket, kept it to her dying day. St. Pambo is commemorated by the Greeks on several days. It was a usual saying of this great director of souls in the rules of Christian perfection: "If you have a heart, you may be saved."

The extraordinary austerities and solitude of a St. Antony or a St. Pambo are not suitable to persons engaged in the world; they are even inconsistent with their obligations; but all are capable of disengaging their affections from inordinate passions and attachment to creatures, and of attaining to a pure and holy love of God, which may be made the principle of their thoughts and ordinary actions, and sanctify the whole circle of their lives. Of this all who have a heart, are, through the divine grace, capable. In whatever circumstances we are placed, we have opportunities of subduing our passions, and subjecting our senses by frequent denials; of watching over our hearts by self-examination, of purifying our affections by assiduous recollection, and prayer, and of uniting our souls to God by continual exterior and interior acts of holy love. Thus may the gentleman, the husbandman, or the shopkeeper become an eminent saint, and make even the employments of his state an exercise of all heroic virtues, and so many steps to perfection and eternal glory.

ST. AGNES, V. M.

A. D. 304 or 305.

St. Jerom says, that the tongues and pens of all nations are employed in the praises of this saint, who overcame both the cruelty of the tyrant and the tenderness of her age, and crowned the glory of chastity with that of martyrdom. St. Austin observes, that her name signifies chaste in Greek, and a lamb in Latin. She has been always looked upon in the church as a special patroness of purity, with the immaculate Mother of God and St. Thecla. Rome was the theatre of the triumph of St. Agnes; and Prudentius says, that her tomb was shown within sight of that city. She suffered not long after the beginning of the persecution of Dioclesian, whose bloody edicts appeared in March in the year of our Lord 303. We learn from St. Ambrose and St. Austin, that she was only thirteen years of age at the time of her glorious death. Her riches and beauty excited the young noblemen of the first families in Rome, to vie with one another in their addresses, who should gain her in marriage. Agnes answered them all, that she had consecrated her virginity to a heavenly spouse, who could not be beheld by mortal eyes. Her suitors finding her resolution impregnable to all their arts and importunities, accused her to the governor as a Christian; not doubting but threats and torments would overcome her tender mind, on which allurements could make no impression. The judge at first employed the mildest expressions and most inviting promises; to which Agnes paid no regard, repeating always, that she could have no other spouse than Jesus Christ. He then made use of threats, but found her soul endowed with a masculine courage, and even desirous of racks and death. At last, terrible fires were made, and iron hooks, racks, and other instruments of torture displayed before her, with threats of immediate execution. The young virgin surveyed them all with an undaunted eye; and with a cheerful countenance beheld the fierce and cruel executioners surrounding her, and ready to despatch her, at the word of command. She was so far from betraying the least symptoms of fear, that she even expressed her joy at the sight, and offered herself to the rack. She was then dragged before the idols, and commanded to offer incense: "but could by no means be compelled to move her hand, except to make the sign of the cross," says St. Ambrose.

The governor seeing his measures ineffectual, said he would send her to a house of prostitution, where what she prized so highly should be exposed to the insults of the debauchees. Agnes answered that Jesus Christ was too jealous of the purity of his spouses, to suffer it to be violated in such a manner; for he was their defender and protector. "You may," said she, "stain your sword with my blood, but will never be able to profane my body, consecrated to Christ." The governor was so incensed at this, that he ordered her to be immediately led to the public brothel, with liberty to all persons to abuse her person at pleasure. Many young profligates ran thither, full of the wicked desire of gratifying their lust; but were seized with such awe at the sight of the saint, that they durst not approach her; one only excepted, who, attempting to be rude to her, was that very instant, by a flash, as it were, of lightning from heaven, struck blind, and fell trembling to the ground. His companions terrified, took him up, and carried him to Agnes, who was at a distance, singing hymns of praise to Christ, her protector. The virgin by prayer restored him to his sight and health.

The chief persecutor of the saint, who at first sought to gratify his lust and avarice, now laboured to satiate his revenge, by incensing the judge against her; his passionate fondness being changed into anger and rage. The governor wanted not others to spur him on; for he was highly exasperated to see himself baffled, and set at defiance by one of her tender age and sex. Therefore, resolved upon her death, he condemned her to be beheaded. Agnes, transported with joy on hearing this sentence, and still more at the sight of the executioner, "went to the place of execution more cheerfully," says St. Ambrose, "than others go to their wedding." The executioner had secret instructions to use all means to induce her to a compliance; but Agnes always answered she could never offer so great an injury to her heavenly spouse; and having made a short prayer, bowed down her neck to adore God, and receive the stroke of death. The spectators wept to see so beautiful and tender a virgin loaded with fetters, and to behold her fearless under the very sword of the executioner, who with a trembling hand cut off her head at one stroke. Her body was buried at a small distance from Rome, near the Nomentan road. A church was built on the spot in the time of Constantine the Great, and was repaired by Pope Honorius in the seventh century. It is now in the hands of Canon-Regulars, standing without the walls of Rome; and is honoured with her relics in a very rich silver shrine, the gift of Pope Paul V., in whose time they were found in this church, together with those of St. Emerentiana. The other beautiful rich church of St. Agnes within the city, built by Pope Innocent X., (the right of patronage being vested in the family of Pamphili,) stands on the place where her chastity was exposed. The feast of St. Agnes is mentioned in all martyrologies, both of the East and West, though on different days. It was formerly a holyday for the women in England, as appears from the council of Worcester, held in the year 1240. St. Ambrose, St. Austin, and other fathers have written her panegyric. St. Martin of Tours was singularly devout to her. Thomas à Kempis honoured her as his special patroness, as his works declare in many places. He relates many miracles wrought, and graces received through her intercession.

Marriage is a holy state, instituted by God, and in the order of providence and nature the general or most ordinary state of those who live in the world. Those, therefore, who upon motives of virtue and in a Christian and holy manner engage in this state, do well. Those, nevertheless, who for the sake of practising more perfect virtue, by a divine call, prefer a state of perpetual virginity, embrace that which is more perfect and more excellent. Dr. Wells, a learned Protestant, confesses that Christ declares voluntary chastity, for the kingdom of heaven's sake, to be an excellency, and an excellent state of life. This is also the manifest inspired doctrine of St. Paul, and in the revelations of St. John, spotless virgins are called, in a particular manner, the companions of the Lamb, and are said to enjoy the singular privilege of following him wherever he goes. The tradition of the church has always been unanimous in this point; and among the Romans, Greeks, Syrians, and Barbarians, many holy virgins joyfully preferred torments and death to the violation of their integrity, which they bound themselves by vow to preserve without defilement, in mind or body. The fathers, from the very disciples of the apostles, are all profuse in extolling the excellency of holy virginity, as a special fruit of the incarnation of Christ, his divine institution, and a virtue which has particular charms in the eyes of God, who delights in chaste minds, and chooses to dwell singularly in them. They often repeat that purity raises men, even in this mortal life, to the dignity of angels; purifies the soul, fits it for a more perfect love of God, and a closer application to heavenly things, and disengages the mind and heart from worldly thoughts and affections. It produces in the soul the nearest resemblance to God. Chastity is threefold, that of virgins, that of widows, and that of married persons; in each state it will receive its crown, as St. Ambrose observes, but in the first is most perfect, so that St. Austin calls its fruit an hundred fold, and that of marriage sixty fold; but the more excellent this virtue is, and the higher its glory and reward, the more heroic and the more difficult is its victory; nor is it perfect unless it be embellished with all other virtues in an heroic degree, especially divine charity and the most profound humility.

ST. JULIAN, ANCHORET.

THIS saint was carried away captive from some western country when he was very young, and sold for a slave in Syria. For some years he much aggravated the weight of his chains by his impatience under them; till having the happiness to receive the light of faith, he found them exceedingly lightened by the comfort which religion afforded him. A right use of his afflictions from that moment contributed much to the sanctification of his soul. Not long after, he recovered his liberty by the death of his master, and immediately in the fervour of his devotion dedicated himself to the service of God in an austere monastery in Mesopotamia. He frequently resorted to the great St. Ephrem for advice and instructions in the exercises of virtue; and that holy man went often to see him that he might edify himself by his saintly conversation. This learned doctor of the Syriac church tells us that he could not forbear always admiring the sublime sentiments and spiritual lights with which God favoured a man who appeared in the eyes of the world ignorant and a barbarian. Julian was of a robust body, inured to labour, but he weakened and emaciated it by great austerities. He worked with his hands, making sails for ships; and wept almost continually at the consideration of his past sins, and of the divine judgments. St. Ephrem tells us that he often admired to find that in the copies of the Holy Bible, after Julian had used them some days, several words were effaced, and others rendered scarcely legible, though the manuscripts were entire and fair before; and that the holy man candidly confessed to him, when he one day asked him the reason, that the tears which he shed in reading, often blotted out letters and words. Our saint always looked upon himself as a criminal, trembling, and expecting every moment the coming of his judge to call him to an account. It is easy to imagine how remote such a disposition of mind was from being capable of entertaining the very thought of amusements. His extreme humility appeared in his words, dress, and all his actions. He had much to suffer from certain tepid and slothful monks, but regarded himself as happy to meet with so favourable opportunities of redeeming his sins, and of exercising acts of penance, patience, meekness, and charity. Prayer was almost the uninterrupted employment of his heart. He made in his little cell a kind of a sepulchre, where he lived retired for greater solitude whenever his presence was not required at duties of the community. He assisted at the divine office without ever moving his body, keeping his whole attention fixed on God, as if he had been standing before the tribunal of his sovereign Judge. St. Ephrem assures us that God honoured him with the gift of miracles. Sozomen writes that his life was so austere, that he seemed to live almost without a body. Thus he spent twenty-five years in his monastery, purifying his soul by patience, obedience, and the labours of penance. He passed to a glorious immortality about the year 370. See his life written by his friend, the great St. Ephrem, Op. t. 3, p. 254, ed. Vatic.

ST. PANTÆNUS,

THIS learned father and apostolic man flourished in the second age. He was by birth a Sicilian, by profession a Stoic philosopher. For his eloquence he is styled by St. Clement of Alexandria the Sicilian Bee. His esteem for virtue led him into an acquaintance with the Christians, and being charmed with the innocence and sanctity of their conversation, he opened his eyes to the truth. He studied the Holy Scriptures under the disciples of the apostles, and his thirst after sacred learning brought him to Alexandria in Egypt, where the disciples of St. Mark had instituted a celebrated school of the Christian doctrine. Pantænus sought not to display his talents in that great mart of literature and commerce; but his great progress in sacred learning was after some time discovered, and he was drawn out of that obscurity in which his humility sought to live buried. Being placed at the head of the Christian school some time before the year 179, which was the first of Commodus, by his learning and excellent manner of teaching he raised its reputation above all the schools of the philosophers, and the lessons which he read, and which were gathered from the flowers of the prophets and apostles, conveyed light and knowledge into the minds of all his hearers, as St. Clement of Alexandria, his eminent scholar, says of him. The Indians who traded to Alexandria, entreated him to pay their country a visit, in order to confute their Brachmans. Hereupon he forsook his school, and was established by Demetrius, who was made bishop of Alexandria, in 189, preacher of the gospel to the Eastern nations. Eusebius tells us that St. Pantænus found some seeds of the faith already sown in the Indies, and a book of the Gospel of St. Matthew in Hebrew, which St. Bartholomew had carried thither. He brought it back with him to Alexandria, whither he returned after he had zealously employed some years in instructing the Indians in the faith. The public school was at that time governed by St. Clement, but St. Pantænus continued to teach in private, till, in the reign of Caracalla, consequently before the year 216, he closed a noble and excellent life by a happy death, as Rufinus writes. His name is inserted in all Western Martyrologies on the 7th of July.

The beauty of the Christian morality, and the sanctity of its faithful professors, which by their charms converted this true philosopher, appear no where to greater advantage than when they are compared with the imperfect and often false virtue of the most famous sages of the heathen world. Into what contradictions and gross errors did they fall, even about the divinity itself and the sovereign good! To how many vices did they give the name of virtues! How many crimes did they canonize! It is true they showed indeed a zeal for justice, a contempt of riches and pleasures, moderation in prosperity, patience in adversities, generosity, courage, and disinterestedness. But these were rather shadows and phantoms than real virtues, if they sprang from a principle of vanity and pride, or were infected with the poison of interestedness or any other vitiated intention, which they often betrayed, nay sometimes openly avowed, and made a subject of their vain boasts.

INDEX.

	PAGE
ST. PAUL, THE FIRST HERMIT	5
ST. ISIDORE, P. H.	11
ST. MACARIUS, THE ELDER, OF EGYPT	12
ST. ANTONY, ABBOT	17
ST. MACARIUS OF ALEXANDRIA	30
ST. JOHN, THE ALMONER	37
ST. FRANCIS OF SALES	43
ST. SYNCLETICA, V.	69
ST. MARY OF EGYPT	72
ST. SISOES, ANCHORET IN EGYPT	80
ST. JOHN, THE DWARF	85
ST. CATHARINE	91
ST. THAIS, THE PENITENT	94
ST. PELAGIA, THE PENITENT	98
ST. FRANCIS BORGIA	99
ST. PHOCAS, GARDENER, M.,	135
ST. ELIZABETH, QUEEN OF PORTUGAL	138
ST. EULOGIUS, PATRIARCH OF ALEXANDRIA	148
ST. MARTIN, BISHOP OF TOURS	151
ST. WILLIAM, CONFESSOR	173
ST. VERONICA OF MILAN	178
ST. ARCADIUS, MARTYR	182

ST. LUCIAN.. 180
ST. FRANCIS OF ASSISIUM, ... 188
ST. ELIZABETH OF HUNGARY, WIDOW........................ 225
ST. IGNATIUS OF LOYOLA, FOUNDER OF THE SOCIETY OF
    JESUS 240
ST. ARSENIUS, ANCHORET 277
ST. PAMBO OF NITRIA, ABBOT 288
ST. AGNES 293
ST. JULIAN, ANCHORET.............................. 297
ST. PANTÆNUS 299

THE END.

www.ingramcontent.com/pod-product-compliance
Lightning Source LLC
Chambersburg PA
CBHW021957220426
43663CB00007B/847